WITHDRAWN

LAW IN A
CHANGING AMERICA

The American Assembly, *Columbia University*

LAW IN A
CHANGING AMERICA

Prentice-Hall, Inc., *Englewood Cliffs, N.J.* A SPECTRUM BOOK

Current printing (last number):
10 9 8 7 6 5 4 3 2 1

Preface

On March 14, 1968, over 100 persons prominent in the legal profession (bench and bar) and in the worlds of education, the clergy, communications, business, and government gathered at the Center for Continuing Education, University of Chicago, for The American Assembly on Law and the Changing Society, a consideration of goals for the legal profession in the years ahead in the light of the social changes of the present and recent past. The Assembly was under the joint auspices of the American Bar Association and The American Assembly of Columbia University. Orison S. Marden served as chairman, with the president of The American Assembly as co-chairman. With them on the Advisory Committee were Sol M. Linowitz, Bayless Manning, Myres S. McDougal, Earl F. Morris, Lewis F. Powell, Jr., Oscar Ruebhausen and Bert H. Early.

For three days the participants, in small discussion groups, considered in depth the issues raised in this volume and on the fourth day in plenary session reviewed a final report of findings and conclusions. The report, printed as a separate pamphlet, may be had from The American Assembly or the American Bar Association.

The papers which follow were prepared under the editorial supervision of Geoffrey C. Hazard, Jr. as advance background reading for the Chicago meeting. They are intended as well for general readership and for use at other American Assemblies on this subject.

The opinions contained herein are those of the individual authors and not necessarily of the American Bar Association, or of The American Assembly, which takes no position on matters it presents for public discussion. The same may be said of the American Bar Endowment, the Rockefeller Brothers Fund and the Danforth Foundation, whose generous grants, gratefully acknowledged herewith, made this Assembly program possible.

Clifford C. Nelson
President
The American Assembly

Table of Contents

8

Richard W. Nahstoll
Regulating Professional Qualification

9

David F. Cavers
Legal Education
in Forward-Looking Perspective

Geoffrey C. Hazard, Jr., Editor

Foreword

This is a book about the problems facing the legal profession in the next decade or so and, in less definite terms, those that will appear in the next generation. It is therefore also a book about social problems facing American society. As De Tocqueville observed, in a modern democracy social problems become translated into legal problems—if the democracy coheres, that is. In dealing with legal problems, the perspectives and skills of trained lawyers have always turned out to be indispensable, notwithstanding the age-old inclination to dispense with them.

Because contemporary social problems have this special connection with law, it is not artificial to treat society as though it were a lawyer's client. Most if not all of the papers contained here do that, not excluding the one by Wilbert Moore, who is a social scientist and not a lawyer. That is to say, the authors of these papers approach a problem or cluster of problems with the aim of finding solutions ("What needs to be done to solve or ameliorate this difficulty?"), and proceed by isolating the problem's internal characteristics ("Precisely what is the difficulty?"), and then suggesting lines of action to deal with it ("Here is what we must do."). This approach is breath-taking in its ambition when applied to problems of the scale described by Mr.

GEOFFREY C. HAZARD, JR., _is Executive Director of the American Bar Foundation at the American Bar Center in Chicago, Illinois, and Professor of Law at the University of Chicago. He has practiced law in Oregon, taught law in California and Michigan, written many articles for professional legal journals and contributed to the American Assembly volume on_ The Courts, the Public, and the Law Explosion. _Professor Hazard is the author of two books on civil procedure._

Gossett (economic relationships in giant enterprise) and Dean Pollak (securing true protection of the law for all American citizens). But these "mega-problems" are just as much legal problems as such more specific questions as providing education in law to students in general education (Mr. Elson), or to law students (Dean Cavers and Professor Goldstein), or to lawyers (Mr. Reichert).

These are legal problems because they are social problems to which legal processes are relevant. And because legal processes will be used in solving them, they are problems for the legal profession. Of course, this is an introverted way to describe social problems. Yet there is value in describing them that way, because to do so raises the question whether the legal profession's perspective of social problems today is in some ways squinted. This question is in turn important because how the legal profession sees and approaches the problems of its social client affects the way those problems are resolved. These are issues dealt with by Professors Kalven (the relation between scientific knowledge and legal decision-making), Jones (economic evidence and analytical technique in regulation of economic behavior), and Yarmolinsky (identifying and probing policy issues that are infused with technically complicated questions). A message in these papers is that substantial segments of the legal profession—like substantial segments of the rest of society—have large intellectual distances to close before they can deal adequately with the fundamental problems society now confronts.

The closure of those gaps will change the character of the legal profession, in ways implied not only in the papers of Professors Kalven, Jones and Yarmolinsky, but in those of Dean Cavers and Professor Goldstein as well. If part of legal education moves along the research-oriented line suggested by Professor Goldstein—and part of it already does—then legal education as a whole will divide in the way stated by Dean Cavers. And that will be both an effect and a cause of changes in the organization and technical content of the professional services provided by lawyers. Some of these changes in organization and content are considered by Professor Schwartz in his treatment of new arrangements for providing legal services to private individuals. In the light of such changes and others considered here, for example by Dean Pollak, the question "What is a lawyer, anyway?" becomes one of serious practical significance, as Mr. Nahstoll gently but relentlessly brings to our attention.

This is the question that the legal profession has to deal with in many different forms and guises now and in the immediate future. Perhaps the greatest error the profession has made in the recent past, and which society has indulged it in making, is to assume that the question has a single answer. The legal profession does not always recognize that it is functionally subordinate to its clientele: the particular problem-solving jobs it does depend on what kinds of problems society has. In the time of the Plantagenets, the main question was that of domestic tranquillity, in the time of King James that of government accountability, and in the time of J. P. Morgan that of industrial organization. Today, it appears to be all these questions rolled into many more. Whatever else it may be, contemporary and future society is complicated.

A legal profession conceived as existing to solve one set of problems, but needed to solve many others as well, will not long exist in robust health for any purpose. The task of the legal profession is to re-direct its energies in the willing service of society's new demands on it. The purpose of these papers is to suggest what those demands may be, and how the profession might move toward solving them. Undoubtedly these are questions of concern to society at large as well.

Bayless Manning

Introduction:
New Tasks for Lawyers

The law has forever had, and will forever have, an endless agenda of unfinished business. There are always tasks for the law newly crying out for attention. We are today surrounded by evident needs for reform and improvement in our judicial process, in the conduct of our administrative agencies, in our legislative machinery, and in our correctional institutions, to name but some. These tasks were new yesterday, are new today, and will be new tomorrow, but they are not the subject of this American Assembly. The topic that has been placed squarely before us here is ourselves as lawyers, and our profession.

Twelve chapters have been prepared. Each is addressed to an aspect of the way in which the legal profession is trained and functions in the United States. Except for one distinguished sociologist, each of the authors is a lawyer of outstanding reputation in his field; each is marked by maturity and experience; each is a man of sober reflection and insight. Each chapter was prepared independently. Yet the chapters, taken together, yield a composite picture that is coherent and self-consistent. And that composite picture is one that should disturb us all. The recurring theme of the chapters is that we lawyers have a

BAYLESS MANNING, *dean of The Stanford University Law School since 1964, was for four years professor of law at Yale University. He has been Special Assistant to the Undersecretary of State, and from 1959–1961 served as Chairman of the Connecticut Commission on Revision of Corporation Laws. Dean Manning is the author of several books and numerous articles on law and legal institutions.*

major new task before us—to make ourselves into modern men and to realign our profession into modern society.

Our law schools are not dealt with gently by the authors. Professor Cavers charges that our law schools proceed in lockstep with each other regardless of local situations and constituencies, and that our students are marched through law school in lockstep in spite of differentiations in their interest and their prospective professional careers. Moreover, the cadence for the lockstep is one that was set more than half a century ago at a time when the social environment of the country was very different, when the mix of the judicial, legislative, and administrative processes was quite unlike its modern pattern, and when we had not yet invented the tools with which to study, and learn from, the legal process in action. Professor Cavers issues a call for a recognition of differentiated functions among different law schools and a change in law school curricula that will thrust students out of the morgue of appellate judicial opinions and into the turbulence of life in contemporary America.

Professor Goldstein's thesis regarding legal education follows a different radius but emanates from the same center as Professor Cavers', and is no less critical. Goldstein calls to our attention that it has been at least forty years since the perception became clear that the legal process is a part of the social process as a whole, but that we have done little with that perception in our law schools other than to talk about it. He sees as a major obstacle the persistent conception of the lawyer as an all-purpose generalist, and argues for greater specialization and deeper concentration on inter-disciplinary work by both faculty and students in our law schools. It will not indefinitely satisfy the inquiring mind of the good student to be told in class by his professor: "Judges may tend to be more lenient in sentencing than juries, or vice versa, but we do not know which it is and someone ought really to find out—but not me." Professor Kalven's study of that very point about jury behavior, and the paper he has contributed to this volume, foreshadow tomorrow's legal scholarship in the world of legal reality.

Mr. Reichert, dealing mainly with the subject of continuing legal education, launches another criticism that we all know to be accurate —that our law schools do not prepare graduates to step into the role of practitioner. And Mr. Elson deplores the failure of the law schools, and of lawyers, to acquaint the rest of society with the workings of the legal process.

These general observations about our professional training institutions are, in my perspective, undeniably true. The nation's approximately 130 accredited law schools, while qualitatively differentiated, are almost carbon copies of each other in their educational programs. Their curricula and teaching methods closely adhere to a model that crystallized at the turn of the century. Training patterns in the law have undergone less development in the last three quarters of a century than those of almost any other discipline and certainly less than any other profession; contrast, for example, the dramatic modernizing changes that have occurred during that period in our schools for training doctors, engineers, and business executives. Only a handful of today's law faculty members have, like Professor Kalven, the methodological skills required to go beyond the study of words to investigate the actual operation of the legal process where it counts— where it makes its impact felt with overwhelming force upon the lives of people. The legal profession as a whole has not generally understood the critical social need for research into the law in action, and has even tended to resist it. Law schools are virtually without research funding. The foundations and governmental sources that support research into virtually every other area of human activity by and large have been predominately inhospitable to legal research. This inhospitality results from a conception of a law school—only partly a caricature—as a place where brilliant, but slightly eccentric law professors alternate between sitting in their offices, where they endlessly read advance sheets of judicial opinions, and standing in their classrooms where they endlessly ask uninformed students unanswerable questions.

And Mr. Reichert is right too. Our law schools have never really been practice oriented, have never been other than theoretical. It is simply a myth, though one that is apparently widely held, that the law schools of the good old days were interested in law for the practitioner while the trend today is to become theoretical. Our law schools have never been other than theoretical—never more so than in the high days of exquisite classroom pursuit of conceptual distinctions between shifting and springing uses, affirmative and negative injunctions, bailments and loans, and contracts of sale and contracts to sell.

But, accepting the validity of these criticisms of our law schools, what shall we do about it?

The doctors, the architects, and the accountants have somehow managed to develop workable, though doubtless imperfect, arrangements in their professions to bridge the gap between theoretical scholastic training and professional proficiency. Is it inevitable in the law that training for the neophyte must be conducted at the expense of the fortunes, and perhaps the lives of his hapless early clients? What institutional rearrangements can be made inside or outside our law schools to provide clinical training for the young lawyer, in his own interest and in the interest of those who need legal help?

Within this century, through basic research in the physical sciences, in medicine, psychiatry, psychology, mathematics, economics, anthropology, archaeology—to name but some—mankind has learned more about himself and his environment than he had learned in his entire prior history. Is it a plausible proposition that the operation of our legal institutions is somehow different and not worth serious research investigation? According to the latest annual report of the university with which I am associated, total university expenditures for research last year amounted to more than 37 million dollars; of that amount more than 10 million dollars was devoted to medical research—and less than 20 thousand dollars was attributed to legal research. These research ratios are nationally typical. Is the health of our legal order today so robust that we can afford such unconcern about it?

It is also nationally typical that the ratio of the number of students to the number of faculty in law schools is markedly higher than that of any other field of graduate study. The ratio is predicated on assumptions, which become self proving, that law students, unlike other graduate students, are handled in large classes and that law professors, unlike other academicians, have no research work to be done. These conditions persist despite the evident fact that, as both Goldstein and Kalven point out, we know remarkably little about how the legal process actually operates, and we also know that with an investment of time and money, we could find out a great deal about it. Until Professor Kalven's study, no one had ever really tried to learn what juries actually do and with what consequences. How is the check collection system operating under the uniform commercial code? What really happens in juvenile courts? Who in fact receives what kinds of criminal penalties and for what kinds of offenses? How is the behavior of investors actually affected by different kinds of securities regulations? What have been the actual effects of the *Miranda* case? What do zoning laws actually do to land values? What is the actual effect of that marvel of ingenuity, the rule against perpetuities? The answer to all these questions, and a million more like them, is that we do not know, that we could find out, and that we are still not trying to find out. As a result, decision makers in our judicial, legislative and administrative institutions continue to follow rules, change rules, and make new rules in what is often virtually a factual vacuum. How should we go about repairing this situation? What kind of a research arm should a modern school of law have? How should people be trained for this kind of social legal research? How can it be financed?

Conceding the particular points made by Messrs. Kalven, Goldstein and Reichert, what should our law schools do to supply a basic legal introduction to those who will become working lawyers? Has our law become so complex, and have legal careers so differentiated, that we must indeed abandon the concept of the lawyer as generalist and embark upon early specialization as has happened in almost very other field and discipline? Or should we create new institutions for that purpose, reserving to our law schools that function which they have undoubtedly performed most successfully, the provision of what Professor Hazard has recently epitomized as "an enlightening theoretical apparatus" and "instruction in the fundamental analysis of legal process"?

The training provided by our law schools has contributed impressively to the leadership, growth, strength and freedom of the American people. Can we identify the essential ingredients of that training system so that we can avoid the risk of throwing away the good, and learn to make it better? All these questions about our legal educational institutions, and many more like them, are before us.

With Mr. Nahstoll's chapter, we move away from the law schools and turn to an examination of our present institutions for policing the qualifications of members of the Bar. Mr. Nahstoll's chapter is severely critical of our existing procedures at every level of the process. He sees the inquiry into fitness of character as pro forma. He points out that bar examinations have little or no relationship to a candidate's competence to hang out a shingle and represent a client. Our licensing system has made no accommodation whatever to the reality of specialization, and affords us no means of recognizing special qualification or upholding standards of competence of the specialist. Bar examinations follow a content pattern substantially identical to that borrowed from law curricula of sixty years ago, and in all but the strongest schools, the pattern of the local bar examination, in turn, strongly inhibits change in educational programs. The reverse proposition is also true: to the extent that a school does move forward toward modernization of its educational program to make its graduates into better lawyers, it places its graduates at a competitive disadvantage in taking a bar examination. In the field of continuing legal education, significant forward motion has occurred and the emergence of new institutions devoted to this function is, as Mr. Reichert observes, encouraging; but our licensing system remains a one-shot affair and we have no institutional means for requiring, or even encouraging, members of the profession to expose themselves to continuing education in the law.

Again, it seems clear that Mr. Nahstoll, like his co-authors, has confronted us with an unpleasant but true statement of things as they are. It would be hard to argue that a bar examination tells us very much about a man's qualifications to be a lawyer; it tells us even less if the examination was taken twenty years ago. Those of us in the profession know something about how to choose a good lawyer; we do it seriously and successfully when our problem is to decide which of the younger associates in our firm we should promote to partner; we would think demented a suggestion that we should base that important step upon the results of a written examination on classical law school curriculum courses. There are other problems about our licensing procedures. It is revolting to contemplate the cram courses that have sprung up through the country as the by-product of the present system for qualifying young lawyers. In preparation for local bar examinations, a vast proportion of the graduates of our law schools—even the ablest students trained at our most distinguished schools—sit through six hours of daily lectures for six to twelve solid weeks memorizing in Chinese fashion endless outlines and gimmicks of local examinationship—outlines and gimmicks that will be erased from their minds within a month after the examination date. Whatever improvement is made in law schools greatly increases the necessity for this kind of cramming unless the bar examinations change too. Just what the bar examinations are examining for is very questionable. It is not plausible that a legal subject matter that was irrelevant to bar admission last year should, by a change of rule, be thought essential to the practitioner this year, while another subject that was essential last year has suddenly become irrelevant. Indeed, it is not even plausible that either subject is essential when not one successful practicing lawyer out of 10,000 could pass an examination in either subject if it were given to him tomorrow. In addition, bar examinations in our largest states are today pressing against the outer limits of administrability as the annual increase in the number of candidates forces use of increasing numbers of graders.

And Mr. Nahstoll's points about licensing specialties are obviously accurate. At present we deliberately clog what meager communications devices we might have, whether by telephone directories or lawyer referral services, so that the public and potential users are prevented from getting at the information we do have about specialization and about specialists. And we do this despite the fact that our increasingly urbanized life pattern has sharply curtailed the informal, word-of-mouth information channels of small town life.

But again, what should be done about it? Should we remit to the law schools the job of examining on basic theoretical subjects (a job they are doing already anyway) and focus the bar examination on something else? Is it within our reach yet to design bar examinations for machine grading? Should the examinations in some way inquire into the candidates' practical qualifications? If not, does our inability to test for practical experience lead to the conclusion that we need some form of internship plan? Are we ready to face the reality of specialization in order to inform the client public? Are we ready to require that members of the profession periodically re-educate themselves?

The only clear fact is that our existing licensing machinery is out of date and not working at all well. One of the tasks before us is to suggest ways to improve it.

Professors Yarmolinsky and Jones present to us in their chapters another aspect of the question of specialization and the intellectual qualifications of the working lawyer. These chapters address themselves to the problems of the legal advocate and the legal decision-maker who is increasingly called upon to find ways to marry the classical processes of legal decision with modern processes, and products, of social science methodology. Once the law is perceived as a massive corpus of policy preferences of the society in which it operates, legal decision-makers are not free to ignore or shut out from their minds data and analytic products that bear upon the issue before them. That matter was decided with the acceptance of the Brandeis brief.

Professor Jones' chapter makes the point vividly: it is apparent that antitrust law has something to do with the social objective of maintaining a competitive economic system; economists have developed an increasingly sophisticated comprehension of the competitive process and of the way in which it works; but how shall the institutions of the law make use of this new learning? And how shall we go about the job of defining and allocating the respective roles to be played by the older processes of legal decision making and the newer empiric approaches? No one as sophisticated as the authors of these chapters believes that the law has become economics, or believes that the older ways of legal thinking have been supplanted by the techniques of the new. What is clear is that the older processes can now be supplemented—are now being supplemented—and that our institutional arrangements of the profession must somehow be adjusted to put this development to practical use.

On the whole, it is fair to say that neither the law schools, the practicing profession, nor the bench has eagerly reached out to inquire whether new tools and new techniques can be put to good use in the law. The computer is a generation old now, and is fully absorbed as an indispensable tool in industry, in government, in the military, in the medical profession and in university life. But our law schools and the general institutions of the law (except, significantly, the Internal Revenue Service) remain largely innocent of the computer's existence. Managerial and organizational techniques, in which America is the world's leader, have undergone a revolution in this country in the last sixty years. But the operating patterns of the legal profession have remained essentially static. Other industries and professions have learned how to make use of technicians and paraprofessionals, and thus to increase the public service product of those whose professional talent and educational investment are the highest. The institutions of the legal profession have not yet worked out such arrangements. In most fields, a keen awareness of the need to remain current, to stay in the forefront of change, is manifested by a close relationship between the practitioner and the research center, by refresher instruction, by leaves and sabbaticals to ward off staleness and the inevitable human tendency to do things tomorrow the way we did them yesterday. But in the legal profession there has been no corresponding emergence of counterparts to these features of twentieth-century American life. I have indeed heard it observed that the only significant innovations in the technology of law practice since the turn of the century are the Xerox and the looseleaf service, both of them efficient allies in the profession's implacable war against the nation's forest reserve.

What should we do about this? How does one go about converting an arrested industry into a modern industry, an old model profession into a new model one? What kinds of organizational changes are needed? What kinds of training and for whom? What kinds of equipment? Others outside the profession seem to have worked out ways to do it. Land title work that was once a mainstay of the legal profession has moved from the profession into the hands of more efficient institutions operated in a modern manner. The same process may be seen at work today in the trust field and, in part, in the tax field. Have we no other resort than to appeal to the bench to restrain the illegal practice of what was law? The endless delays, heavy legal costs and blizzards of papers involved in probate administration contribute significantly and almost universally to public disesteem of the profession and have recently made a poor book an instant best seller. Can the way of doing business in the law remain indefinitely in a nineteenth-century mold when all around us is changing?

Professor Schwartz and Dean Pollak force us to look at another facet of the profession as it is presently organized—our capacity to serve the public—as they turn to the topic of group legal services and legal services for lower income groups. The profession's traditional set toward the solo practitioner and fee for services has made it virtually inevitable that the profession should have little contact with the legal needs of lower and even middle income groups. This generalization is somewhat mitigated by Legal Aid programs and by the tradition of judicially appointed counsel in criminal trials of serious degree but the substance of the point remains valid.

The time seems to be upon us when shifts in the tides of prevailing public opinion are overtaking or have overtaken, the bar's institutional attitudes in these areas. Professor Schwartz and Dean Pollak review the development in their papers, and Mr. Reichert too invites us to speculate further upon the effects of the new federal anti-poverty programs. The recent decision of the Supreme Court in *United Mining Workers v. Illinois State Bar Association* may have a portentous impact upon the structure of the profession. And, as Mr. Reichert puts it bluntly,

> The new leaders of the poor . . . want proper legal care, and the indications are that sooner or later, Republicans or Democrats, they will get it. I suspect that they will constitute a primary force in compelling the legal profession to face, much sooner than we anticipate, a plethora of problems about which we have long been aware but with which we have yet to come to grips.

Again, it seems to me, we must face up to the problems presented by Messrs. Schwartz, Pollak and Reichert. The effort of the profession to cling to an earlier structural model seems likely to be overtaken by a new diversity of institutional arrangements, as currents of change in the society sweep ahead. The American Bar Association itself has responded flexibly and constructively to the emergence of the new legal services programs, but the same cannot be said uniformly of state and local professional organizations. What should we do about it, and must we wait until we are pushed from the outside?

To Mr. Gossett, president-elect of the American Bar Association, and Professor Moore, we are indebted for two chapters that provide a broad substantive backdrop to our consideration of possible institutional modifications in the legal profession. No abatement appears in prospect in the national trend toward increasing urbanization and toward a society increasingly characterized by large-scale organizations. As both Dean Pollak and Professor Moore observe, the development of these large-scale structures will put increasing pressure upon the sense of significance of the individual and upon his freedom of mobility and expression. And, as Mr. Gossett demonstrates in an example drawn from the field of collective bargaining in a major industry, large-scale organizational units will, by force of their mass and momentum, increasingly cut across and infringe upon the interests of the public as a whole. In such an interdependent and close knit society, new legal balances will have to be found between the public interest and the latitude of mobility left to such organizations, argue the chapters, and new vehicles must be designed for countering the submergence of the individual. Manifestations of the trend may already be seen in recent auto safety legislation, in wage-price guide posts, and in community legal service programs.

Once more, if we survey the scene around us, it is difficult to disagree with the prediction made by these authors. If the past may be taken as a guide, we in the legal profession will play an active part in the emerging reconfiguration of American life and in the design of new social instruments and programs to respond to that reconfiguration. We shall be intimately involved as representatives, spokesmen and advocates for the individual and for collectivities, and as legislators and judges. If we are to perform these functions perceptively and effectively, our training as lawyers must make us sensitive to the realities of modern society around us and our own institutional arrangements must be in tune with it. Are we meeting those requirements?

In conclusion, I should like to suggest that for a moment we back away from our twelve chapters sufficiently far to see them as a whole rather than as individual pieces. Seen from this perspective they appear to me to state and restate a single, unified, powerful theme. They summon us to discern clearly the basic typology of modern American society and to contrast it with the basic typology of the legal profession. They depict in vivid color a rapidly evolving American society characterized by large scale units of organization, by a high degree of specialization, by rapid change, by emphasis upon research and innovation, by educational differentiation by the orchestrated use of different skill levels and by an ever widening circle of the members of the society who are able to assert a claim of right to participate in *all* the benefits of an affluent society. By contrast, the legal profession in the United States is seen to be characterized by a slow rate of institutional evolution, a small-unit organizational pattern, an absence or even denial of specialization, a unitary rather than differentiating conception of what it is to be a lawyer, a monolithic educational system without a clinical component, a static professional training pattern, an almost total absence of research and managerial innovation, tension between practitioners and centers of intellectual inquiry, only a rudimentary pattern of continuing education participated in by only a small fraction of the potential users, the absence of a recognized and utilized class of paraprofessionals, and an economic reward system that is strongly predisposed to service the needs of those who are best able to pay.

This typological disparity may be misleading. It may be possible to demonstrate that despite the apparent institutional incompatibility the legal profession is in fact able to perform, and is performing, in a responsive and satisfactory way in response to the needs of America's modern society. But the task before us, as I see it, is to tackle that precise question, to weigh and critically assess the chapters before us, and their implications, and to make our own judgment as to whether the time has come when changes in the institutional apparatus of the legal profession are in order and what those changes should be.

To borrow from Harrison Tweed, "I have a high opinion of lawyers. With all their faults, they stack up well against those in every other occupation or profession. They are better to work with, or play with, or fight with, or drink with than most other varieties of mankind." We of the legal profession have a reputation, which in my judgment is deserved, for possessing a special capacity for dispassionate analysis, a clear-eyed regard for the facts, an open-minded willingness to look at a problem from every side, a human historical perspective that enables us to perceive problems in their full context, a nose for detecting trouble in advance, and a talent as conceptual architects to design imaginative adaptations to head it off.

When a non-lawyer effectively tackles a problem with a similar set of instincts and skills, we pay him tribute; we say that he handled the matter in a very lawyer-like way. The problem before us in this Assembly is ourselves, the institutional arrangements of our profession and in a significant degree, the future of the legal order of the people of the United States. I do not doubt that later observers will say that the participants in this American Assembly handled their task in a very lawyer-like way.

Wilbert E. Moore

1

Forthcoming Patterns of Social and Political Structure

The art of prophecy now commands considerable attention. The American Academy of Arts and Sciences has a Commission on the Year 2000; there is a British Commission on the Next Twenty Years; a periodical called *The Futurist;* a French series of papers called *Les Futuribles;* and these represent only samples. No government agency, no large private corporation, and no important professional group is without its own corps of forecasters, nor will they be—to make yet another prophecy—in the foreseeable future.

The interest in the future arises from the perception of present social change of unprecedented scale and speed. The future is interesting and challenging because it is uncertain. I do not refer to the uncertainty about whether mankind will even have a future, although that question adds bite to any attempt to see ahead. Rather, my reference is to such less apocalyptic questions as how our polity, economy, living arrangements, and styles of life will differ from those of today. These are puzzling enough to concern us all.

The attempt to descry the future would be easier were we better equipped with reliable knowledge of the causes and course of social change. Speculative and intuitive analysis of processes of social change is an art of long standing—witness De Tocqueville, Holmes, and Veblen. Yet the processes of social change have become the subject

WILBERT E. MOORE *is Sociologist of the Russell Sage Foundation. He taught sociology at Princeton University for more than twenty years. A past President of the American Sociological Association, Dr. Moore is the author of numerous books, including* Industrial Relations *and* The Social Order *and* Social Change.

of more disciplined consideration only recently. For example, attention to system dynamics was long suppressed in such fields as my own discipline of sociology. Our conceptual models of society led us to ask questions about interdependence, equilibrating mechanisms, and possible deviance, but not about sequences. Similarly our methodology, including our efforts at quantitative precision, has been oriented to cross-sectional views of social relationships and not to examining their trends. The same is perhaps true, broadly speaking, of economics, jurisprudence and political science.

It is to be hoped that intellectual resources of the social sciences may be improved in this respect, but doing so is not our mission here. The issue is raised, rather, as a matter of caution: the array of verified principles relating to the paths of change in contemporary complex societies is in fact meager. We are in the curious position of being better able to stipulate what "must happen" in the modernization of traditional societies (though mostly without precise sequences in mind) than we are to formulate what will continue to happen once a specified degree of modernization has been attained.

Although the most prudent advice is thus to be cautious, since it is also important to predict and control outcomes, it is equally necessary to be brave.

Forecasting: Methods and Rationale

Unless forecasting is to rest solely on supernatural revelation, it must be based upon assumed relations between the past and present, and present and future, and upon the assumption of some order or system of interacting elements. In retrospective analysis, which is to say history, we have felt a confidence about assuming such relationships that is markedly stronger than is felt when the system of assumed relationships is projected forward. Nevertheless, there are components of forecasting that correspond to the components of historical analysis. In the paragraphs that follow we shall outline some of the tools of the prophetic trade.

THE COMPONENTS OF FORECASTING

Despite the conspicuousness of social change, important characteristics of the social order are likely not to change, but rather to *persist* into the future just as they have persisted from past to present. Many of our customs and institutions demonstrate hardy powers of survival. Illustrations particularly relevant to our main concerns here include the processes of composing differences in attitudes and interests through democratic processes, compromises in inter-group negotiations, and judicial processes of litigation. Insofar as such processes have persisted over long periods in the past, it is to be assumed they will persist in the future.

A second basis of prediction is the *continuation of orderly trends.* For example, age-specific mortality rates of various age-groups have declined at a remarkably regular rate; so also has there been a regular increase over time in the proportions of youths of relevant ages attending secondary schools and colleges. Some trends are straight-lined, others are not. The rate of urbanization, for example, must slacken as the proportion of the population living in urban areas approaches unity. The point is that orderly trends can be identified in the past that can be expected to continue, within varying margins of uncertainty. Trends of this sort are the basis for predictions about population size, economic productivity, air pollution, oil consumption and the like. And such predictions are ones in which we may have a reasonably high degree of confidence.

Predicting *discontinuous change* presents much more severe problems. These difficulties cannot be fully explored here. But whatever the difficulties of predicting discontinuous change, the problem is not always one of sheer conjecture. Some changes in long-term relationships may represent the completion of a process. For example, there used to be an inverse relationship between relative affluence of families and the number of children in them, a relationship that no longer holds securely. The effacement of this relationship seems to signify the virtual completion of a process, that of diffusing knowledge of contraceptive techniques and attitudes favorable to their use throughout all sectors of society. For all income levels, children now compete with other possible consumption expenditures as a matter of deliberate choice, rather than representing ignorance and error. A similar phenomenon is the failure of the hours of work to fall much below 40 per week over the last 25 years, even though in industrial countries they had steadily fallen over the previous century.

Finally, much of the course of social change is not truly mindless or autonomous. On the contrary, a very large proportion of contemporary change is the outcome of planning, ranging from planned technology through research and development expenditures to planned urban environments or modes of political organization. To have a fairly accurate picture of the future of social activity that is the subject of planning, it is necessary only to know what the plans are and what is the likelihood of their fruition. It is tolerably clear, for example, that information processing will be quite different 10 years from now because IBM, AT&T and others plan to make it so and have every prospect of carrying out their plans.

TELEOLOGY AND TELEONOMY

The great and growing importance of planning brings us to the rationale of forecasting. In this regard, there is a helpful conceptual distinction between teleology and teleonomy. Teleology is the description of a future goal and the behavior oriented to achieve that goal; teleonomy consists of predicting that part of the future which probably *cannot* be controlled and making prior ameliorative or adaptive adjustment to that state of affairs. The essence of the relation between forecasting and planning is the effort constantly being made to increase the teleological capacity—planning—and to reduce the effects of inevitability in future situations.

As to certain dimensions of the future, the degree of uncertainty can be sharply reduced by paying close attention to the implications of facts now known, and laying plans accordingly. The most conspicuous of these dimensions is population. Society has extremely small power over the effect of both death rates and birth rates on the labor force, short of inhumane measures. The labor force of the year 2000 is pretty much at hand and its age structure is predictable with very little margin of error, short of catastrophe. The size and age structure of the labor force in that year can thus be taken as a given factor in a whole variety of projecting and planning such as that required to deal with urban congestion, demand for schools, labor input, and various kinds of economic production. This is possible because we may assume, as a factor of social *persistence,* that repugnance to genocide will continue, and therefore that people born today will be living and breeding tomorrow and for years to come.

A SELECTIVE FOCUS

Post-industrial societies will differ from each other, and not just in details, because they will reflect different histories and will continue to rely on differing forms of social control and tension-management. Our principal focus in what follows will be American Society, without explicit attempts at wider generalization. Moreover, the range of structural change in America itself is too large to permit an adequately brief summary. Among several possible ways of focusing selectively, the most appropriate for present purposes is perhaps to concentrate on certain pervasive *processes of change*—processes that impinge on all such institutions as the family, the economy, and the polity. These processes include differentiation, organization, and participation. Each of these at the same time comprises several sub-sets of social transformation and intersects with others.

Differentiation

By "differentiation" I mean the tendency of individuals and groups in the social community to be different from each other in attitudes, styles of life, special interests, and other respects. Despite mountainous mole-hills of prose from subterranean critics of contemporary society, I can find no substantial and credible evidence for the dismal doctrine of "mass culture." The supposedly stultifying standardization produced by the mass media has resulted at most in some superficial commonalities: fashions, fads, and the transitory "in" vocabulary and status symbols. Yet even language, which would seem most subject to standardization, retains its authentic regional accents, and all sorts of other differences abide and abound. In countless other aspects of life, beneath superficial similarities lie important and perhaps increasing tendencies toward differentiation. These tendencies can perhaps be summarized in the word "specialization."

GROWTH AND SPECIALIZATION

Continuing specialization of roles and organizations is often taken as a datum in the analysis of social change, a kind of prime mover not itself explained. Yet the phenomenon of specialization is by no means inexplicable. I suggest that in American society we can identify three sources of specialization:

1. The growth and increasing density of population, providing opportunities for specialization and virtually assuring it;
2. The rapid growth of knowledge and of rational technique, so that any individual can command only a small portion of the total stock;
3. The rapid expansion of options in both products and practices, permitting discretionary choices and novel combinations by eclectic mixture.

Occupational specialization is certainly the most conspicuous form of rapid differentiation of adult roles. An aspect of technical changes in productive processes, and the one that invited the most critical comment, has been the *dilution* of skills through the subdivision of tasks. But this is only part of the picture. At no time has this form of specialization been the unique or sovereign tendency, since an increasingly complex productive system has also demanded new skills and new skill combinations. The long-term trend, indeed, has been toward an *upgrading* of the minimum and average skill levels, and the most modern productive technology requires production workers who have a large measure of machine mastery rather than subservience.

Occupational specialization reflects the intersection of two phenomena, the increased size of units (business organizations, government structures, urban communities, etc.) and the increase in useful knowledge (various sciences, technologies and sub-technologies). Occupational specialization is the process by which the possibilities and imperatives of advancing useful knowledge are translated into productive tasks in the context of increasingly large social units. Yet just as the less-skilled worker is threatened by actual displacement by mechanization, the highly skilled worker and the professional are threatened by technical obsolescence if he fails to keep pace with the expansion of relevant knowledge, and the modern manager or adviser is by no means exempt from the demand to be a learner throughout his career. Indeed, the manager and top echelon professional are now faced with unprecedented complexity, for in most instances they can no longer pretend to be leaders and exemplars by being more skilled than their subordinates. Their prime roles now are that of coordinator of specialists and integrator of related bodies of specialized knowledge. In performing these roles, the manager and high-level professional suffer impairment of their authority in proportion as their tasks of coordination become more complex.

Specialization is also exemplified in the wondrous range of organizational forms, not only to produce and distribute goods and services or to govern and maintain order, but also to prosecute special interests or indulge various recreational and expressive activities. Although many organizations may "just happen," much time and energy is now spent in inventing organizations. Organizational specialization has gone so far that it is difficult to find a broad-purpose—the sociological term is "functionally diffuse"—organization beyond the family. Some genuine neighborhoods exist, and a few genuine communities, such that their inhabitants find within them a full range of residential, occupational, cultural and political resources. But such social units are becoming increasingly exceptional, and few are immune to the divisive or at least fractionizing effects of specialized organizations—from the multiplication of government agencies at all levels to McDonald's refinement of the quick lunch counter.

Still another type of specialization is that in what may be called style of life—housing, recreational habits, cultural interests. Styles of life will continue to permit eclectic choice. For the lowest income sectors, market choice is of course radically restricted. For all others, the tremendous variety of alternative goods and services permits wide discretion. This means that income is a poor predictor of life styles, and that education and occupation will predict part of the differences better than income levels. This in turn means that present ways of describing the needs and preferences of various sectors of the community in terms of income groupings will become less and less reliable as guides for action and for planning. There are not high, low and middle income groups, but there are myriad sub-groups cross-cutting income levels.

Specialization, whether of occupations or organizations or styles of life, poses problems of coordination, of greater or lesser severity. Among the instruments of coordination are of course law, legal process and legal institutions, so that the burden of effective coordination can be expected to fall ever more heavily on them as on other coordinating agencies. We shall return later to the problem of organization, for coordination is by no means automatic or self-regulating.

INEQUALITY, OLD AND NEW

The notion of America as a "classless" society has been pooh-poohed by scholars, but, in my view, with decreasing justification. Not that the United States has ever had a genuinely equalitarian social order, nor is that precisely the direction of change. Rather, the semblance of hereditary strata, never absolute, has been steadily eroded by strong social and economic mobility from one generation to the next and by the lack of wide gaps in most status distributions in our society. The closest approximations of genuine strata are found at the very top and very bottom of income or other status differentials. Neither of these "classes" is impermeable, but there are strong tendencies to self-perpetuation. For the substantial majority of the population, however, social groupings are interpenetrating. Although the term "middle class" is used to describe this majority, that term suggests a homogeneity which does not exist. Rather, there are multiple gradations on one or another bases of ranking, the distinctions are often fine and somewhat arbitrary, inconsistencies abound, and mobility is widespread between generations and within careers. Again, the tendency of Americans to identify themselves in polls and sample surveys as "middle class" may be more accurate than the views of critics who find this behavior amusing. In light of this perceived sense of basic similarity and equality, the subtler differentiations between individuals and groups according to various forms of specialization become more significant.

We should not leave the subject of inequality without a comment on poverty, now so much in public discussion. Aside from the aged and those having some sort of disability—which constitute a fair portion of the poor—the problem of poverty mostly involves the hereditary poor. As long as there is a range of income distributions, those at the lower end are of course relatively poor. But if the range is relatively narrow, the minima tolerably high, and the avenues of mobility by merit open, the inequality would be relatively consistent with our professed values. The present concern arises because these conditions do not exist for some clearly identifiable sectors of the community precisely at the time when they are increasingly characteristic of most sectors of the community.

Current and prospective difficulties include:

Urban Negro protest—The general rise in levels of income and opportunities has left some segments of the population behind—mainly Negroes and some rural whites. As poverty became distinctively a minority problem, it has become increasingly invisible to substantial portions of the population. Renewed visibility, however, has arisen from the concentration of the Negro poor in central cities, and from political protest and civil disorder. But this sort of visibility excites anxiety rather than sympathy in much of the majority population and hence inhibits collaborative efforts toward amelioration rather than promoting it. In any case, it must be expected that protest and unrest will *increase* as the most abject poverty is alleviated, as long as relative deprivation remains conspicuous.

The false promise of formal education—The increased reliance on formal education as a mechanism of mobility may have actually decreased the opportunities for the members of one generation of an impoverished minority to escape the social and economic limits of their parents. To the degree that formal education displaces mechanical aptitudes, athletic ability, or entrepreneurial skill as mobility opportunities, the occupational system becomes less open despite other expanded opportunities. To an increasing degree the failure of youngsters to do well in school is both a personal tragedy and a social waste, for the educational system is not well designed to identify and develop the talents of those who are not "bookish." To avail the benefits of formal education requires access to a highly motivated environment, and want of access to such environments is the salient characteristic of cultural deprivation, which in turn is what formal education is supposed to overcome. Considerable social ingenuity will be required to remedy this structural defect in American society.

GEOGRAPHICAL REDISTRIBUTION

Another form of social differentiation, beyond specialization and the differentiations within the broad middle class, is that represented in geography. The geographical relocation involved in urbanization, so dominant a tendency in recent decades, might at first glance appear to represent a force for increasing homogeneity of our population. Certainly the rapid pace of rural-urban migration, together with the impact of modern transportation and communication on towns and villages, has radically reduced the "cultural" and even the organiza-

tional differences between city and country. (This is another example
of "completion of process," discussed earlier.) However, the urbanization process has led to new forms of differentiation that seriously
challenge the capacity of "inherited institutions" to cope with the
complexity of the megalopolis.

The "invasion" of central cities by Negroes (and, especially in the
East, by Puerto Ricans) partially duplicates a long-established pattern
of ethnic concentration by successive immigrant groups. However, the
assimilation of ethnic groups into the main stream of American life
has proved to be conspicuously more difficult where "racial" distinctions
are drawn. Dispersion of Negroes, occupationally and especially res-
identially, appears to be a very slow process. Meanwhile, and in some
part owing to the concentration of Negroes in central cities, the process
of suburbanization goes on apace. In larger metropolitan complexes,
the Balkanized political structure of suburbia is preserved as a hoped-
for barrier against the vicissitudes of the urbanization process. Moreover, as between separate suburban political sovereignties further
differentiations take place, not only by income level but also by other
social characteristics; some suburbs are quiet, some "swinging," some
"cultural" and some frankly recreational. Yet the common problems
of metropolitan areas—air and stream pollution, traffic congestion,
the provision of public services—are difficult or impossible to solve
by traditional modes of political organization. Again, substantial
social inventiveness will be required to avoid an increasingly chaotic
style of social differentiation.

PLURALISM

The notion of American Society as a "melting pot," assimilating diverse national and ethnic stocks into a single, homogeneous amalgam,
had the disadvantages of most metaphors: exaggeration. Traditional,
regional, ethnic, political, and religious differences persist. These differences are of course partly effaced by the appearance of new axes of
differentiation—witness the fractionizing of the Boston Irish when
elements of their progeny moved up professionally, educationally and
financially. But the traditional sources of differentiation have not disappeared, so that the result is an even more fast-growing pluralism than
before, as the cases of Louise Day Hicks and Robert Kennedy indicate.

Much of the growing pluraliism is manifested in socially neutral
preferences, such as those in cuisine, artistic taste, or form of recreation. Other aspects are tolerable disagreements that can be worked out
through established processes of articulation and negotiation, chan-
nelled through regularized divisions—as in political parties. If alle-
giances shift on successive issues, and regroupings of position are made

fluidly, the society is not threatened with divisions that would be dangerous to collective survival. But the proliferation of divisions may result in subdivisional pockets whose ties to others are too weak and too few to permit their participation in alliances. This condition, for which the overused term "alienation" is not inappropriate, can be explosive. Watts, the white "ethnic" neighborhoods in some Northern cities, and the Klan-dominated towns in some Southern states are illustrative of this condition, and critically challenge the capacity of our conflict-resolving mechanisms.

Organization

Virtually everything that engages more than one person's interests gets organized in American society. The independent craftsman, tradesman, or professional is a diminishing category; many a repairman handles the accounts of franchised dealers, and many a professional nominally in private practice is in fact in group practice or partnership, and thus not operating in solitary splendor (or squalor). As William H. Whyte complains in *The Organization Man,* traditional individualism becomes steadily eroded by the conformity-demands of organizations, which exist prior to the individual's tour of duty, and which will survive his possibly disruptive acts. This tendency is unmistakable and carries with it perplexing and even sinister implications. Yet it is important to be clearer than we often are about the character and value of the "individualism" that we see being displaced.

To a very large extent, the traditionally treasured individualism was not a pure and simple ideal, but had its highest relevance in the notion of an atomistic and impersonal market for goods and services. And since organized production and organized distribution have been characteristic of industrialism since its inception, "individualism" often came to mean little more than the privileged irresponsibility of exploitative employers. At most it often meant individualism by default, rather than a design to accommodate individuals who did not exactly fit into the conventional arrangements. If we are to take seriously the threats to individualism that organizations present, we shall have to embrace a more sophisticated and purposive concept of individualism than we have in the past.

Why should organizations multiply, and become more complex? Certainly a major part of the answer lies with social differentiation, already examined. And the character of contemporary differentiation is such that common understandings and unspoken consensus must be increasingly rare. In such circumstances it becomes increasingly necessary that aims be stated clearly, that means for their achievement be worked out, and that formal groups be set up for mobilizing effort and assigning tasks to participants. It used to be difficult to distinguish between apathy and simple contentment with ongoing arrangements; now apathy means a genuine withdrawal, for informal arrangements do not serve, and formal ones require positive participation. Development of formal arrangements for positive participation, in the conventional term of political sociology, is the process of bureaucratization.

BUREAUCRATIZATION

Bureaucracy is not to be equated with an evil, do-nothing complex of offices uniquely characterizing national governments. It is a type of organization to be found wherever numbers of specialized task-performers are coordinated in a system of graded steps of authority. The simplest measure of bureaucratization is the proportion of wage and salary earners—as compared with proprietors and the self-employed—among those gainfully occupied. It will be scarcely surprising that this ratio is highly correlated with level of economic development: in the United States this proportion exceeds four-fifths of the labor force. By this and any other standard tests, private corporations are at least as bureaucratic as public agencies, and the United States one of the most bureaucratized societies of all time, and becoming more so.

The reason is that size and specialization do produce formalization of rules and procedures, of job specifications and the jurisdictions of organizational divisions. Public and private bureaucracies share some irrational tendencies, which I cannot here document in detail: overstaffing with needless subordinates, who merely add to the entourage of administrators, but not to the efficacy of performing the mission; overstaffing with advisers of dubious value, on the chance that their magic will work, or on the grounds that some competitor has seen fit to add such an advisory function; a proliferation of essential silly rules and controls, based originally on some real or imagined human frailty, and mindlessly applied thereafter to otherwise conscientious and possibly creative bureaucrats. And they face the perennial, and insoluble, problem of balancing centralization for the sake of uniformity and decentralization for the sake of efficiency.

Perhaps the most important feature of contemporary bureaucratic organization—and that feature grows apace—is its endeavor to predict, cause, and control social change, and not merely to react to environmental alterations. "Research and development" accounts for a growing proportion of corporate budgets, whether from their own funds or on governmental contracts. Universities, too, have greatly expanded research activities, to the degree that in most of the nominally private institutions more than half of the annual budget comes from Federal sources. To these components of "the knowledge industry" we must add research agencies within government and a great proliferation of not-for-profit organizations engaged exclusively in research. Technology has become a major component of investment policy, both private and public.

There is a very popular notion abroad in the land that technology is an automatic, autonomous, and indeed sovereign source of social change. This idea is, of course, much admired by technologists, for after all that makes them leaders, but it will not pass muster as a social theory. To a remarkable degree, in the modern world every economy or society gets about the technology that it deserves, or at least what it is able and willing to support. We have weapons rather than clean streams, moon shots rather than efficient urban transit, packaging machines but no depackaging machines because real decision-makers have allotted resources and mobilized talents for some changes and not for others.

In the allocation of resources to technology, the bureaucracies of today and tomorrow aim at two interrelated types of change. One is change in the organization of the organization itself—exemplified by management surveys, computerization of internal information systems, corporate and government agency reorganization. The other is change in the organization's relationship to "outsiders"—most significantly other organizations—exemplified by government agencies' development of new regulatory or programmatic schemes, corporate merger and diversification, new product lines of goods, services and power. Both types of technological development involve reformulation of rules and procedures, of job specifications and jurisdiction—questions of critical normative and ultimately legal and political significance. The technological restlessness represented by the size of "R and D" investment thus implies a continuous dynamic in bureaucratic structure and relationships, and hence a continuous dynamic in legal and political issues concerning bureaucracies.

There is another, and specially troublesome, aspect to the pervasively organized character of American life. To a growing degree decisions are "collective," made on behalf of others by persons in essentially fiduciary positions. Consider assets. Certainly the major part of our total national assets are held by units of government or by private corporations and various non-profit organizations. They are held in one form or another of trust, so that decisions about them are not made in the first instance by beneficiaries. Such powers in trust raise, as they have since the idea of the trust was invented, questions of conflict of interests, duty of diligence, and standards for exercise of discretion, all inherent in managing "other people's money." I do not suggest that we attempt to turn the clock back, to return to days that were better only through nostalgic distortion. I do suggest that the conduct of fiduciaries, whether public officials or corporate executives, is not clearly governed by rules that will assure equity to the various interests properly involved. One can confidently expect successive attempts to clarify rights and responsibilities, to make power "responsible."

VOLUNTARISM

The bureaucratization of productive tasks does not end the pervasive character of organization. Both interest-oriented and expressive associations appear to multiply faster than the general growth of population, and undoubtedly reflect the increasing formalization of relationship associated with urbanization, and the increasing differentiation of positions and life styles. Though organizations do offer new forms of social participation, a point to which we shall return, the voluntarism that they exemplify is not untainted. The interest-oriented association is *for* some cause and thus against others. Those whose interests would be adversely affected by the association's success are virtually forced into a counter-organization. The right to be a non-joiner is being steadily eroded, and about that we may perhaps be allowed a faint note of regret.

Participation

American society has always fallen well short of the democratic ideal of universal adult participation in political processes. Aside from residential, educational, and property qualifications for the franchise —qualifications gradually liberalized over the long term—the citizenry has exhibited considerable apathy. Some of the apathy certainly has been associated with lack of local community ties, poor education, and poverty, even if those impediments do not constitute forms of disqualification. The extremely low participation by urban Negroes in anti-poverty programs designed to elicit some sharing of decisions is now widely known, though civil rights activities have attracted somewhat wider participation. Indeed, there may be justifiable suspicion that conventional political organizations, and even novel ones that are externally sponsored, aim at co-opting rather than genuinely representing Negroes and other underprivileged sectors of the population. Yet, because the effort to achieve broader participation is recognized as a social and political necessity, we may continue to witness various forms of unconventional politics. New forms of participation may well challenge the constituted order, and may indeed here and there go well beyond the tolerable limits for the maintenance of public safety. Nevertheless, they do bespeak involvement rather than apathy, and may lead to genuine improvement in the society's operation.

There is a further development in all post-industrial societies that merits attention. All such societies have become "welfare states" in various forms and degrees. One consequence of such welfare policies is to enlarge the scope of rights and privileges that are regarded as incidents of citizenship to include things—often expressed in terms of money—that previously were allocated by competitive or essentially chance sources (such as property inheritance). What was before more or less opportunity is now regarded more or less as a right. Education has long since passed this route, as has the right to political participation. The right to participation in the labor force is now asserted by minority groups such as Negroes and majority groups such as women. And the claim of right is being extended to various services, including medical and legal ones.

Creeping socialism this may be—though many private corporations have long recognized certain uniform claims on services. I should prefer to call it creeping democracy as long as we keep private alternatives to public programs. Indeed, the nature of private alternatives may be the most critical task for those who would preserve as much of the "opportunity state" as possible in face of "welfare state" demands.

The very rapidity of contemporary change may lead to the mistaken impression that all is in flux. Yet some change remains gradual and essentially evolutionary. The family's emergence as the major source of personal integrity has been gradual. Our political system is also essentially evolutionary, though it could be argued that its change has been unduly slow in the management of such problems as those confronting metropolitan areas.

We should also note that some values and rules have a hardy survival power. Aside from such collective values as national patriotism and such commonly held individual values as longevity, health, and economic well-being, we also share such expectations as punctuality and trust. Perhaps even more important than these enduring values and expectations, and particularly in view of continuous differentiation, is the continuing reliance on the procedures for resolving differences. According to circumstances we rely on the democratic vote, bargaining and negotiation, and, if necessary, judicial processes that provide for litigation of disputes through advocacy on the part of adversaries. On the whole, these prove to be effective "tension-management" devices. Even if we may have to invent new ways of coping with problems, these are likely to endure.

William T. Gossett

2

Balances and Controls in
Private Policy and Decision-Making

Man's vision of the law changes with the changing facts of life—the perceptions, fears and aspirations by which the consensus of the nation assigns priorities to the basic purposes of the law. Ten years ago, we could have been directing our attention to "Law and Social Justice"; thirty years ago, to "Law and Social Security"; forty years ago, to "Law and Prosperity"; and, before that, to whatever was uppermost—federalism, states rights, national union, protectionism, expansionsism—in the national consciousness. Today we are concerned with social change itself.

If American democracy has a genius, it is the readiness with which its legal institutions and practices have accommodated shifting objectives without profound or radical change in fundamentals. Much of this has been due to insight into the broad social and economic context of the law, and to a general recognition that the law as applied must reflect rather than contest the expressed aims of the people. Much of it has also been due to instinctive processes in the democratic experiment—those processes that stem more from social faith than from a political system.

There is a silent consent among the self-governed as to the direction in which they are moving, the uneasinesses that they experience and

WILLIAM T. GOSSETT is President-elect of the American Bar Association and a past president of the American Bar Foundation. He has been General Counsel of Bendix Aviation Corporation and Vice President and General Counsel of the Ford Motor Company. In 1962–63 he served as Deputy Special Representative for Trade Negotiations. He now practices law in Detroit.

the restraints that they feel; and these things are spelled out in law-making, decision-making, and rule-making, only after they have surfaced from deeper and more irresistible currents. As Woodrow Wilson had it, with more than Calvinist orthodoxy, "Law records how far society has got—it is not a process of regeneration."

Mystique is repugnant to the legal mind. But it is not mystique that felt convictions, as distinguished from legislative acts or judicial opinions, are decisive legal events in an open society. This extra-institutional character of the law as a social instrument has been intrinsic to democracy in America in a way that is almost *sui generis*. It was implicit in the ventures that brought the colonial settlers here in the first place, and in the purposes and devices of the Constitution-makers. It is evidenced in the terms such as "covenant" and "compact" that cropped up in our earliest civil history—words that would never be found in the political lexicons of such institutionally pure democracies as those of ancient Greece. Democracy in America has been a social contract from the beginning—not just a method and structure of government—implying ideas of inherent right, inherent obligation, inherent restraint and inherent tolerance. As Charles Evans Hughes said, "Success in the democratic experiment lies in the extent to which the strong are harnessed, with bits and reins and blinders, and are induced to pull the democratic cart on a straight road without running away or upsetting it."

Balances and Controls

All this presupposes "balances and controls"—a phrase useful in pondering the relationship of the law and social order in those areas of industrial order and progress with which, as a lawyer, I have been most familiar. Balances and controls in themselves are neither legal ideas nor social ideals; in themselves they are not even instruments either for articulating the one or for realizing the other. They are at most approximations of desired effects, because if they were clear or absolute their result would be only stagnation: in perfect balance, by hypothesis, there is no movement at all. And everybody knows that "control" excites resentment in free men as a political or social technique, and apathy as a political and social program. It is significant that the Constitution-makers were more interested in "separation" of powers than "balance" of powers, and it probably was not accidental that the word "control" appears nowhere in the document they authored.

Nevertheless, balances and controls are relevant to the democratic quest. They serve not as rigid braking mechanisms but, so to speak,

as cam wheels—permitting complicated and sensitively adjusted movement in a complex social machine where the application of direct
power could cause (and has caused in the past) fearful havoc. The
need for adjusting mechanisms does not derive from inadequacies of
social conscience, which seems to me generally more, not less, acute
than in the past. It derives from the intricacy of social machinery. And
both the demands and the opportunities of the age in which we live
demand social machinery of unprecedented intricacy. Sometimes these
cam wheels will be made by the same forces that give rise to their
need. Cardozo observed in *The Growth of the Law*, that "sooner or
later, if the demands of social utility are sufficiently urgent, if the
operation of an existing rule is sufficiently productive of hardship
or inconvenience, utility will tend to triumph." But when "later" is
not soon enough, conscious effort is required to redress balances. Some
such effort may be necessary in certain kinds of conflicts involving large
organizations in our society.

Third Parties to Disputes

In our devotion to traditional concepts of contract law, we are
apt to think of all legal relationships in terms of parties to a contract;
and our instincts dictate that any resolution of a conflict should
result in an equitable consideration of the interests of each of the
contenders. But the emergence of the large corporate enterprise as a
force in national life has brought a third factor into the matter—the
public interest—not a party to the contract, but having a very real
stake in the matter. The outcome of a bargaining contest between
an eighteenth-century wheel manufacturer and his journeyman could
hardly affect the general economy of the Confederation; the outcome
of a bargaining contest between General Motors and the United Automobile Workers could carry implications national and international
in scope.

As far back as 1934, Mr. Justice Stone, no iconoclast about traditional economic concepts, could observe, in full awareness of a changed
world, "Today what the Wall Street banker does may have serious
consequences on the fortunes of a cotton planter in Mississippi and
the farmer in Iowa. The textile manufacturer of New England is at
the mercy of the employer of child labor or underpaid labor in the
South." Today third, fourth and fifth parties—lookers over the shoul-
der—demand seats at the conference table and a friend in court: The
stockholder, the dealer, the consumer, the supplier, the press, the in-

nocent bystander—the elusive participants, passive or otherwise, that we call the public.

This is the crux of the matter. So far as social order goes, neither the giant corporation, a necessary creation of our age, nor the industry-wide labor union, an inevitable counterpart, depend for their survival on external balances or controls to contain each other's power or to survive. In the plausible phrase of a perceptive contemporary economist, they "countervail" each other—but in the process third parties risk being ground to dust. When that risk becomes strong enough, either the principles of their own accord and in their own interest, must envision adequate horizons, construct adequate safeguards, and establish adequate restraints, or face having it done for them, ordinarily by government.

And that has often been the case. Controlling organization power indeed, has been the major continuing preoccupation of our domestic history since the Civil War. When all else fails, the establishing of balances, often involving controls, is a task thrust upon government, whether it likes it or not, and which it can ignore only at its own risk. Performing that task is an exercise in constitutionalism, because achieving realistic balances and exercising effective controls is the essence of constitutionalism. Arthur N. Holcombe has put the case well: "A good constitution means at least for a time a stable equilibrium of forces. The best constitution would provide an opportunity also for the gradual readjustment of the balance between forces, changing in strength at different rates and in different directions, without ever disturbing too much the general equilibrium."

"A stable equilibrium of forces," as Professor Holcombe indicates by his judicious use of the *caveat* "at least for a time," is never a *fait accompli*. One generation's equilibrium is another generation's imbalance. General external pressures, sensed rather than defined, swelling up in the local, regional or national community are a powerful factor, not necessarily in determining the policy of private entities, but in public judgment as to whether that policy unduly disturbs the equilibrium among the forces concerned.

The enlightened policy-maker or negotiator will take this very seriously into account, or he may find that he has won a battle but lost a war. For there are always articulate and watchful outsiders ready to undertake remedial action. Whether their motive is genuine concern, political opportunism, or social crusading is beside the point; if their thrust meshes with that of a third force in the community, either the private policy will be changed and decisions modified, or the third force will express itself in legislative or administrative action, possibly in litigation, and occasionally in consumer resistance or other private action.

Management vs. Labor

My own participation in this perpetual struggle for an equilibrium of forces that characterizes the free industrial society has been most considerably in the automobile industry. For a long time, it was assumed that the major forces to be brought into some kind of tolerable and workable balance within this huge industry were management and labor. The direct confrontations in contract negotiations epitomize and dramatize this—even though any negotiator worth his salt knows about how far his side is prepared to go before he begins the talks. (So, of course, does the negotiator on the other side.) The arrival at these positions, which follow extremely intricate analyses, calculations and planning, constitutes the making of policies that can have far-reaching effects, for the company or union directly involved, for the industry as a whole and for the entire economy—not excepting, in some instances, the world economy.

These implications are recognized by the participants. Negotiations are not entered into lightly; they are hard-headed sessions, conducted by serious and responsible men, and they are basically decision-making mechanisms—deciding the fundamental economic question of wages, working conditions, and employee benefits for a specified future period. This bargaining process seems on the surface in itself a balance and control, for it removes a very major decision from the exclusive domain of either management or labor and forces each to take into account the other's position, with due regard, of course, for general economic conditions and the public attitude toward the parties. But the process, on the whole, has not worked well.

In the first place, across-the-table bargaining can break down. One side's "final" position may be so far from the other's that the gap can never be closed. If so, economic brinkmanship on both sides may be involved. But factors other than economic expectations on one side or the other often are responsible—the internal politics of union leadership, for example, or managerial intransigence. Here the balance of forces can and often does result in stagnation, with a strong union and a resolute management equally determined to impose its will on the other. Strikes and suspension of operations result—the bankruptcy of industrial diplomacy.

There is, however, a major flaw in across-the-table bargaining even when it avoids a breakdown and consequent strikes and cessation of production; and in my observation it is inherent in the process. The flaw is the inclination to escape the immediate conflict by agreeing to terms that set off a never-ceasing spiral of wage and price increases. The progression and the context in which it occurs have become commonplace. As a contract approaches its expiration date, union leaders make public, to one degree or another, their demands in wages, fringe benefits and other working conditions. Management counters with the statement, with varying degrees of indignant emphasis, that the demands are impossible. Theoretically, the two sides enter into negotiations, as equals, to find out what is possible. But in actual practice management has no instrument on its side nearly as powerful as the strike.

Under the common law, the worker's right to quit working was balanced by the employer's right to discharge him. In the realities of twentieth-century industrial life, the old equation has become unworkable. The witholding of employment by an employer to enhance its bargaining position—denominated a lockout—is subject to practical limitations, especially in the case of a large employer. Since the employer cannot find replacements for its thousands of discharged employees, a lockout results in a work stoppage and consequent loss of production no different from a strike. The only advantage an employer secures by a lockout is tactical control of the manner and timing of the work stoppage. Then, too, although lockouts are legal when invoked for proper purposes in the bargaining process, they have not entirely lost the stigma that attached to them in the days when they often were used to undermine the union. In the public mind, therefore, lockouts tend to be regarded as beyond the pale of decency in labor relations, especially when used by one of the industrial giants. It appears as a practical matter, therefore, that the lockout is not readily available to the large industrial manufacturer, and no other instrument has evolved or been devised as an effective balance to the right to strike.

In these circumstances, bargaining almost invariably results in escalating the economic returns to labor, it being wholly outside probability that a union leadership could survive if its demands simply preserved the status quo, however acceptable that might be economically. Management, on the other hand, generally could not enter negotiations with proposals that wages and fringe benefits be reduced. Management is thus on the defensive from the outset and knows very well it is going to end up by making concessions to one degree or another —although it often knows very well, too, its concessions are not going to be quite so damaging to its own interests as claimed.

Generally speaking, contemporary collective bargaining results in settlements involving increases in wages and fringe benefits that are beyond the employer's capacity to pay in its existing earnings position and beyond its technical capacity to offset by improved efficiency. To meet the situation, management must resort to price increases. In an increasingly efficient operation and with expanding sales, these sometimes turn out to be more than adequate to meet the rise in labor costs and produce inordinate profits—which labor, of course, seeks to use as the basis for further increases in wages and fringe benefits during the next round of negotiations.

The Public Interest

This whole process seems to me a predictable inflationary influence in our economy, with consequent disturbing effects on the social order.

The inflationary pressure generated in the bargaining process in giant industrial manufacturing industries is transmitted to other areas of the economy; wages and prices in less vulnerable industries go up, then those in service enterprises, then those in the government service, and then the "price" levels in taxes and welfare benefits, such as Social Security. The chain of reaction is not always straight-line, but the general pattern has been unmistakable in the last two decades.

Beyond these effects, which are all disturbing socially as well as economically, there are others that can be more far-reaching in their consequences. There is no question, for example, that persistent rises in labor costs (along with the adoption of uneconomic shop practices imposed upon management by powerful unions) have been a contributing factor in reducing the number of daily general newspapers in New York City from seven in 1963 to three in 1966 and in eliminating competition among evening papers in that city altogether. It seems evident also that "cost-push" inflation in the construction industry, where relatively small employers are dominated by relatively powerful building trades unions, has been a contributing factor in pushing housing costs further above the ability of low-income groups to afford decent housing.

The public interest in these effects on journalism and housing, to confine attention to these illustrations, is very specific and very real. Preserving competition in journalism, meaning here the preservation of competitors, has always been a special concern—because it fills a special need—in the United States as a self-governing nation. Jefferson went so far as to say that "were it left to me to decide whether we should have a government without newspapers, or newspapers without

a government, I should not hesitate a moment to prefer the latter."
The decline of metropolitan press competition may have brought us
closer to government without newspapers than Jefferson might have
imagined. And, so far as the housing market is concerned, we know
that grievances over the cost and quality of housing are part of the
tensions in our cities that have brought them to the flashpoint.

In an age inhospitable to many kinds of small enterprises, there is
no reason why labor should pay the cost, in low wages and other sub-
average economic benefits, for a service essential to the entire community, whether it is newspapers or housing or anything else. And in the
case of the press, the possibility that the service can be supplied or sub-
sidized by government if it proves economically unfeasible for the
private sector is no answer, given the reasons for our concern about
the press. There was a solution in the case of the New York papers:
automation, with a resulting reduction in mechanical jobs on a sufficient scale to make possible wages for mechanical workers commensur-
ate with those paid for similar jobs in other printing operations. But
the unions would have none of it. As a result, all the jobs—mechanical,
editorial and clerical—were lost on four papers, which disappeared in
the wake of extended collective bargaining sessions that were deeply
injurious to the public although it possessed neither a determining
nor even a participating voice. Somewhat similar if less drastic consequences have been felt in the construction industry, railroads, and
shipping.

Under present conditions, to return to the title of this paper, apparently there is no effective balance or control that can prevent the kind
of damage to the public interest that was brought about by contesting
private parties either in such cases as the New York newspapers or in
the economic escalation that charaterizes the bargaining rounds in most
large industries. Presidential guidelines have tended to collapse because
there are political inhibitions that disincline an incumbent administration or a Congress to make them effective. That occurred in 1967
when a wage increase guideline figure of 3.2 per cent which the
Johnson administration had established was shattered disdainfully in
several industries as new labor contracts were written to anticipate
improved efficiency and to provide for increases in the cost of living.
On the other hand, in the automobile industry, among others, automatic cost-of-living increases had been written into the old contracts
and had, in fact, provided increases every year during the lives of the
contracts. Nevertheless, increases far in excess of the guidelines were
sought and received, the government being or feeling powerless to
counter the clearly inflationary threat.

The Device of Arbitration

There is strong and understandable pressure from the public to establish arbitration machinery to resolve labor disputes that may bring about strikes having repercussions endangering the public good. This pressure is especially strong in labor disputes in public transportation systems. It would be comfortable, indeed, to submit such matters to truly impartial arbitrators. But even if we had arbitrators who were in fact impartial—a difficult thing in itself—the arbitrators' task would be essentially that of fixing wages and working conditions. And it is hard to see how arbitrators could decide those questions without also determining prices and profit margins as well. In that case, of course, the countervailing powers of management and labor exerted as built-in controls through the bargaining process would be neutralized and abandoned.

Mr. Justice Brandeis seems to have foreseen this comparatively early in the evolution of labor-management relations when he wrote,

> Arbitration implies and involves the shirking of responsibility by the chief parties to the dispute. The burden of the task of adjustment is shifted onto the shoulders of some alien tribunal. The result is that employer and workman fail to get the discipline they ought to have, and they are prevented from obtaining that intimate insight into one another's needs and difficulties without which essential justice is likely to be missed. But beyond that, the arbitrators are rather likely, from the very nature of the task, to hand down a wrong award. They may easily miss the heart of the difficulty, because they are not in the midst of the actual struggle.

Mr. Justice Brandeis' thought that arbitration would be an insignificant factor in the prevention or settlement of disputes was expressed at a time when industrial power was still unilateral—on the side of industry. With his enormously sympathetic insight into the unhappy plight of the workers of his own generation, he apparently did not foresee that labor would one day wield a power in many ways equal to that of the corporation and in some ways its superior. Certainly, the major preoccupation of progressive democracy during his period on the bench, from 1916 to 1941, was curbing the excessive powers of the business elite whose decisions, though privately made and privately accountable, could affect the lives of everyone. Countervailing power that could curb corporate power or bring it unwillingly to terms was not yet enough of a reality to pose the dilemma that currently makes arbitration a seemingly attractive avenue of escape.

The "shirking of responsibility" feared by Mr. Justice Brandeis refers, I think, to the propensity of the parties, when arbitration is in the offing, to make excessive demands on the theory that the arbitration will result in down-the-middle compromise of opposing positions. In any event, arbitration is essentially authoritarian inasmuch as it ends up telling private entities the policy they must follow and the decision that has been made on their behalf. In a free society this is a novel and worrisome device, born of desperation, perhaps, but nevertheless hardly congenial. Yet because industrial bargaining is organized as a bilateral process, and treated as though it involved only a bilateral conflict, no alternative to arbitration seems to appear.

There is an essential paradox in the push, as it seems to be, toward arbitration of strategically important labor-management disputes. The whole thrust of industrial democracy since the reforms of the first Wilson administration was directed—and appropriately so—toward the reconciliation of political freedom with economic freedom, on the ground that the former without the latter is empty and barren. Yet the effect of arbitration is to substitute, in place of democratic safeguards and controls, the application of administered decisions to questions that can affect everyone's economic prospects. These decisions are not always arrived at under procedures consonant with due process, are not generally subject to review, judicial or otherwise, and in their nature cannot be justified or criticized by reference to rule or principle. It seems no exaggeration to say that resort to arbitration for industrial disputes could lead to the same "freedom," full in political form but empty of economic substance, that Wilson's New Freedom undertook to reform.

In a society as complex and industrialized as ours is today, there seems to me to be a danger that easy resort to the device of arbitration might very well deter us from more venturesome and creative efforts to bring into closer accord our democratic aspirations and our economic development. Any movement toward more arbitration, whatever its form and whatever its surface conveniences, would turn us away from the main direction of our political development, which has been the slower process of adapting or extending traditional safeguards to new problems, new situations and new opportunities as they arise. It would turn us away, too, I think, from a realistic and comprehensive approach to the fundamental problems of assuring justice to both sides in disputes and at the same time assuring that the public interest, convenience and necessity will not be done permanent violence by the outcome.

Legislative Intervention

The impulse to intervene by arbitration in relations between major industrial and labor organizations has been ad hoc—through executive action or, less often, by special legislation. But the idea of intervention in private organizational conflict by general legislation has not been ignored, particularly in areas outside labor relations. This is not surprising. In view of the permeating effect that decisions of private entities such as major corporations can have upon the total life of the nation, there is little dispute anymore that they are appropriate objects of governmental concern. This has been reflected in the growing willingness of the American electorate to intervene through law in the workings of the economy and in the affairs of private business.

The reason for this is neither punitive nor suspicious; it is basic: the concentration of economic strength in the hands of a relatively small number of large corporations. It has been estimated that the two hundred largest American companies now control one third of the manufacturing assets, not just of the nation, but of the entire world. Obviously, such corporations, and hundreds of others approaching them in importance, are so big, so powerful and make so large an impact on the welfare of society that they must come under public scrutiny and governmental attention. Indeed, today though we speak of "private" policy or "private" decisions, decision-making by the great industrial complexes is not regarded as private except in the strictest technical sense. (Even in that sense corporate business is hardly "private": more individuals are qualified as shareholders to vote for the directors of our largest corporation than are qualified in forty-four states to vote; in the third largest corporation, there are more shareholders than there are voters in twenty-one states.)

Both legislatures and courts now look at industrial corporations as quasi-public institutions—arms of the state, subject to some of the legal principles that control the conduct of public utilities and government agencies. This view of the large corporation opens up broad vistas for legal control over business, its policies and decisions as well as its actions. For all practical purposes, this means that the government can and will take action when specific problems arise that appear to jeopardize community welfare. If existing law is involved, litigation may be initiated or administrative hearings convened. If there is no apposite law or judicial decision, a legislative inquiry is likely: and it is almost axiomatic that new laws will be enacted in the wake of any Congressional investigation inspired by the complaints of enough people that they have suffered some real or imagined damage. The alleged injury may be to individuals or groups having a special relationship to the corporation, as has been the case, for example, with the automobile dealers in their relationships over the past decade or so with the manufacturers. It can involve relations between the corporation and the public at large, as is the case with the recent automobile safety campaign or that concerning "truth in packaging."

During the 1950's, the automobile dealers revolutionized their legal relationship with the industry, diminishing the rights of the manufacturers and enlarging those of the dealers. At the beginning of the decade, the manufacturers had the right to terminate the dealer's franchise substantially "at will," to increase the number of dealers in a market area, to choose successor dealers for existing dealers, to approve or discourage buying and selling agreements between outgoing and incoming dealers, to allocate products among dealers during periods of shortages—virtually to conduct their affairs with their dealers as they saw fit.

Largely through litigation, legislative innovation and administrative procedure, in the ensuing decade the range of freedom open to the corporation in formulating and executing policy in these areas was cut back severely. Committees of the Congress, in the five-year span between 1955 and 1960, held no less than thirteen different hearings to elicit testimony on bills to regulate in one way or another the distribution of products in the automotive industry; and in August of 1956, The Automobile Dealer Franchise Act was enacted. This had a salutary effect upon the policies and attitudes of the manufacturers and upon the terms of dealer franchise agreements. In addition, during the same period of time, fifteen states adopted laws designed to pass from the manufacturers to the dealers control of policies regarding automotive distribution within the state. In effect, they require motor vehicle manufacturers, factory branches, factory representatives and distributors to obtain special licenses each year in order to engage in business in the state.

Generally speaking, all these developments in the legal climate of manufacturer-dealer relationships came about either in response to new conditions or in reaction to claimed abuses. For one thing, in earlier decades of the motor industry, a dealer had a score or more manufacturers from whom he could choose to do business if he found conditions with one manufacturer onerous or objectionable. Today he does not have the same range of choice—at least for domestic products —and is often in the position of clinging to the franchise he has or being left with an expensive establishment and no domestic product. For the dealer just going into business in a new market area, the growing concentration of production has also narrowed the franchise choices.

As to abuses, there is probably little question that in the years following World War II and during the Korean War, when there was a shortage of products, some manufacturers showed insufficient understanding of their dealers' problems and too little restraint in dealing with them. As a result, the dealers, lacking sufficient strength individually to cope with the manufacturer on equal terms, did so collectively by forming strong trade associations under militant leadership—a very interesting parallel to the path that labor took in American industry generations earlier. Characteristically, they resorted to legislation, or threat of legislation to gain concessions from the manufacturers, or to correct imbalances of power that they could not achieve through direct bargaining. It requires modest powers of prophecy to predict that this pattern will repeat itself in other industries and under other circumstances in years to come.

Boomerang and Public Opinion

If a partisan group overreaches in its effort to rectify an imbalance of power, it runs the risk of suffering setbacks from the very sources from which it sought relief. In the course of the struggles described above, the automobile dealers suggested that the Federal Trade Commission be given fuller legislative authority to regulate factory-dealer relations. But they withdrew their support of the legislation upon realization that it would lead, in addition, to FTC regulation of dealer relations with the public. Nevertheless, the legislative intervention they had invited had its effects on them, as evidenced by the legislation requiring the "manufacturer's suggested price" to be shown on a label on each new car—a device aimed at improving the public's bargaining position as against the dealers'. And it is evident that the dealers cannot expect permanent immunity for their servicing and used car sales policies, to say nothing of the possibility of regulation of dealer activities in products other than automobiles. In short, once an area of imbalance is drawn into public attention, the public concern is unlikely to abate until all broadly shared grievances have been considered.

Public opinion is also a powerful factor in its direct effects, that is, aside from influencing legislation. This is a slow and evolutionary process, but it has a pendulum quality that produces reactions against excesses or abuses at either end. To instigate effective control of activity in the private sector, public opinion need not originate or culminate in mass uprisings. If there is a sore spot, a solitary crusading journalist can spark political action. It will be recalled that Lincoln, when he met Harriet Beecher Stowe, the author of *Uncle Tom's Cabin,* commented, "So you're the little woman who wrote the book that made this great war." It was also "a little woman," Rachel Carson, who wrote *The*

Silent Spring, instigating broad-scale investigation and regulation of the use of insecticides, and not so much reflecting as creating public concern. And a striking example of the capacity of a single book to mobilize public opinion is Ralph Nader's scathing denunciation of modern motor car design, *Unsafe At Any Speed*. It led to widespread airing of the problem of rapidly accelerating highway fatalities, to dramatically re-opened hearings before a Senate Subcommittee, and ultimately to the enactment of sweeping new legislation in the National Traffic and Motor Vehicle Safety Act of 1966.

Before Nader's impassioned and skillful piece of advocacy, there had already been hearings before the Federal Trade Commission, several Congressional committees, and the General Service Administration. A number of major bills were pending in Congress, including provisions for a national highway traffic safety center, a federal safety car project to serve as a prototype for manufacturers, the application of GSA safety standards to all cars whether government-ordered or not, and the establishment of federal standards and grades for tires. In a field new to federal intervention, action remained in suspense, however, until the Nader book struck with powerful impact upon the press and the public and provided decisive impetus to the legislative initiative. And it was recognition of the force of public opinion that transformed the automobile industry's position on the legislation from resistance to acquiescence.

Private industrial policy-making and decision-making that affects labor and consumers is ultimately controlled in one way or another by the pressures that formulate public policy and inspire public decisions. Insofar as it succeeds in shaping private decision-making to the expectations of general public sentiment, it is clearly preferable to more direct forms of bringing private interest in line with the public interest —such as arbitration or legislative controls. This is so because private adjustment is both more flexible and more consistent with the ideals of an open society. The process may be slow and halting, but it is nonetheless inexorable. Yet, preferable as this process may be, there is some doubt in my mind that it is good enough. For it is essentially a trial and error process that must have time on its side. Where time is not on the side of private "voluntary" adjustment, it runs the risk of precipitating extreme measures where the public mood is impatient or the trend of events does not admit of delay. Nor do I find the theory of countervailing power—concentrations of power neutralizing one another or forcing them in the right channels or checking their excesses—any more adequate. This strikes me as a simplistic natural history approach to a problem that has social subtleties unsusceptible of solution by what amounts to accident.

In the broadest sense, we are dealing with a constitutional problem, and we should treat it with corresponding seriousness. Both in the internal systems of large corporations and labor unions and in their external relationships, technical and economic developments have created such vast power concentrations that we may need to develop new applications of constitutionalism to keep them in gear with the broader public interest. In the apt phrase of Professor William G. Andrews, they are Leviathans that might become Frankensteinian monsters. The aim is to afford these gargantuan entities which are so necessary to modern life the freedom they need to act, to interact and to react, without leaving the effects they may have on society wholly to chance, to improvised political countervention or to arbitrary ad hoc edicts. It is the classical problem of seeing that no power is granted that is not also checked. No trustworthy solution to this problem has been found except constitutionalism.

The Need for Constitutionalism

For the purposes of this discussion, constitutionalism may be defined as an internally applied system of granting, limiting and checking of powers. Frequently these powers are implicit rather than explicit, accidental products of socio-economic evolution, for the most part unfettered by rules or built-in safeguards. The suggestion here is that it may be time to explore possible mechanisms within the internal organizational structures of corporations and unions to bring about effective limitations and checking of powers. This is by no means to imply that a general revision of the external limitations and checks embodied in the statutes relating to business and labor may not also be required in due course.

Many students of corporations see some form of constitutionalism to be no less essential to the interests of shareholders. Shareholders have become a kind of third party in the affairs of the corporation—looking over the shoulders of management but without much more authority than complete outsiders. This view, first clearly set forth thirty-five years ago by Adolph A. Berle, Jr., and Gardiner C. Means, has been well summarized by Professor Wilbur G. Katz, of the University of Chicago Law School:

> Stockholders of the modern corporation think of themselves as passive investors, like bondholders, and not as owners. Most of them have no thought of actually participating in the selection of management. In the modern corporation, management is in practice a self-perpetuating oligarchy. It is management which selects the board of directors and not the other way around. Meetings of stockholders and the proxy solicitation

machinery are no more than elaborate rituals by which management nominations for the board are ratified. The rare outbreak of a proxy war and the even rarer unseating of management serve only to highlight the absence of political responsibility in most modern corporations.[1]

Similar reservations have been expressed about accountability in the exercise and transfer of leadership in labor unions. The late Professor Selekman, of Harvard, observed,

> . . . although union officials and corporate management start from opposite sides of the pole—one elected, the other appointed—they end up pretty much at the same point: both are highly centralized, authoritarian governors of power systems. . . . And often the trade-union president, like the corporation president, may have a decisive voice in his succession. In what we might call personality structures, too, union and corporate presidents have a striking resemblance. They are both strong men, enjoy power, and do not suffer dissidents gladly.[2]

As in the corporation, unions now have effective power in private decision-making and policy-making that bears importantly upon the lives of millions, both within the unions and outside them. Unions have the right, upheld by the courts, to decide the conditions under which new members will be admitted or excluded. They fix policy with regard to huge pension funds that can exert powerful influence in the investment community. They can also wander far afield of matters of direct economic self-interest in pursuit of causes that will rally support of their leaderships and give their organizations point and purpose. As Gus Tyler, long associated with the International Ladies Garment Workers Union, put it, "To keep the membership in line, the union needs issues, hot issues, daily issues." Such aggressive and adventurous spirit in organizations having great economic and social influence constitutes a force no less potent than that of the giant corporation.

Both corporations and unions have gone through enormous transformations in the last quarter-century. On the whole, their decision-making and policy-making have been responsible and conscionable. Yet their private choices are fraught with public significance, frequently more sweeping in their reach and more forceful in their impact than legislative acts, judicial decisions or executive orders. As the situation stands, these choices are still treated as essentially private ones—private in origin, private in method, private in accountability. We have been trusting to natural countervening pressures and increasingly to arbitration to keep the forces of private choice in balance, under

[1] Wilbur G. Katz, "Responsibility in the Modern Corporation," 3 *Journal of Law and Economics*, 75 (October, 1960), 75–76.

[2] B. M. Selekman, *A Moral Philosophy for Management* (New York: McGraw-Hill, Inc., 1959), p. 182.

control and responsive to the public need and interest. But we may have been crowding our luck. We are certainly putting a strain on the capacity of our democracy to remain open and truly autonomous. The time has come, perhaps, to extend constitutional safeguards to private entities that rival government instrumentalities in the expanse and intensity of their powers. Perhaps also these entities will see that they should share the initiative in bringing this about.

Louis H. Pollak

3

To Secure the Individual Rights of the Many

We have come a long way, and not in all respects a forward way, from our constitutional beginnings. Today, to be sure, we are masters of a continental domain, and are better fed, more productive, more literate, and vastly more numerous than we were one hundred and eighty years ago. (*All* our shots are heard—and many are fired—around the world.) And as we look to the coming decades, we can, with confidence, chart further increases in every quantifiable category, save one—the land we live in and are rapidly filling up. But what is less than clear is whether our capacity for making the substance of our lives approximate our aspirations—our system, as it were, for the production and distribution of values—is not becoming dangerously attenuated. We have food enough for almost everyone, and, if we use more wisely the skills we already possess, we should be able to create more jobs and build more and better houses and schools and hospitals; but it is not at all certain that, in the course of developing more processes and programs to service more and more people, we are not cutting down the per capita share of freedom.

In venturing these concerns one perhaps may postpone, as premature, Orwellian anxiety about the Big-Brotherism of the future (though

Louis H. Pollak *is Dean and Professor of Law at Yale Law School, where he has specialized in constitutional law. He has practiced law and served in the State Department. A director of the NAACP Legal Defense Fund and Chairman of the Board of the National Office for the Rights of the Indigent, Dean Pollak is the author of* The Constitution and the Supreme Court: A Documentary History.

present planning for national data banks does little to calm the nerves); and one may even pretermit (in the hope they will prove transitory) the stresses currently introduced into our national life when large numbers of young men are ordered to military service in a cause which arouses their deepest skepticism. But, on more prosaic levels, we certainly can take little pride in such shabby despotisms as, for example, the denial of unemployment compensation to claimants whose sabbatarian convictions compel the refusal of Saturday employment (see *Sherbert v. Verner*, 374 U. S. 398 [1962]), or the withholding of welfare payments from mothers whose non-compliance with the degrading "man in the house" rule is detected through midnight searches. See Reich, *Midnight Welfare Searches and the Social Security Act*, 72 Yale L. J. 1347 (1963). To scotch such dangers—indeed, to foster emancipating institutions—is a matter of paramount political concern. A thesis of this paper is that our traditional paladin—the judiciary—cannot be expected to patrol the full length of our ever-extending ramparts. We need re-enforcements, including some who are equipped to venture outside the walls and wage offensive warfare.

"All Virgil Wants Is to Be Let Alone"

This is not meant to suggest that our judges are failing to fulfill their protective function. Quite the contrary: by and large, our judges have, ever since the *School Segregation Cases* (347 U. S. 483), and on a wide number of fronts, displayed an increasingly firm commitment to the realization of our democratic values. The problem is one of institutional competence: courts are too limited in manpower, and their eighteenth-century arsenals are too unsophisticated, to keep pace with the range and complexity of today's and tomorrow's governmental functions. Our principal tribunal—the Supreme Court—operates not very differently from the way it did one hundred and sixty-five years ago, when Marshall decided *Marbury v. Madison* (1 Cranch 137); and that was a time when most of those who staffed state governments and the other branches of the national government believed, with Jefferson, that "that government is best which governs least." In such a setting, the role of judicial review was expected to be one of intervention by negation in those instances in which other agencies of government (whether state or national) were venturing beyond their authority. It is to be remembered that even Jefferson—least hospitable to judicial power—contemplated that the judges would play such a role. "In the arguments in favor of a declaration of rights," he wrote Madison in 1789, "you omit one which has great weight with me, the legal check which it puts into the hands of the judiciary. This is a body, which if rendered independent & kept strictly to their own department merits great confidence for their learning & integrity. "

The notion of the ideal government as the non-doer, the leaver-alone of citizens, has long since vanished, never to return. Yet the myth-picture—with government and citizen at opposite ends of a see-saw, and the court as the fulcrum—retains its powerful appeal. Consider this recent news dispatch from Round Mountain, California:

> For two months mountaineer Virgil Gray has stood off U. S. marshals and govrenment surveyors with an arsenal of shotguns and rifles to keep them from "trespassing" on his 40 acres near this Northern California hamlet.
>
> Government agents have approached Gray's primitive cabin on Buzzards Roost Rd., from time to time only to take off when the 53-year-old wood-chopper pointed a gun in their direction.
>
> Three weeks ago Gray took pot shots at a team of surveyors when they crossed his property line 30 miles northeast of Redding. No one was hit.
>
> The stubborn mountain man, believing the government is doing him wrong, is holding up completion of a $700 million 900-mile power line from Bonnerville [sic] Dam on the Columbia River to Southern California. It had been scheduled for completion early this year.
>
> But Gray refuses to let the Federal Government run the power line over his land.
>
> Asst. U. S. Atty. Rodney Hamblin declared: "Come hell or high water that power line is going to be built through Gray's 40 acres."
>
> "We believe the U. S. government is offering a fair and reasonable amount of money—$1,200—to use four and one-half acres of Mr. Gray's land for the line."
>
> The mountaineer was ordered to appear in Sacramento federal court in November regarding the matter. He never showed up. Although an order was issued for his arrest, no one has been able to serve it.
>
> Gray doesn't have a phone. The U. S. Attorney's office in San Francisco wrote him a letter informing him that he would have to negotiate or be jailed.
>
> He ignored the letter.
>
> U. S. District Judge Thomas J. McBride finally ruled last week: "Gray simply cannot stop agents of the federal government from a project which Congress has directed shall be built."
>
> The judge gave Gray until Jan. 1 to allow a representative of the government on his property for a conference or U. S. marshals would encircle the 40 acres, move in and arrest him.
>
> Wednesday Hamblin extended the deadline two days.
>
> Gray is adamant. And his wife, Jane, insists:
>
> "He ain't gonna budge. The way he figures, he bought and paid for the property. He don't want the power line on his land."
>
> "It's a free country. It ain't Russia. All Virgil wants is to be let alone.

And I don't blame him." [*New Haven Register*, Jan. 4, 1968, p. 35, cols. 2–3.]

The dispatch goes on to explain the background of Mr. Gray's difficulties:

> Gray has refused to discuss the matter with anyone since the impasse began two months ago. He won't talk about it with friends, relatives, newsmen or federal agents.
>
> When anyone comes to his tar-papered log cabin, he grabs a gun or two and runs into the woods.
>
> "That man's been took all his life, ever since he was a young boy. He don't trust nobody."
>
> "Virgil had to quit school in 6th grade to help support his folks. He got crippled in a mill accident. Never got a penny out of that."
>
> Gray's oldest son, Ronald, 20, explained: "My father couldn't draw insurance on a back injury because the mill said it happened when he was in the Navy during World War II."
>
> "The Navy claimed it happened when my father worked at the mill. So he was laid up for years with a bum back, in and out of hospitals and stuck with all the bills."
>
> Mrs. Gray continued: "We had a place up the road at Burney before this one. Virgil got throwed in jail in an argument with neighbors over the property line. Nobody listened to Virgil's side of it then. They never have. So what's the sense in talking about the power line." [*Id.*, at col. 3.]

Far from blaming Virgil Gray, one can't escape a grudging admiration for that beleaguered man. And one pities him, for he will most assuredly lose the unequal contest, and the power lines will be strung across his forty acres. But before the issue is foreclosed, Virgil Gray is entitled to compel the government to satisfy a federal judge that a substantial public purpose does justify the taking and that the proposed compensation is fair. For Virgil Gary, no demonstration of necessity will be persuasive, and no compensation will suffice. And he and Mrs. Gray may even come to the rueful conclusion that we are no freer than the Russians. However, the judicial inquiry and assessment are also important to the Grays' fellow citizens, who have come to rely on the "learning & integrity" of an independent judiciary as somehow setting our country apart from the totalitarian nations.

Today, no depth of forest, no mountain fastness, can insulate Virgil Gray from the claims of society. In the three-quarters of a century since the closing of the frontier, the power lines of the nation and the states have spun their inexorable web across the land.

But the almost-certainty that Virgil Gray cannot keep his forty acres inviolate does not mean that the right he cherishes—to be "let alone" —has disappeared. What has disappeared is the right of spatial isolation. But a more important right, or group of rights, has begun to emerge in its place. "The makers of our Constitution," wrote Brandeis forty years ago,

> undertook to secure conditions favorable to the pursuit of happiness. They recognized the significance of man's spiritual nature, of his feelings and of his intellect. They knew that only a part of the pain, pleasure and satisfactions of life are to be found in material things. They sought to protect Americans in their beliefs, their thoughts, their emotions and their sensations. They conferred, as against the Government, the right to be let alone—the most comprehensive of rights and the right most valued by civilized men. *Olmstead v. United States,* 277 U.S. 438, 478 (1928) (dissenting opinion).

Brandeis' insistence on the sanctity and centrality of "the right to be let alone" was more than rhetoric. It was argument in support of the proposition that the Supreme Court should set aside criminal convictions obtained in callous disregard of the individuality and self-respect of those who are the targets of the law-enforcement process— in the particular case, convictions based on the testimony of government agents who, covertly and without judicial authorization, listened in on the incriminating telephone conversations of the accused. As was not uncommon, Brandeis was writing in dissent. But within the last few months, the Supreme Court has turned that dissent into prevailing constitutional doctrine. *Katz v. United States, 36* U. S. Law Week 4080 [Dec. 18, 1967].

This instance of fresh judicial response is representative of many decisions in recent years in which the Justices have shown themselves to be increasingly sensitive to the importance and ubiquity of "the right to be let alone." Some of the examples which spring immediately to mind are likewise drawn from the realm of criminal procedure: the addition, to the arsenal of defensive weapons available to the accused in state as well as in federal trials, of the Fourth Amendment's exclusion of unlawfully-seized evidence and the Fifth Amendment's privilege against self-incrimination; also, the newly-strict insistence, in state and federal prosecutions, that in-custody interrogation be hedged around by rights of silence and access to counsel.

But avowal of the sanctity of the individual is, in the judicial view, more than a catalogue of courtesies to be observed in the station-house and the courtroom. It is also a reminder that there are limits to the regulatory authority vested by the people in their governments, state and national—limits which must be observed if our governments are to remain both republican in form and democratic in spirit. Among the plainest examples of this are the Court's insulation of marriage from anti-birth control and anti-miscegenation laws. But to distill from these instances the familiar warning that one's home is one's castle, says both too much and too little.

Too much because, as a moment's reflection reminds us, the home is not and should not be impervious to all community superintendence: the home is not a sanctuary in which one can with impunity hoard gold or explosives, or abuse one's children. Too little because, as further reflection suggests, one does not surrender his individuality by leaving his own threshold—be it to pray, to read, or simply to wander. What the Court said in *Katz* of the Fourth Amendment (in rejecting the claim that the *publicness* of a phone booth robbed the occupant of protection against official eavesdropping) seems generally applicable to the protective provisions of the Constitutions—the amendment "protects people—and not simply 'areas'. . . ." 36 *U. S. Law Week* at 4081.

But the promotion of individuality has further public dimension. A society which is at once republican and democratic depends upon individual (sometimes alone, sometimes in concert with others) assertion in a host of public forums—the common; the town meeting; the marketplace; the church; the library-museum-auditorium. And, as Charles Black has pertinently intimated in "The Lawfulness of the Segregation Decisions," 69 *Yale L. J.* 421, 429 (1960), the constitutional concept of *citizenship* should be regarded as carrying with it immunity from official insult or constraint in whatever public precincts one is entitled to enter—an observation which seems to have *a fortiori* weight with respect to those public activities one is *required* to participate in. Plainly enough, governmentally-mandated racial segregation in public schools and in the armed forces constituted such official trespasses on the private integrity ("the hearts and minds") of persons participating in the community's public processes. And it may be ventured that public school programs of released time, flag salute, and prayer, foundered on a contiguous reef.

It would disrespect Brandeis to argue that he contemplated each of these problems, and each of these solutions, when he propounded a constitutional "right to be let alone." But it does not seem impertinent to suggest that what for him was "the most comprehensive of rights" implied a core idea: a freedom to cultivate one's own garden, heedless of the surrounding landscape which others (indifferent; hostile; or, perhaps worst of all, well-meaning) may have designed.

As Brandeis was zealous to define and protect the most precious liberties, he was also scrupulous in insisting on the limited competence and authority of judges. He would have been among the first to recognize that traditional judicial capacity to protect identifiable individuals against conventional forms of state coercion may not connote judicial aptitude to mitigate, on behalf of thousands, the state's omnivorous benevolence. Certain current examples of problems judges can only deal with marginally may illustrate the difficulty.

STOP AND FRISK

In the Supreme Court's 1967 Term, there were pending before the Court certain criminal cases which challenged the increasingly common police practice of "stop and frisk." Under this practice, a policeman may detain and search someone he finds on the street in a slum neighborhood—someone who looks "suspicious" but whom the policeman has no basis for arresting. The cases before the Court were criminal prosecutions growing out of "stop and frisk" episodes in which the process did in fact yield evidence of crime—e.g., a weapon, narcotics, etc. The validity of the challenged convictions turned on the admissibility at trial of incriminating evidence taken from one with respect to whom, prior to the "stop and frisk," the state confessedly had no adequate grounds for arresting or obtaining a search warrant. The question before the Court was whether the obvious infringement on a citizen's dignity and freedom of movement could be validated to the extent of sanctioning those criminal convictions which flow from that fraction of "frisks" that are fruitful. But, because the Court has power to deal only with those isolated "stop and frisk" cases which result in prosecution and conviction, the issues confronting the Justices seem shrouded in unreality. Fred Graham, of *The New York Times,* explained why:

> This shifting police emphasis from convicting criminals to preventing crimes suggests that the Supreme Court may be reaching the point of diminishing returns in its efforts to police the police by excluding illegally obtained evidence. According to the [American] Bar Foundation's experts, big-city police officials are coming to the conclusion that prosecution is often so cumbersome and punishment so inadequate that their manpower is better spent in "aggressive patrol" than in trying to get convictions. "Since there is no particular police concern with prosecution, evidentiary standards enforced by the threat to exclude the evidence illegally obtained do not deter the police from engaging in these practices," they concluded.
>
> This attitude on the part of the police seems to reflect a shift in public concern from "enforcing the law" to "reducing crime." Few people know what the conviction rate is in their community, but each year as the percentages climb, more people worry about the crime rate. The discovery that "aggressive patrol" can actually reduce the crime rate has had a sharp impact on big-city police emphasis.
>
> Thus, it seems likely that aggressive patrol will persist in the ghettos, despite what the Supreme Court says about stop and frisk. If so, a new and chilling element is entering the controversy over the "coddling of

criminals" by judges. For if the Supreme Court is losing some of its power
to "coddle criminals," then even those who have damned the Court for
placing itself between the police and the accused must wonder who now
remains with the strength and courage to do this when it should be
done. . . .[1]

DISCRIMINATION

Years of litigation conducted by the N.A.A.C.P. Legal Defense Fund
led the Supreme Court, in the *School Segregation Cases* and their
sequelae, to invalidate all governmentally ordained regulations keyed
to race. As the Justices well knew, not only up to but for many years
after the 1954 decisions, the Legal Defense Fund's systematic courtroom assault on segregation was substantially the only way of bringing
national power to bear on this most deeply corrupting of our social
ills. This judicial awareness doubtless played a shaping role in the
Court's recognition, a decade ago, that litigation is a form of political
action protected by the First Amendment. Thus armed, the Legal Defense Fund (which is the real forebear of our effective law-offices-for-the-
poor) broadened its programmatic litigation. Today it is asking courts
to exercise a far more extensive and continuing surveillance of other
branches of government. Recently, for example, the Legal Defense
Fund undertook

> . . . a suit to enjoin the construction of a link of Federal Interstate
> Highway 1–40 that would wipe out 80–90% of Negro-owned business in
> Nashville and isolate Fisk, Maharry, and Tennessee A. and I., Negro uni-
> versities, from the rest of the city. . . . The LDF is proceeding with its
> case against construction of the New Jersey College of Medicine which
> would wipe out homes in which 10,000 Negroes live, in Newark, New
> Jersey, without providing adequate relocation. . . . Similar cases are pro-
> ceeding against the Department of Housing and Urban Development with
> regard to an urban renewal project which would destroy a Negro and
> Japanese community in San Francisco without furnishing relocation, and
> with respect to a state road building program in Ossining, New York, that
> skirts all residential areas in its route until it reaches Negro sections which
> it is projected to destroy. To assist in these and other cases, the LDF has
> engaged the services of city planners in order to base the cases on housing
> and economic surveys of affected areas.[2]

The kinds of skills the Legal Defense Fund will deploy in preparing
its cases suggests the degree to which the cases may be expected to
reach beyond the normal judicial ken.

[1] "The Cop's Right (?) to Stop and Frisk," *N. Y. Times Magazine*, Dec. 10, 1967,
Sec. 6, p. 44.
[2] Legal Defense Fund Press Release, Jan. 1968, pp. 1–2. Cf. *N. Y. Times*, Jan. 16,
1968, p. 44, col. 3.

DE FACTO SEGREGATION

Possibly the most dramatic, and frustrating, index of the confining scope of judicial power is to be found in Judge J. Skelly Wright's heroic attempt, in his recent opinion in *Hobson v. Hansen,* to grapple with the inhumanities of the District of Columbia public school system (269 F. Supp. 401 [1967]). Judge Wright's starting point was, of course, the unassailable premise that legally ordained segregation is unconstitutional. From this he moved to an arguable, if not self-evident, condemnation of *de facto* segregation acquiesced in by school authorities. But Article III of the Constitution limits the remedies he can ordain; regrettably, he lacks authority to widen the boundaries of the District to bring in an appreciable number of white students. Similarly, there is great weight in Judge Wright's indictment of the "track" system as a callously administered device which consigns tens of thousands of (overwhelmingly Negro) children to systematic non-education; but the Judge is without power to appropriate the hundreds of millions of dollars needed to turn the District's school system from a custodial into an educational institution.

[To some extent, limitations on the institutional competence of the judiciary may be reflected in doctrines of "standing" asserted as barriers to judicial inquiry. But, although frequently overlapping, these functional and doctrinal considerations are by no means coextensive. See, e.g., *Flast v. Gardner,* 271 F. Supp. 1 (S.D.N.Y., 1967), rejecting on standing grounds (but with no attempt to show that courts were *incompetent* to try the issues) a citizen-taxpayer challenge to federal appropriations in aid of secondary education which were said to constitute impermissible assistance to church-related schools. In his dissent, Judge Frankel noted that "some non-logical nerve may tingle when the stark proposition is put that concededly unlawful or unconstitutional action is in effect immune from judicial scrutiny." *Id.* at 5 n. 4. In 1968 the *Flast* case reached the Supreme Court.]

These three examples by no means exhaust the instances in which courts are being asked to assert authority over unfamiliar and unfenced domains. The examples were selected as presenting certain common characteristics which may help to define a pressing problem in the design of political institutions.

In each of these three instances a court has been asked to assume the difficult role of making, and setting the stage for implementing, certain critical choices of social policy. [It may be urged that the "stop and frisk" cases, which test the propriety of a particular law-enforcement strategy, present the kinds of problems conventionally committed to judicial supervision. This is unquestionably true, to the extent that the issue before the Supreme Court is regarded as confined to the validity of the convictions under review; but if the "real" issue includes the propriety of "stop and frisk" procedures which do not result in arrests, the Court is being asked to resolve far more general questions about the power of the state to trammel citizen mobility. These are questions the Court may feel impelled to resolve in the state's favor or (perhaps more likely) avoid altogether, unless the Court feels able and ready to authorize widespread injunctions against patterns of police behavior it regards as oppressive.] Normally, democratic theory tells us, critical choices of social policy should be determined in the political rather than the judicial arena. But—someone will promptly be heard to say—there is nothing new in judicial choices which have the effect of changing social policy. From *Dred Scott* [19 How. 393] to *Carter Coal* [298 U. S. 238] (on the debit side), from *Milligan* [4 Wall. 2] and *Pierce v. Society of Sisters* [268 U. S. 510] and *Near v. Minnesota* [283 U. S. 697] to the *School Segregation Cases* [347 U. S. 483] and *Baker v. Carr* [369 U. S. 186] (on the credit side), the Supreme Court has been making fundamental social choices in substitution for those made by officials more directly responsible to the electorate. And of course this is true—and, we have come to believe, necessary and proper.

But there is a difference. In most of the great cases (whether "good" or "bad")—in, for example, *Dred Scott* and *Carter Coal,* and in the *School Segregation Cases*—the Court was asked to displace policy determinations wittingly arrived at by legislators and/or their accredited executive agents. In the cases which currently engage our attention, courts have been asked to act in situations in which, typically, responsible elective or appointive officials have made little or no effort to arrive at a comprehensive resolution of competing interests (except, perhaps, on so high a level of abstraction—['New Jersey has to have a state medical school, and it ought to be in one of the large population centers' or 'We ought to group high school children by aptitude']—or so low a level of particularity—['We'll have to add five acres to the medical school site for off-street parking' or 'We'll have to cut the budget for reading specialists by 25 per cent']—as to amount to abdication with respect to the real issues). In short, we are considering instances in which, typically, appeals are made to courts not *against* but *in default of* deliberate political decisions on central questions of policy.

This is not to say that no policies animate highway engineers, school superintendents and school board members, redevelopment administrators, HUD officials, and police commissioners. It is to say, however, that highway builders, state and federal, have as their single mission the building of highways to connect and/or circumvent large cities: from this perspective, plans which arouse the ire of middle-class neighborhoods had best be modified, not because the plans are wrong but because the objectors have some capacity for creating substantial political roadblocks; but plans obnoxious to slum-dwellers, or to bird-watchers, are bull-dozed ahead because the objections seem *irrelevant*—and the objectors lack power. It is to say that police commissioners are, for the most part, quite understandably more interested in raising the "clearance" rate and lowering the number of reported major crimes than in being civil to black drop-outs lounging on city streets. It is to say that school superintendents, while not unconcerned with imparting skills to "disadvantaged" children, have no real hope of making any headway until middle-class constituencies—constituencies with political muscle—recognize that appropriations for public education have to be doubled or trebled. It may be a palliative to appoint an associate highway commissioner for environmental equilibrium, a deputy police commissioner for police-community relations, an assistant superintendent of schools for "inner city" programs. But such official special pleaders are quickly isolated if they move beyond their limited, and often ephemeral, political base. Consider the difficulties encountered as civil rights gave way to crime-prevention in the hierarchy of politically appealing issues, by Harold Howe, of the Office of Education, and by Sargent Shriver, of the Office of Economic Opportunity.

The Claims of the Future

Our governmental mechanisms are caught in an acute dilemma, and one which is bound to increase in intensity year by year. Up to the 1930's, we were able to "make do" with a system of government which assumed that most people could manage their affairs on their own, or could help one another (through trade unions, charities, etc.) as necessary. The role of government was chiefly interstitial, providing services—schools, post offices, roads, licensing procedures— well understood to be beyond the scope or interest of the private sector. Direct governmental responsibility for support and care was confined to limited constituencies—e.g., the mentally ill, veterans, the blind, criminals. Just as the two great political parties made relatively modest demands on government (other than the privilege of office-holding), so too their rivalry with one another, although keen, was carried on within relatively narrow limits of social choice: the parties tended to divide more on geographic and vocational (and to some extent ethnic) lines than along lines of class or ideology. It was an era in which one could have talked with some accuracy about a politics of consensus, had the phrase then been fashionable.

Depression, war, rising population, and the desire of Negroes for more than technical emancipation, have changed all this. Belatedly, we have come to realize that government—the United States, jointly and severally, acting on behalf of the entire population—has and will increasingly have manifold and pervasive responsibilities to insure the housing, schooling, employment, medical care, income maintenance, and dignity, of the entire population. Our bureaucracies are not yet adequately trained or funded—nor centralized and decentralized enough—to perform these jobs. Our political parties are still prisms of narrow range, ineffective to refract a widening spectrum of claims. And, indeed, our outmoded legislative institutions are not equipped even to receive and in some intelligible way identify those claims which filter through, let alone equipped to resolve them in a deliberate way. Our task is to minister to tens of millions, in accordance with their democratically-arrived-at precepts, and with unremitting concern for the respect the entire community continuously owes to each individual member. We may not be ready for that task, but we have not the luxury of deferring it until our political institutions are in better repair. We must mend and amend those institutions even as we work within them.

Priorities and Principles

To make the various political institutions work will of course require major structural overhaul. With respect to one of the vital elements—the design (including what might be called the self-concept) of our legislatures—the drive for reapportionment is a real, if modest, first step. It was not by chance that it was the Supreme Court—the body which has so long exercised quality control over the legislative product—which took the lead in a process which should encourage the law-making branches, state and federal, to exercise their own responsibilities in better fashion, and to that extent diminish the Court's supervisory burden. Nor was it by chance that the Court chose as the premise of legislative reform the precept that "Legislators represent people, not trees or acres" [*Reynolds v. Sims,* 377 U. S. 533, 562]—a precept echoed by the Court's recent admonition to all government officials that the privacy enshrined in the Constitution "protects people—and not simply 'areas'. . . ." (*Katz v. United States,* 36 U. S. Law Week 4080, 4081 [Dec. 18, 1967]).

The people whom legislators must learn to represent, and administrators must learn to serve, are people hitherto substantially ignored by our political institutions. They are Negroes, Mexican-Americans, and Indians; they are the elderly; they are the poor of the slums and the poor of the tenant farms; they are those old enough to drop out, to be unemployed, to be drafted, but not to vote; they are those just old enough to vote, and far too old to give a damn. In the past, they have not asked enough from their country to have much interest in doing anything for their country. They have asked so little because, up to now, nobody has bothered to listen.

Listening and responding to those who live in the other America do not mean assuring the inhabitants some participation, even maximum participation, in the government of their alienated land. They mean assuring the maximum participation of all citizens in the government of their common and united land. Nor should we be deterred from insisting on the comprehensiveness of the nation (and of the constituent states) by separatist demands of those we have hitherto ostracized. Our history outlawed secession once, and with finality; neither bias nor guilt should induce us to vacate that judgment.

But our collective oneness with our country must not be permitted to obscure our individual inviolability—"the right [of each of us] to be let alone." We have long relied on the judiciary to protect this "most comprehensive of rights"; we must continue to place reliance, as Jefferson did, on "the learning & integrity" of that branch precisely because it has been "rendered independent." And, for however long our political institutions lag behind full awareness and full exercise of their responsibilities, we will have to continue to ask the courts to engage in a more searching surveillance than they find congenial. But, as people and programs multiply, we will be in growing jeopardy if judicial watchfulness is thought to be our single safeguard. It may well be that added watch-dogs—the ombudsman, for example, or a domestic strain of that fashionable breed—would be of help. But more is needed: the high resolve of political officials, law-makers and law-implementers, to take affirmative steps to protect and enlarge the liberties of those they govern. To the extent that the availability of judicial review has, over the course of our history, worked attrition in legislative and administrative vigilance to secure individual liberties, now is the opportune time for congressmen and aldermen, and for cabinet members and mayors and police commissioners and school superintendents, to begin to view their official obligations in more spacious terms. They must see it as their responsibility to exercise the liberating, as well as the regulating, powers of the charters they work under. Fidelity to the supreme law of the land requires no less.

4

The Quest for the Middle Range: Empirical Inquiry and Legal Policy

Law, in the shadow of science,
has given rise to great expectations.
—Edwin W. Patterson,
Law in a Scientific Age 3 (1963)

And gradually, very gradually,
the law might once again become
a learned profession.
—Robert M. Hutchins,
The Autobiography of an Ex-Law Student,
1 *Univ. Chi. Law Review* 511, 518 (1934).

I have two firm convictions, neither of which I will be able to follow, as to how best to proceed with a topic as old and as frustrating as the relationship between law and science. The first is that law and science each cover so much ground and touch at so many points that the topic can only sensibly be pursued in the seriousness and the spaciousness of book-length treatment. The second, taking a leaf from the case method, is that insight will best be gained by examining in rigorous detail an instance of the scientific study of legal phenomena to see at close range what scientific inquiry can and cannot do for law.

HARRY KALVEN, JR. *is Professor of Law at the University of Chicago. In addition to many articles for professional journals, he is the author and co-author of several books, including, with Hans Zeisel,* Delay in the Court *and* The American Jury.

My sense of dismay has been increased by the circumstance that in preparation for my current task, I elected to read the Carpentier lectures delivered at Columbia Law School in 1962 by Professor Edwin W. Patterson, entitled *Law in a Scientific Age* (New York: Columbia University Press, 1963). Professor Patterson was a most distinguished scholar, a dedicated and serious man, a master of private law, and one of the most influential students of jurisprudence of his time. One could not hope to come to the task with better equipment or more talent than he had. And yet as I read his book, it yields small insight and one comes away with a sense of the singular difficulty of the task.

Despite these misgivings, this is perhaps a good time to re-examine the issue. There has been a marked change in the past ten years. We have the beginnings of a literature, book-length legal studies with an empirical bent. The relevant shelf—which is still well under five feet—now includes such items as Jerome Carlin's two studies of the legal profession and Erwin Smigel's study of the Wall Street lawyer; the study of auto accident reparation in Michigan by Alfred Conard and his associates; the participant-observer study of the Oakland police by Jerome Skolnick, and the study of police procedures in arrest by Wayne LaFave; the experimental study of the pre-trial conference by Maurice Rosenberg; the studies of court congestion by Professor Rosenberg and his colleagues at Columbia, by Leo Levin and E. A. Woolley at Pennsylvania, and by Hans Zeisel, Bernard Buchholz and myself at Chicago; the study of the American jury by Hans Zeisel and myself; and the experimental study of the jury and the insanity defense by Rita James Simon. (At such list is inevitably somewhat arbitrary by way of inclusion and exclusion; some additional items are listed in the Bibliography.) Taking these dozen studies together for the moment, there are three remarkable things about them: they all were published in the past ten years; they represent sustained research efforts involving often five to ten years of work; and, finally, they are books. There has been nothing like them previously, and their existence marks a major change in the relationship of law and science.

Moreover, there have been a number of institutional developments. There are now social scientists who are full-fledged members of law faculties; for over ten years law teachers have been included in the select group of social scientists who spend a year at the Center for Advanced Study in the Behavioral Sciences at Palo Alto. There has come into existence a special association of lawyers and social scientists, the Law and Society Association, with its own journal. There are the American Bar Foundation, and the Walter Meyer Institute to sponsor interdisciplinary researches. There have been summer training institutes under the auspices of the Social Science Research Council, and the joint auspices of the American Association of Law Schools and the Russell Sage Foundation. And so on.

In brief, things are looking up.

Yet despite these good tidings and despite its shrewdness about the differences between law and science, my point put bluntly is that the law on the whole remains today gratuitously unscientific. Put less bluntly, we in the legal world need some literacy as to scientific method and as to the scientific idiom of exposition. Most important we need to develop some *taste,* and I use the word advisedly, in scientific inquiry. We are fond of talking about getting "the feel" of a rule of law; we need also to get "a feel" for empirical inquiry in law.

Since legal tradition dictates that one look back before he looks ahead, I shall first glance at the past relationship of law and science before attempting to confront the current moods, difficulties and prospects.

A Short, Fitful History of Science and Law

I would like to extract three themes from the history. First, to note the pattern of oscillation between optimism and skepticism; second, to consider whether we really have been "talking prose" for forty years, that is, doing empirical inquiry without naming it; and, third, to appraise the earlier hope that social science disciplines could be married to the law by collating existing social science texts with legal problems.

A short history of the flirtation between law and science can be written in terms of oscillation between simplistic optimism followed by chilling skepticism followed by a decade or so of silence and inaction, with the cycle then repeating. [This "historical" sketch is borrowed directly from Kalven, "Some Comments on the Law and Behavioral Science Project at the University of Pennsylvania," 11 *Journal of Legal Education* 94 (1958). Citations of the articles mentioned below as well as a few other references on the general theme are given in the Bibliography.] Thus, at the turn of the century we have Münsterberg announcing a grand prospectus for the wonders psychology would perform in making law, particularly the law of evidence, scientific. There is still a certain excitement in the dream he put forward in 1908 in *On the Witness Stand.* But he is promptly shot down in a merciless and funny law review piece by John Wigmore, *Professor Münsterberg and the Psychology of Testimony.* Time passes and presently the dream reappears. This time it is the Yale Law School psychologist, Edward Robinson, and this time it is the whole law that is to be revamped and made rational with the aid of science.

The book, delightful in its optimism, is entitled *Law and Lawyers,* and the date is 1935. The killer of the dream is Philip Mechem, then a professor of law at Iowa, and the counter essay is entitled significantly, *The Jurisprudence of Despair.* Another decade passes and a great law teacher, Underhill Moore, publishes his New Haven traffic studies, a heroic effort to take nothing for granted and to establish at least for one small corner of law some scientific truth about the relevant human behavior. The title is *Law and Learning Theory,* and the date is 1943. This time there is not even a rebuttal; there is simply silence. We come then down to 1950 with perhaps the most optimistic call to arms yet—Frederick Beutel's *Experimental Jurisprudence.* The skeptical rejoinder for the legal fraternity this time is made by David Cavers in a piece entitled *Science, Research and Law.*

This is of course neither a serious nor a fair history of the prior efforts, but highlighting the pattern of challenge and response may help make evident several points. Too often the dream of science in law has been put forward by those in flight from law. Law has been seen as a museum of irrational procedures and untested assumptions of social fact and behavior; science has been seen as the home of rationality; the shortcomings and hesitancies of science have been brushed aside in the conviction that anything would be better than what we have now. There are at least two difficulties with this stance. First, it is not the way to make friends and influence other lawyers, and, second, it is profoundly wrong. Indeed, it is profoundly unscientific. As FCC Commissioner Lee Loevinger has urged in a recent thoughtful piece on the theme of law and science, they are complementary not rival systems. Certainly one reason the rapprochement of law and science has been so slow is that the case for science has been put with a crusader's fervor, with science offered as the rival and superior way of managing practical human affairs. It is little wonder then that proposals to turn law upside down with the aid of science have met with a chilling response. The millenium will come sooner when the cause of science is embraced by those with a respect for the wisdom of durable institutions and procedures and a respect for seasoned experience; in brief, a respect for what the law already knows.

Moreover, the advocates of science have usually put forward prospectuses rather than concrete instances of fruitful collaboration. It was not what the scientist now knew but what he would find out if we gave him all our problems. This gave the point to Mechem's title *The Jurisprudence of Despair:* if we had to wait until science had the knowledge that was said to be rationally required, if we had to wait until then before making credibility judgments or handling criminals, the message of hope filled him with despair.

My second point about the past requires a brief autobiographical note. Some years ago I was invited to talk at a panel on law at the annual meeting of the American Sociological Association. I thought it would be a good stunt to go back to some traditional pieces of legal writing to show the sociologists that the law had really always had an empirical base, and that a large amount of undramatic factual inquiry had long been part of good professional legal scholarship. I selected some items that I recalled from memory as having a neat factual premise. The results on re-reading were harrowing.

One item was Roscoe Pound's speech before the American Bar Association in St. Paul in 1906 on *The Cause of the Popular Dissatisfaction with Administration of Justice* [reprinted in 8 Baylor L. Rev. 1 (1956)]. The speech is singularly famous in legal circles —for enthusiasts of judicial administration it approaches the status of William Jennings Bryan's Cross of Gold speech. Pound's address, which still retains considerable power, examines four grounds of criticism: difficulties that relate to all legal systems, difficulties peculiar to Anglo-American law, difficulties stemming from the American court structure, and finally difficulties arising from the environment of judicial administration.

In the course of his broad and generous review, Dean Pound sweeps through the waste of judicial manpower, the evils of concurrent jurisdiction, apathy toward jury service, the diseconomy of law in the form of case law, the degeneration of the law into a trade, etc. For our purposes, however, three features clamor for attention. First, he makes absolutely no effort to establish that there is any special popular dissatisfaction with the administration of justice. In a remarkable sentence in the second paragraph of the article we are told: "*It will be assumed then* that there is more than the normal amount of dissatisfaction with the present-day administration of justice in America." That is that; no need for Gallup, Roper or Lou Harris to inquire. Second, many of the reasons he offers, while a basis for rational expert criticism of the system, could not conceivably be causes of *popular* dissatisfaction in the sense that they were the sort of thing the man in the street would complain about. Finally, there is an eccentric burst of empiricism when he turns to the proliferation of appeals. He counts a sample of appellate cases and reports in exact percentages the sources of appeal: we are solemnly told that in 19.3 per cent of the cases in the volumes 129 to 139 of the *Federal Reporter* the issue was one of federal jurisdiction.

The speech is thus a monument to a certain legal attitude. It has an aura of empiricism but displays literally no interest in finding out whether its topic as defined has any reality, or whether its diagnosis has any validity. It is, of course, a speech on the causes of Roscoe Pound's dissatisfaction with the administration of justice and it is, therefore, not foolish despite its gross failure to provide factual basis for its central thesis. Moreover, its rhetoric of empiricism is effective.

One other item will suffice. It relates to a problem in the law of defamation and to an article in 1914 by Jeremiah Smith, a greatly admired Harvard law teacher and scholar, entitled, with the literary felicity of those days, *Conditional Privilege for Mercantile Agencies*. The problem was that arising when a credit agency, which for a fee furnishes to subscribers the credit rating of individuals, makes a mistake prejudicial to the subject's credit. Was this to be treated as libel, making the agency answerable to damages? Or was the agency to be given a conditional privilege, being exonerated so long as it had not deliberately falsified the report, a technique the law had employed to protect and encourage various other instances of useful communications? In 1908 the House of Lords in *McIntosh v. Dun* decided there should be no privilege, reaching a result contrary to that of several American courts. The English judges reacted with an amusing fastidiousness against what they regarded as no business for a gentleman, and accordingly held that the agency should bear the full risks of erroneous credit reporting. "The trade," said the Lords, "is a peculiar one."

Professor Smith wrote in criticism of the decision. As I remembered it, he had rested his case in part on the failure of the English court to recognize the importance of the credit reference in modern society, that is, on a sociological fact of contemporary life. On revisiting, however, I discovered that in a long article he had devoted only two sentences to the credit customs of the day and that his documentation was confined to a footnote reference to two cases in which *judges* had made the point.

Smith, who was always scrupulously exact in his legal analysis, did not feel it necessary to document social fact seriously. And yet, as with Pound, power of the article is not really weakened by this shoddy empiricism.

On analysis, it turns out, in the case of the Smith article, that no sensible purpose would have been served by a careful inquiry into the role of the commercial credit agency in modern life. As a matter of common observation we already know enough for the purposes of the problem. But the point for the moment is simply that like Pound so rigorous an analyst as Smith saw no need to confront and check his factual premise seriously.

We have after all been talking only law for forty years!

My last historical theme requires briefer comment. One strategy for rapprochement between the fields has been to attempt to collate law and science, to fit science texts to legal problems. This approach has special appeal to the lawyer scholar, because it means he can continue to work in the library where he feels at home and because he can continue to produce casebooks, although now they will be interlineated with non-legal materials. The most famous effort to utilize this strategy was that of the Columbia Law School during the late twenties and early thirties, an effort whose history has been definitively traced for us by Brainerd Currie. [Another noteworthy effort was that by Pennsylvania in the mid-fifties; see comments by Watson, Foote, Levin, & Kalven in 11 *Journal of Legal Education* 73–100 (1958).]

The collating strategy invites several reflections. There was never any reason to anticipate that the social scientist would have been putting the law's questions, and of course he was not. There is always, therefore, a considerable distance between social science learning and a given legal problem and the dream of systematically making one-to-one connections was bound to be defeated. For example, in psychology there were arresting studies of rumor which at first blush appeared to be just what the evidence scholars had been looking for to test the hearsay rule and its exceptions. But the studies dealt with the distortions caused by repetition of a given story, say, ten times. The law did not need to be told about hearsay ten times removed; its concern was with hearsay only once removed.

In a similiar fashion, the application of existing social science learning to a legal problem may become apparent only after research has been done directly on the legal problem. In our jury studies, for example, one of our findings is that juries do not hang if they are *initially* split 11 to 1, although they may sometimes end up hanging with only a single juror hold-out. A hung jury requires an initial faction of two or three, the minority juror apparently needing reenforcement to withstand the pressure of contrary group opinion. He cannot stand alone. The result is strikingly congruent to the well-known Asch and Sheriff experiments showing that a man could be made to doubt, or disavow, his own perceptions when placed in a group of role-players all of whom dissembled as to their perceptions. If, however, the subject was given at least one companion, he was likely to stick stubbornly to his opinion regardless of the group pressure. We knew ahead of time of the Asch and Sheriff studies but could not sense their application to the problem of the hung jury.

The upshot is that collation of texts will not take us very far and that if science is to help on legal problems, research will have to be done freshly. This means that there is still a long road indeed to travel.

There is a postscript to this. We may have said too quickly that no one should have expected the social scientist to have put the legal questions. Does not the failure of law and social science to mix more zestfully require some explanation from the social science side too? Why has not the law as phenomena seemed of sufficient interest to the social scientist to move him to put *his own* questions to it and to study it not as law but as part of his study of society? There is thus the possibility that we may have a kind of no-man's land between law and social science—a potentially rich field for inquiry which neither side cultivates.

Law and the Management of Scientific Doubt

We turn then to the present scene.

It will be helpful to put to one side the application of science in the litigation of particular cases. The trial of an issue of fact is not simply a scientific exercise but a practical affair conducted with stringent deadlines and without the scientist's prerogative of suspending judgment until further evidence is in. A trial is an exercise in the management of doubt, for which the law has rules about the burden of proof that science does not need. And we might note that the proposals for impartial medical experts in personal injury litigation appear to have been the result more of a desire to ameliorate court congestion by increasing settlement pressures than the result of a desire to make the law more scientific. In short, the use of science to establish particular facts in the litigation of individual cases seems to me like the use of other resources for the same purpose, and altogether unexceptionable. It is not here that we find difficulties in the relation of law and science.

Our concern rather is with the utilization of science in the law-making process, that is, to the establishing of legal norms through the documenting of social facts. While science may occasionally have its impact on the common law-making process, we are perforce dealing primarily with its possible relevance to constitutional adjudication and to direct legislation.

It may prove safest to begin with an example, taken, not surprisingly, from *The American Jury*.

It has been a major point of criticism of the jury that it did not understand the case. The challenge, inferred from the fact that the jury has no special training for its task, was presented most strongly some twenty years ago by Judge Jerome Frank. Frank, pointing up the random sequence of proof at a trial and the belated giving of instructions, argued that a trial of any complexity imposed on the jury heroic feats of memory and judgment which he thought must be clearly beyond its members' competence. The upshot he felt was that trial by jury was a process in which the jury applied law it did not understand to facts it did not get straight. The jury system was thus a supreme instance of the law's irrationality.

In *The American Jury*, Hans Zeisel and I marshall several lines of proof which persuade us that Judge Frank this time was wrong. The main research strategy of the study was to secure hypothetical verdicts from trial judges on cases which had actually been tried to them with a jury, and to match the judge and the jury verdict for the same case. This was done for a national sample of some 3576 criminal jury trials and it is from this data that our argument against Judge Frank is derived.

We first noted that the basic pattern of agreement and disagreement between judge and jury is at odds with the Frank thesis. They were found to agree in 78 per cent of all cases. Moreover, the disagreement was highly directional: in 19 per cent it was occasioned because the jury was more lenient than the judge and in only 3 per cent was it the result of the judge's decision being more lenient than the jury's. If the jury did not understand the case, the inference was that it would be deciding a different case than the judge so that agreement would be a matter of chance. The pattern of judge-jury verdicts, however, was not to any appreciable extent random.

Second, we drew on explanations furnished by the trial judge for the cases in which there was disagreement. In the hundreds of instances in which the judge offered explanations for disagreement, we found only one in which he suggested it was because the jury did not understand the case.

Finally, we argued from cross-tabulation. The judges had rated all cases in the sample in terms of whether they were "easy" or "difficult." We then advanced the hypothesis that if the jury had a propensity not to understand the case, the propensity should be more evident in the cases the judge had classified as difficult than in the ones he had classified as easy. If Frank were right, it should follow that the rate of judge-jury disagreement should be higher in the difficult cases than in the easy cases. In fact, the disagreement rate for each group was the same.

The three lines of evidence together made, we thought, a pretty persuasive case that the jury did understand, and that Judge Frank was wrong.

The example suggests many inviting themes including the importance of developing a statistical sense about the performance of an institution, and the irony that it was Jerome Frank, our most realistic, non-dogmatic scholar who in this instance appears guilty of cavalier fact-finding. I cite it, however, to point up a major source of legal caution. Our conclusion depends not only on these lines of proof but equally on questions affecting our whole methodological strategy. *If* our sample of judges and jury trials is askew, *if* mail questionnaires are unreliable, *if* the judge cannot be taken to have made a meaningful rating of cases as easy and difficult, *if* our cross-tabulation gives a spurious non-correlation because of failure to control hidden variables—any of these "ifs" and our conclusion is endangered. We observed earlier that a trial involves the management of doubt. Contemporary social science knowledge is going to be circumstantial and inferential and its reception by the law world also involves the management of doubt. It is a kind of doubt which is peculiarly awkward for the law man to field. The lawyer is an expert in handling the imprecision of law; he has to get to feel comfortable with the imprecision of social science. And this does not mean that all the dangers are in his being gullible and uncritical. A naive inflexible skepticism is worse. A little methodology is a dangerous thing.

The jury example invites a moment's further reflection. We do not fully know how the jury manages to "understand" so well. We suspect from juror interviews and from mock jury deliberations that what is involved is a process of collective recall. It is not necessary that each individual juror remember and refresh the others. And it will turn out that different jurors will recall different facts so that the collective recall of the group will be far superior to the *average* recall of the individual jurors. The jury, as we have said, is likely to be as strong as its strongest link. Here we can dimly see fascinating *general* questions about human arrangements which neither law, nor anyone else, studies.

The Middle Range

Recognizing the necessary imprecision of contemporary social science brings us to another issue which has received widespread attention in the context of the segregation cases. Are there some value judgments in law which can only be trivialized if social science is brought to their support? This was, as I see it, the point behind Edmund Cahn's challenge to the Supreme Court's footnote in *Brown v. Board of Education* which cited a series of studies purporting to show that segregation in education is prejudicial to Negro school children. "I would not," said Professor Cahn,

> have the constitutional rights of Negroes—or of other Americans—rest on any such flimsy foundation as some of the scientific demonstrations in these records . . . (s)ince the behavioral sciences are so very young, imprecise,

and changeful their findings have an uncertain expectancy of life. Today's sanguine asseveration may be cancelled by tomorrow's new revelation—or new technical fad. [30 *N. Y. U. Law Review* 150, 157 (1955)]

Professor Cahn had a point, although not quite the one he was making. His fear was that scientific fact having been tendered on the issue, the merits would be thought to stand or fall with it, so that a shift tomorrow in the fashions of science would force a shift in the conclusions about segregation. The fear now seems to us unfounded, not because the scientific fact might not change, but because it has become clear that neither we nor the Court rested our conviction as to the evils of racial segregation on the scientific proof. That judgment had deeper and perhaps less rational sources.

Much the same point holds, I suspect, for the death penalty, or will hold if it is finally abolished either on constitutional grounds or by legislation. Belief about the death penalty in the end will rest not on oblique evidence as to its capacity to deter, nor on public opinion polls of community conscience, nor on proof of the difficulties it creates in selecting a representative jury, nor finally on the awkwardness of selecting from among those the legislature has made eligible for the death penalty the few who are in fact to die. Conviction will turn on something harder to reach with prosaic facts—the ugliness and cruelty of the cool, deliberate killing of another human being.

It seems clear the law does, and should, embody value judgments that are beyond the reach of factual impeachment. When these profound premises are involved, there will necessarily be an embarassing distance between the premise and any facts modern social science can offer in its support. Perhaps this means, as Professor Cahn went on to indicate, that social science cannot after all play much of a role in lawmaking at the constitutional level. The values at that level are too fundamental.

The image of high level premises which are beyond the reach of fact suggests the converse phenomenon, premises so mundane and commonplace as not to need any systematic confirmation. There is a considerable domain in law where common experience and amateur factfinding provide the knowledge that is needed; professional social science inquiry in such areas will be viewed as an expensive way of telling us what we already knew. Fixing the boundaries of this domain is a treacherous business, for there is a psychological quirk of retroactive recognition which makes people think that a fact once heard is something they had always known. Furthermore, precision often generates fresh insight. We always knew, I suppose, that in criminal jury trials sometimes defense counsel was better than prosecution and sometimes not, and that in some cases they roughly balanced. *The American Jury* after elaborate inquiry and quantification tells us the same thing. But to see that in 76 per cent of all trials the lawyers appear equally matched, that the imbalance in favor of the prosecution (13 per cent) is roughly the same as that in favor of the defense (11 per cent), and that the system is essentially in balance, is to see something new.

Whatever such qualifications, it remains true that a considerable number of legal premises do not need professional empirical buttressing and that the legal system may not be irrational in declining the invitation to research them seriously.

Robert Merton some years ago observed that in their current state the social sciences could aspire only to theories in the middle range. We can adapt his remark to the application of social science to legal problems: it can only aspire to facts in the middle range. Some premises are too deeply held for actual footnoting, and some facts are too well and accessibly known for professional inquiry. What remains then as the critical area is the middle range where the premises are not that unshakeable and where the facts are not that accessible.

It is for this reason, I suspect, that both sides in any ideological dispute about bringing social science empiricism to law tend to overshoot the mark. On the one hand, it is simplistic to urge that because law makes factual assumptions, there should be a one-to-one linking and testing of the underlying social facts, an endless dropping of empirical footnotes to points of law. On the other hand, it is nonsense to say that better documentation of fact cannot ever be relevant to law because the final business of law is not truth but political preference.

Our metaphor of the middle range does not dispose of the perplexities about facts and values which have so haunted discussions of law and science. We would note three further points. First, even when the norms or values are not the ones most deeply held, it remains true that facts do not per se resolve value issues, or, as Professor Patterson put it, that purely factual premises cannot yield a normative conclusion. Their relevance is oblique. They serve to narrow the controversy by eliminating certain points of disagreement or by suggesting unsuspected connections to other points. To take a simple example. There has been a good deal of controversy in recent years over the retention of the jury in civil cases. One point of criticism has gone to the jury's contribution toward court delay because it takes longer to try a case to a jury than to a judge alone. We were able to make an informed estimate of just how much longer a jury trial was, and the "scientific" answer was 40 per cent. This fact alone surely does not resolve the value-ridden controversy about the retention of the jury in civil cases, but it does help to focus the argument and reduce exaggerations on either side. Moreover, having established this 40 per cent figure it was possible to relate it to other strategies that would have approximately the same impact on delay, such as taking two weeks off the summer vacation of judges, speeding up jury trials to the New Jersey level which was 40 per cent faster than New York, or utilizing the split trial procedure.

Next, as the jury example suggests, there is the familiar point that law has a multiplicity of ends and that we can always escape the thrust of factual impeachment by shifting the grounds. The point is one most likely to dismay our social scientist colleagues who wish to pin down a legal premise for testing. Legal rules and especially legal institutions do not have a single avowed end or purpose against which their performance can be tidily measured. We appear to say, for example, that the jury's official function is to decide issues of fact—certainly a social scientist looking at cases would find endless statements to that effect. If, then, he elects to test how well the jury finds facts, we are likely to smile and tell him its real function is to introduce equity and the community sense of justice into the legal system, or to guard against the corruption or bias of American judges, or to provide a lightning rod for community resentment in the disposition of hard cases, or to provide civic education for the juror citizen. One can almost hear the exasperated social scientist shouting, "Stand still for a minute, damnit!" But while this multiplicity of ends may be a profound point about the nature of practical action and about law in particular, it is a shallow point in the relation of science to law. At most, it is a warning against too simplistic a scientific approach. To say the purposes of law are multiple is not to say they are indeterminate or Hydra-headed. The Rosenberg study of pre-trial, for example, tested the procedure not only against its ostensible settlement function but against such other purposes as speeding up trials, improving the quality of trials, or affecting the outcome of cases.

The third familiar theme is that law deals with preference, not truth, and we wish to make the policy choices ourselves and not delegate them to the scientific expert. We want the expert for his facts not for his values. This is part of a problem larger than that of the social scientist in the democratic process. However clear the principle for the division of labor, it is, as we see with the use of the psychiatric expert in insanity pleas, awkward to apply cleanly in practice. What interests us at the moment is not so much this point as the closely related one it leads to. For social science learning to have an impact on the living law, will it first have to become *popular* learning and thus enter law via the normal political process? In a way that is the moral of the pre-trial studies. Until they become more widely shared among the public of judges, they cannot have their impact on the law. And that, too, I surmise, is the moral of the regulation of marijuana. Until the public generally accepts the view of the differences between it and heroin, the science is not likely to make much difference. Here again we can dimly see a fascinating general topic about the role of science in forming public opinion on matters that affect law.

Some Good News about Methodology

A few further reflections on methodology serve to bring us back to the point with which these ruminations began: the inevitable limitations and uncertainties of modern social science learning. I return to the point this time, however, to strike an optimistic note.

There are two chief difficulties—the inability of social science to rely on the controlled experiment, and the difficulties of obtaining access to data when a living institution is the subject of study.

Most all the methodological strategies of the social sciences can be understood best as a response to the obstacles to using the technique of the controlled experiment. Everyone presumably has some idea about the logic of the controlled experiment. A situation is produced in which everything is known to be constant and comparable except for the single factor at issue—the experimental variable. If there is a difference in result between the experimental group and the control group, the inference that the difference must be the result of the experimental variable is hard to beat. The experiment has also the advantage that it can be replicated by someone else, and that it in no way depends on the skill, sensitivity or personal style of the experimenter.

There are, of course, problems of experimental design: making certain that the experimental variable is unambiguous and precise, that no foreign factors are inadvertently introduced in the course of executing the experiment, and that there is a valid index for reading the differences in result. Beyond this, experiments in the social sciences may have some special shortcomings of their own—they are relatively expensive and require repetition over a broad range of small changes in the variable in order to attain generalization of any scope. (In this respect they are strikingly like precedents with narrow holdings.) But whatever the qualifications, the experiment is the preferred method of empirical inquiry and the social scientist would use it if he could.

But one should not exaggerate the crippling consequences to the social sciences of their inability to commandeer controlled experiments. Cross-tabulation of survey data, "the retroactive experiment," under proper statistical etiquette can closely approximate the strength of the experiment. While it is a second best, it is not always a hopelessly outclassed second best. Moreover, facsimile approaches to the true experiment have proved possible. Thus, in Rita James Simon's book on the jury and the insanity defense, she was able, as one strategy of the jury project, to do experiments with mock cases but with real jurors assigned to this duty by the courts. Hence, a plausible facsimile technique of experimenting with jury reactions to different instructions, or different evidence emerged. Again, in *The American Jury*, we were able to approximate the heroic experiment of having a random sample of cases tried once to a jury and once to a judge in an effort to compare the over-all decision-making patterns of each.

Hence, though he may not be able to do real life experiments the social scientist is not entirely prevented from using the logic of the experiment. More important, the justification for official experiment —an experiment conducted by the legal system itself—is substantial, as my colleague Hans Zeisel has persuasively argued, even though the deliberate introduction of differences in legal treatment would appear to violate the norms of equal protection of law. And, most important, in at least two striking recent instances, *official experiments* have in fact been conducted: the Rosenberg study of the pre-trial conference in New Jersey, and the Vera Foundation studies of releasing suspects on bail.

The discussion of experiments has anticipated the question of access to data. It is here that the existing studies carry the greatest message of encouragement. It was, after all, possible to persuade the legal system itself to cooperate in the pre-trial and bail experiments. It was possible for Jerome Skolnick to persuade the Oakland police force to let him participate in raids with them; it was possible for the jury project to persuade judges to assign to them real jurors from the existing jury pool for our experimental studies; it was possible for the jury project to persuade a formidable sample of American trial judges to fill out mail questionnaires on actual jury trials and to report to us their hypothetical verdicts in the cases.

It is not only possible to secure high level cooperation, if one is willing to take time for the necessary diplomacy involved; it is also possible with scientific ingenuity to reach issues thought to be inaccessible. Thus, to borrow again a striking point of method from Hans Zeisel, in both the bail experiment and in the pre-trial study, as well as in the study by Zeisel and Callahan of split trials, it was not necessary to have the experimenter control the experimental variable—to have, for example, a group subject to mandatory pre-trial and a control group relieved altogether of pre-trial. So long as at the outset the groups had been randomly selected, it was sufficient to have mandatory pre-trial for the one and to leave it to the option of the litigants themselves whether or not to have pre-trial in the other. Since the two groups would be the same except for the fact that in the one all cases had been pre-tried whereas in the other only some cases had been pre-tried, the logic of experimental inference was still operative. The important result is that the practical difficulties of such real life experiment can thereby be greatly reduced without undermining its logic.

Finally the technique of secondary analysis, the reanalyzing of existing records, can often yield important findings. That is, the researcher can make a given set of records yield more information than the custodian of the records has discovered in them. The existing social order need not be disturbed by the researchers' effort to collect the data; it has already been collected officially or semi-officially. Three instances of recent work of this sort may be cited: the Rosenberg study of closing statements in New York which provided much insight into the economics of contemporary personal injury litigation and reparation; the exploratory study of claims consciousness in *Delay in the Court* which utilized existing insurance company data; and finally a study by Allen Barton of the administration of the jury system in Peoria, which utilized only existing court records.

Taste in Empirical Inquiry

I have in this meandering way attempted to reflect on the plusses and minuses in the current mood about law and social science. I announced at the outset that it was a frustrating topic; it has proved to be that and an elusive one as well. There are good reasons why the law will not and should not overdo the use of science; and there are good reasons for criticizing it for being too unscientific in stance. I have tried to phrase the Aristotle-like golden mean of not too much and not too little science by saying that the law needs to develop *taste* in empirical inquiry. It needs also to develop an understanding of and an appreciation for the kind of informed guess social science can offer it today.

We need a critical mass of empirical legal studies which are widely shared in the legal culture so that a sense of the liberating possibilities of scientific inquiry into social fact can develop. The studies of the past decade make prospects for the law better in this respect than they have ever been. The "golden era" will come when such work has become routine, and is seen as simply another resource for legal scholarship.

Finally I suspect that one ought not push too hard for practical applications and immediate results. There certainly appear to be inviting theoretical concerns implicit in the current studies. At our best we want the social scientist as a full-fledged partner in scholarship and not as an applied mechanic.

It is not inappropriate to end soliloquies of this sort with a slogan for the future. I have one to offer: let us "empiricize" jurisprudence and intellectualize fact finding.

Bibliography I

Beutel, Frederick K., *Some Potentialities of Experimental Jurisprudence as a New Branch of Social Science.* Lincoln: University of Nebraska Press, 1957. 440 pages.

———, and Tadeo Negron Medero, *The Operation of the Bad-Check Laws of Puerto Rico.* Rio Piedras: Editorial Universitaria Universidad de Puerto Rico, 1967. 158 pages.

Carlin, Jerome E., *Lawyers' Ethics.* New York: Russell Sage Foundation, 1966. 267 pages.

———, *Lawyers on Their Own: A Study of Individual Practitioners in Chicago.* New Brunswick: Rutgers University Press, 1962. 234 pages.

Cohen, Julius, Reginald A. H. Robson, and Alan Bates, *Parental Authority: the Community and the Law.* New Brunswick: Rutgers University Press, 1958. 301 pages.

Conard, Alfred F. *et al, Automobile Accident Cost and Payments: Studies in the Economics of Injury Reparation.* Ann Arbor: University of Michigan Press, 1964. 506 pages.

Handler, Joel F., *The Lawyer and His Community: The Practising Bar in a Middle-sized City.* Madison: University of Wisconsin Press, 1967.

Kalven, Harry, Jr., and Hans Zeisel, *The American Jury.* Boston: Little, Brown and Company, 1966. 599 pages.

LaFave, Wayne R., *Arrest: the Decision to Take a Suspect Into Custody.* Boston: Little, Brown and Company, 1965. 540 pages.

Levin, A. Leo and Edward A. Woolley, *Dispatch and Delay; a Field Study of Judicial Administration in Pennsylvania.* Philadelphia: Institute of Legal Research, University of Pennsylvania Law School, 1961. 426 pages.

McIntyre, Donald M., ed., *Law Enforcement in the Metropolis.* Chicago: American Bar Foundation, 1967. 219 pages.

Newman, Donald J., *Conviction: the Determination of Guilt or Innocence Without Trial.* Boston: Little, Brown and Company, 1966. 259 pages.

Oaks, Dallin H., and Warren Lehman, *A Criminal Justice System and the Indigent: a Study of Chicago and Cook County.* Chicago: University of Chicago Press, 1967.

Rosenberg, Maurice, "Comparative Negligence in Arkansas: A 'Before and After' Survey," 13 *Ark. L. Rev.* 89 (1959).

———, *Pretrial Conference and Effective Justice: a Controlled Test in Personal Injury Litigation.* New York: Columbia University Press, 1964. 249 pages.

————, and Robert H. Chanin, "Auditors in Massachusetts as Antidotes for Delayed Civil Courts," 110 *U. Pa. L. Rev.* 27 (1961).

————, and Myra Schubin, "Trial by Lawyer: Compulsory Arbitration of Small Claims in Pennsylvania," 74 *Harv. L. Rev.* 448 (1961).

————, and Michael I. Sovern, "Delay and Dynamics of Personal Injury Litigation," 59 *Colum. L. Rev.* 1115 (1959).

Simon, Rita J., *The Jury and the Defense of Insanity*. Boston: Little, Brown and Company, 1967. 269 pages.

Skolnick, Jerome H., *Justice Without Trial: Law Enforcement in a Democratic Society*. New York: John Wiley & Sons, Inc., 1966. 279 pages.

Smigel, Erwin O., *Wall Street Lawyer: Professional Organization Man?* New York: Free Press of Glencoe, Inc., 1964. 369 pages.

Tiffany, Lawrence P., Donald M. McIntyre, Jr., and Daniel L. Rotenberg, *Detection of Crime: Stopping and Questioning, Search and Seizure, Encouragement and Entrapment*. Boston: Little, Brown and Company, 1967. 286 pages.

Walter E. Meyer Research Institute of Law, *Dollars, Delay and the Automobile Victim: Studies in Reparation for Highway Injuries and Related Court Problems*. Indianapolis: The Bobbs-Merrill Company, Inc., 1968. 470 pages.

Warkow, Seymour, and Joseph Zelan, *Lawyers in the Making*. Chicago: Aldine, 1965. 180 pages.

Zeisel, Hans, Harry Kalven, Jr., and Bernard Buchholz, *Delay in the Court*. Boston: Little, Brown and Company, 1959. 313 pages.

Bibliography II

Cavers, David, "Science, Research and the Law: Beutel's 'Experimental Jurisprudence,'" 10 *J. Legal Ed.* 162, 1957.

Currie, Brainerd, "The Materials of Law Study III," 8 *J. Legal Ed.* 1, 1955.

Loevinger, Lee, "Law and Science as Rival Systems," 19 *Univ. of Fla. L. Rev.* 530, 1967.

Mechem, Philip, "The Jurisprudence of Despair," 21 *Iowa L. Rev.* 669, 1935.

Moore, Underhill, and Charles Callahan, "Law and Learning Theory," 53 *Yale L. J.* 1, 1943.

Münsterberg, Hugo, *On the Witness Stand*. New York: Doubleday & Company, Inc., 1908. 269 pages.

Patterson, Edwin, *Law in a Scientific Age*. New York: Columbia University Press, 1963. 87 pages.

Riesman, David, "Law and Sociology: Recruitment, Training and Colleagueship," 9 *Stn. L. Rev.* 643, 1957.

Robinson, Edward S., *Law and the Lawyers*. New York: The MacMillan Company, Inc., 1935. 348 pages.

Strodtbeck, Fred, "Social Process, the Law and Jury Functioning," in Evan, ed., *Law and Sociology*. New York: The Free Press of Glencoe, Inc., 1962.

Wigmore, "Professor Münsterberg and the Psychology of Testimony," 3 *Ill. L. Rev.* 399, 1908.

Zeisel, Hans, "The Law," in Lazarsfeld *et al*, eds., *The Uses of Sociology*. New York: Basic Books, Inc., 1967.

————, "Social Research on the Law: The Ideal and the Practical," in Evan, ed., *Law and Sociology*. New York: The Free Press of Glencoe, Inc., 1962.

William K. Jones

5

Legal Regulation and Economic Analysis

One of the principal tasks of American legal institutions and processes is the regulation of economic activity. In performing that task, it is necessary to refer to economic theory and economic evidence in formulating policy objectives and, once policy has been expressed as law, in determining how the policy objectives may be fulfilled. Economic theory is not policy, but rather a set of more or less definite concepts about causal interactions in economic systems. Nor are economic data self-evident in their implications; like all matters of evidence their significance depends on some supporting theory of relevance. Yet much legal regulation of economic activity proceeds on unexamined theories of relevance and is aimed at objectives stated only in vague terms. As a result, policy questions are frequently obscured and their resolution is often a matter of unguided official discretion or even simple default.

Until legal institutions are better equipped to deal with the economic policy issues involved, this condition will persist. As long as it persists, legal regulation of economic activity will fail to exhibit the coherence and responsibility that should be expected of any legal process.

Patterns of Economic Regulation

Economic activity in the United States—the provision of goods and services for the nation's 200 million people—is conducted through

WILLIAM K. JONES *is professor of law at Columbia School of Law. He has served as a consultant to the Department of Justice, the American Law Institute, the Administrative Conference of the United States, and The Ford Foundation. Professor Jones is the author of* Cases and Materials on Regulated Industries.

a large number of organizations. Some of these are government instrumentalities, which provide schools, roads, mail deliveries, scientific research, and a wide variety of other services. Government operations are financed largely by tax revenues (although service charges are exacted in some instances); controls over these operations are primarily political (although competitive pressures are sometimes experienced). Most economic organizations, however, are "private" businesses—corporations, partnerships and individual proprietorships—which enter into countless purchase and sale transactions in a variety of markets, and finance their operations from the revenues derived from these transactions (and occasionally from government subsidies). Private business organizations are subject to two types of control in the conduct of their economic activities: (a) the competitive pressures of the markets in which they buy and sell; and (b) regulations of government instrumentalities. Industries are typically classified as "regulated" or "unregulated" depending on the nature and scope of applicable regulation.

The "regulated" industries are subject to government controls distinctive from those applicable to the economy at large. These controls are concerned with achieving broad economic objectives, as contrasted with those more limited legal restrictions which are encountered in many sectors of the economy and are designed to guard against unsafe, unhealthful, or dishonest practices. The controls apply in a pervasive manner to limit the business discretion of "regulated" companies on such vital matters as price changes and expansion or contraction of operations (although both types of restriction are not present in all instances). Regulated sectors of the American economy include about half of agriculture (price support programs and cartel cooperatives); the production of crude oil, natural gas, and anthracite coal; public transportation facilities such as railroads, trucks, buses, airlines, pipelines, and shipping; public utility services such as telephone, telegraph, electricity and gas; radio and television; and banking, insurance, and securities and commodities exchanges.

"Unregulated" industries are subject to two important forms of legal regulation. First, there are laws applicable to specific industries, but concerned with limited objectives such as safety, health, or the prevention of fraudulent and dishonest practices—the operations of the Food and Drug Administration provide an example of this type of regulation. Second, there are regulatory measures of general applicability, such as the corporation, labor and antitrust laws. The antitrust laws include the Sherman, Clayton and Federal Trade Commission Acts, together with such amendatory legislation as the Robinson-Patman and McGuire Acts. These laws provide an extensive network of controls reaching such practices as cartels and other cooperative arrangements among competitors; mergers of separate firms; "price discrimination" (charging different prices to different customers for the same product of the same firm); and vertical relations between supplier and customer (resale price maintenance, exclusive dealing, tying arrangements, territorial franchises, reciprocity, and refusals to deal). The antitrust laws apply to a limited extent to the "regulated" industries, but have their greatest impact in the "unregulated" sector of the economy.

To provide some perspective on the relative sizes of these sectors of economic activity, a comparison may be made of the national income generated by each. In 1964, 13.8 per cent of national income (exclusive of "private households" and "rest of world") originated in federal, state and local government instrumentalities; 13.5 per cent originated in the "regulated" sector (as defined above); and the remaining 72.7 per cent originated in the "unregulated" sector (some of the activities in this sector were conducted pursuant to government contracts and thus were subject to political controls having a possible regulatory dimension). The present discussion is addressed chiefly to the "unregulated" sector, but the problems involved are also encountered in the other two sectors.

The role of economic analysis in legal regulation will be considered in two stages. First, a specific instance will be set forth in some detail to provide a concrete illustration of the process. This will be followed by a consideration of the characteristics of legal regulation as revealed by the specific example and by other data.

The Von's Grocery Store Case

In March, 1960, Von's Grocery Company merged with Shopping Bag Food Stores over the objection of the Department of Justice that the merger violated section seven of the Clayton Act, which prohibits a merger "where in any line of commerce in any section of the country the effect . . . may be substantially to lessen competition, or to tend to create a monopoly." Von's and Shopping Bag both operated supermarket chains in the Los Angeles area; it was agreed that groceries and related products constituted an appropriate "line of commerce" (sometimes also described as the "relevant product market"), and that the Los Angeles area was an appropriate "section of the country" (sometimes also described as the "relevant geographic market"). In 1958, the year for which most extensive data were available, Von's operated 27 supermarkets, had a sales volume of $93,703,000, and accounted for 4.7 per cent of grocery store sales in the Los Angeles area. In the same year, Shopping Bag operated 34 supermarkets in the area, had a sales volume of $84,164,000, and accounted for 4.2 per cent of area grocery store sales. Von's ranked third and Shopping Bag sixth among Los

Angeles supermarket chains; together, they would have ranked first. Annual grocery store sales in the Los Angeles area amounted to approximately 2.5 billion dollars.

The District Court, writing in September 1964, held that the merger did not violate section seven. It relied on the following factors:

(a) At the time of the merger, there were 4,000 separate concerns operating more than 4,800 grocery stores in the Los Angeles area. To be sure, the number of grocery stores in the area had declined from 6,221 to 4,548 between 1950 and 1963, but this decline had been associated with the development of supermarkets, the growth of shopping centers, and the demise of many small neighborhood grocery stores. Business failures stemming from a variety of causes also had led to the elimination of many stores. Notwithstanding this decline in total number of stores, the District Court observed that scarcely a single household in the area was without a choice of from three to ten competing grocery stores.

(b) The grocery store business in Los Angeles was characterized by ease of entry. Between 1953 and 1962, the number of concerns operating two or three stores in the area had increased from 56 to 104, and the number of concerns operating more than three stores had increased from 40 to 46. In 1960, 246 new grocery stores had been opened in the Los Angeles area: 128 "single outlet" stores; 67 new stores belonging to the top twenty chains; and 51 new outlets of smaller chains.

(c) The grocery store business in Los Angeles was one in which smaller firms could prosper and expand. A number of specific instances were cited by the District Court, which also observed that buying cooperatives made it possible for smaller enterprises to obtain merchandise on terms competitive with larger firms.

(d) By contrast, some of the leading grocery firms in Los Angeles had seen their market shares reduced in recent years. In 1948, the two largest chains had accounted for 21.1 per cent of Los Angeles grocery sales; by 1958, their share had been reduced to 14.3 per cent. The District Court also observed that between 1952 and 1960 concentration in the Los Angeles grocery market either had increased only slightly or had declined; but elsewhere in its opinion the Court indicated that concentration in the market had increased between 1948 and 1958. The Court further noted numerous changes in the identities of the companies comprising the top twenty firms in the market: seven of those in the top twenty in 1960 had not been in existence as chains in 1948.

(e) The outlets of Von's and Shopping Bag were located in different parts of the city so that for the most part they did not compete directly with one another. However, the District Court found that direct competition, where it did exist, was "intensive," and that both Von's and

Shopping Bag were part of the general competitive structure of supermarket sales in Los Angeles.

(f) The motives for the merger were legitimate. They included the need for better management for Shopping Bag, whose earnings had been slipping and whose existing management was thin; the greater efficiency and lower operating costs that combination of functions would make possible; the complementary geographical territories of the two firms; and the broadening of the stockholder base of the surviving firm, which would facilitate the transfer of company shares and the listing of the stock on a national exchange. Neither Von's nor Shopping Bag had engaged in any previous mergers.

(g) The history of prior mergers involving other grocery retailers in the Los Angeles area was not disturbing because the mergers mostly fell into one of three categories: (1) they had been market extensions by companies not previously doing business in the area; (2) they had been offset by the subsequent failure of the acquiring firm and the disposal of its store; or (3) they had been largely or entirely offset by sales of the acquired stores or other stores by the acquiring company.

(h) Subsequent to the merger, competition continued to be vigorous, and was intensified by the introduction of new food merchandising techniques in the Los Angeles area, such as discount houses, bantam stores, and drive-in milk depots. Moreover, Von's-Shopping Bag, despite their 1958 combined market share of 8.9 per cent, did not become the market leader after the merger. In 1960, Von's-Shopping Bag, with 7.5 per cent of Los Angeles grocery store sales, trailed Safeway, which had 8 per cent of sales.

The Government appealed from the adverse decision of the District Court. In the United States Supreme Court, the Government's theory was this:

The reason for restricting horizontal mergers is to prevent the emergence of oligopoly—a condition "characterized by the concentration of market power in the hands of a few companies."

> Where the major sellers in a market are few, a price cut by one is likely to have so drastic and immediate an adverse effect upon the sales of the others as to compel them to respond promptly with matching cuts, thereby wiping out any competitive advantage won by the initiator of the reduction. Realizing this, competitors in an oligopolistic market have little incentive to cut prices. Oligopoly thus promotes price rigidity and discourages vigorous price competition. . . .

The process by which mergers transform a market from a dispersed one to a concentrated one is gradual, and no single merger is likely to be decisive. Remedial action is therefore required against a series of

mergers, even though each viewed in isolation might seem relatively
harmless. The "most pertinent question in a merger case is not, what
is the immediate impact of the merger upon competition, but, rather,
what is the likely future direction of the market's development if the
merger is permitted?"

The Government observed that predicting the long-term future
effects of a merger is "very difficult," calling "more for an economic
prophecy than for a conventional legal judgment." Accordingly, it emphasized the need for general standards to govern the legality of mergers
in accordance with the underlying purposes of the law. The Government urged that "a merger should be deemed presumptively illegal
when it (1) occurs in a market where there is a significant tendency in
the direction of undue concentration and (2) appreciably increases the
existing level of concentration." The Government rejected the idea
that "a merger need not be forbidden unless it actually creates oligopoly," because "[n]o one can say—at least not without an inquiry far
broader and deeper than practical law enforcement permits—at precisely what point a particular market will exhibit oligopolistic behavior."

In applying its proposed test to the facts of the pending litigation, the
Government observed:

1. At the time of the merger, "a small number of large chains accounted for a relatively large share of the market." The three largest
had 19.1 per cent, the four largest 23.5 per cent, the eight largest 39
per cent, and the ten largest 43.6 per cent. Although concentration
"had not reached a level at which price rigidity or other characteristic
competitive ills of oligopolistic markets were evident," the "combined
market share of the leading sellers was at a level that economists would
consider characteristic of at least a loose oligopoly." That is, the leading
firms in the market "identified each other as major competitors whose
actions and responses must be carefully considered in planning price
and other competitive moves." On this point, the Government referred
to evidence in the record that the major chains "were accustomed to
study carefully the prices charged by competing major chains, and that
each strove to maintain the same prices as the others."

2. At the time of the merger, concentration in the Los Angeles retail
grocery market was increasing. Between 1948 and 1958, market shares
increased:

from 33.7 per cent to 40.9 per cent for the largest eight;
from 38.8 per cent to 48.8 per cent for the largest twelve;
from 41.6 per cent to 53.4 per cent for the largest sixteen;
and from 43.8 per cent to 56.9 per cent for the largest twenty.

"Mergers were largely responsible for the increases." Between 1949 and 1958, nine of the leading twenty chains in the Los Angeles area had acquired 126 grocery stores from concerns outside the top twenty chains. The Government discounted the apparent absence of any showing of increased concentration between 1952 and 1960 (as noted by the District Court) on the ground that the 1960 statistics were unreliable.

3. "The merger eliminated a major competitor . . . which was clearly one of the market's leaders." And the merger substantially increased the aggregate shares of the largest firms:

> from 14.4 per cent to 16.9 per cent for the two largest;
> from 19.1 per cent to 23.3 per cent for the three largest;
> from 23.5 per cent to 27.7 per cent for the four largest;
> and from 38.9 per cent to 41.6 per cent for the eight largest.

Comparing the share of the top eight to their share in 1948, the increase was from 33.7 per cent to 41.6 per cent.

4. The presumption of illegality that should attach to the merger could not be rebutted by showing ease of entry into the Los Angeles retail grocery market. The Government argued, first, that the alleged ease of entry relied on by the defendants and the District Court was overstated. Second, the Government contended that ease of entry was not a defense in any event because: (a) while the threat of new competition might restrict oligopoly pricing to a more narrow range, it would not eliminate such pricing; and (b) new entry had not been sufficient to prevent increases in concentration in the market in the recent past.

The Government accordingly argued that the merger should be held to be unlawful even though competition apparently had continued to be vigorous in subsequent years.

The Supreme Court, in May of 1966, held the merger unlawful. Its approach differed substantially from that of the Department of Justice and placed principal reliance on the reduction in total number of grocery stores in the Los Angeles area (although the Court also referred to the merger activities of the larger chains and the size and successful character of the merging companies):

> [T]he number of owners operating a single store in the Los Angeles retail market decreased from 5,365 in 1950 to 3,818 in 1961 [and to 3,590 in 1963]. During roughly the same period from 1953 to 1962 the number of chains with two or more grocery stores increased from 96 to 150. While the grocery business was being concentrated into the hands of fewer and fewer owners, the small companies were continually being absorbed by the larger companies through mergers. . . .
>
> Despite this steadfast concentration of the Los Angeles grocery business into fewer and fewer hands, the District Court [found that concentration

in the market had not increased]. This conclusion is completely contradicted by . . . the steady decline in the number of grocery store owners. . . . It is thus apparent that the District Court . . . used the term "concentration" in some sense other than a total decrease in the number of separate competitors which is the crucial point here.

[The purpose of section seven of the Clayton Act] was to prevent economic concentration in the American economy by keeping a large number of small competitors in business. [The fear was expressed by the Act's sponsors that] concentration was rapidly driving the small businessman out of the market. . . .

. . . This merger cannot be defended on the ground that one of the companies was about to fail or that the two had to merge to save themselves from destruction from some larger and more powerful competitor. What we have on the contrary is simply the case of two already powerful companies merging in a way which makes them even more powerful than they were before. . . .

. . . It is enough for us that Congress feared that a market marked at the same time by both a continuous decline in the number of small businesses and a large number of mergers would slowly but inevitably gravitate from a market of many small competitors to one dominated by one or a few giants, and competition would thereby be destroyed. . . .[1]

Before considering the soundness of the several approaches adopted in the *Von's* case, it is useful to consider two general aspects of legal regulation: (1) the volume of transactions covered by various regulatory programs, and (2) the generality of legislative standards applicable to such transactions.

Volume of Transactions

A merger is not part of the ordinary course of business operations. Yet mergers in the unregulated sector of the economy have been occurring with some frequency. In 1965, 1,893 mergers were recorded by the Federal Trade Commission; in 1966 there were 1,746. Most of these mergers were not challenged by either the FTC or the Department of Justice, the two federal antitrust enforcement agencies. In recent years, these agencies have commenced proceedings against approximately 2 per cent of all reported mergers (and blocked some additional ones by threat of suit). Yet even the merger proceedings

---

[1] Justice White concurred in the Court's opinion, but added a short opinion of his own which drew upon some of the concentration data presented in the brief of the Department of Justice. Justices Stewart and Harlan dissented, relying largely on the grounds advanced by the District Court. See *United States v. Von's Grocery Co.,* 384 U. S. 270 (1966), reversing 233 F. Supp. 976 (S. D. Cal. 1964).

instituted involved a substantial amount of governmental activity, especially if one considers the nature of the cases involved (as illustrated by *Von's*).

Turning from mergers to price changes and contractual relations, the number of transactions subject to antitrust restraint is impossible to compute or even to estimate. Suffice it to say that antitrust limitations on price discrimination and vertical relations have enormous potential reach. The regulatory activity in this area is miniscule in relation to this potential, but is still substantial. In fiscal 1965, the Antitrust Division instituted 486 investigations into alleged antitrust violations, commenced 43 antitrust prosecutions, and terminated 52 cases. In the same year, the Federal Trade Commission initiated 242 formal investigations into antitrust matters, issued 26 antitrust complaints and entered 39 orders to cease and desist. These figures include merger matters as well as other antitrust violations; but, with the exception of Department of Justice investigations, the non-merger cases preponderate.

The regulated sector of the economy is smaller than the unregulated, but the intensity of government activity is much greater. The Interstate Commerce Commission, for example, regulates railroads, trucks, buses and other instrumentalities of domestic surface transportation. In 1964, all of these activities originated less than 4.5 per cent of national income. Yet in fiscal 1965, the ICC received a total of 220,818 tariffs or schedules embodying new or changed rates. Of these, 9,341 tariff publications involving 4,627 rate adjustments were considered by the ICC's Suspension Board, which decided to "suspend" (postpone the effectiveness of) 1,872 rate adjustments. Many of these suspended rates were discontinued before the Commission could consider them on the merits, but in fiscal 1965 it adjudicated some 561 rate controversies. In the same year, the Commission acted on 6,842 applications for new operating authority, of which over 3,800 were granted in whole or in part. Controversies involving mergers, securities, service, abandonments, and a variety of other matters competed for the attention of the Commission.

Two institutional requirements are generated by the fact that a large volume of transactions are subject (or potentially subject) to regulatory control.

First, the enforcement agencies (or others) must develop standards for determining which transactions will be challenged. If, for example, the FTC and the Department of Justice are to challenge 2 per cent of recorded mergers, they must have some method of determining *which 2 per cent*. It would not make much sense simply to bring an action against every fiftieth merger coming to the attention of the authorities.

Similarly, the Suspension Board of the ICC must have some standard for determining which tariffs it will suspend. Selection of cases may be simplified somewhat by the presence of protests from other interested parties. But this factor can hardly be controlling, since some meritorious transactions may provoke frivolous protests, and some harmful transactions may not affect any private party with sufficient immediacy to produce an objection. The need to economize on the resources of government in the face of substantial volumes of transactions—to direct the attention of government agencies to areas which most require their attention—calls for the development of standards for the initiation of regulatory proceedings.

Second, rendering decisions in those cases in which proceedings have been instituted requires the development of standards for decision. The volume of proceedings is so great that an effort to decide each case "on its own facts"—as if it were a unique and nonrecurring problem—would lead to a breakdown in the regulatory system. At the same time, it is important to avoid decision-making that is wholly arbitrary—decisions which provoke comments of the type voiced in the dissenting opinion in *Von's:* "The sole consistency that I can find is that in litigation under Section 7, the Government always wins."

That standards are required seems clear. The nature and source of these standards turn on other aspects of the legal regulation of economic affairs.

Generality of Legislative Standards

Most transactions subject to regulatory control are governed by statutes embodying highly generalized standards of illegality. The lawfulness of a merger under section seven of the Clayton Act depends on whether its effect "may be substantially to lessen competition, or to tend to create a monopoly" "in any line of commerce in any section of the country." A similar standard governs the legality of exclusive dealing contracts and tying arrangements under section three of the Clayton Act. Price differentials within the scope of the Robinson-Patman Act are unlawful if they offend this same standard or if they may "injure, destroy, or prevent competition" with the party granting or receiving the discriminatory price (unless the price differential is justified by the cost savings of the seller or by the seller's need to meet competition in "good faith"). The other major antitrust provisions are even more general in their terms. The Sherman Act, which prohibits combinations or agreements in restraint of trade, has been interpreted to apply only to "unreasonable" restraints, the judiciary exercising the power to classify restraints as reasonable or unreasonable. The Act's prohibition against monopolization is surrounded by similar judicially administered limitations. Finally, the Federal Trade Commission has a mandate to proscribe "unfair methods of competition" whenever it finds that it is in the "public interest" to do so.

In the regulated sector, the statutory standards are similarly general. The Interstate Commerce Act's provisions governing rates of regulated carriers contain a measure of specificity—e.g., the proscription of discrimination where the carrier's service to different customers is substantially similar (section 2). But the basic provisions of the Act (as they apply to railroads) require "just and reasonable" rates, based upon Commission consideration of the movement of traffic, the need for low-cost service by shippers, and the need for adequate revenues by carriers (sections 1, 15a); and they forbid rates which give "any undue or unreasonable preference or advantage" to any party, or subject any party to "any undue or unreasonable prejudice or disadvantage" (section 3). New service is to be permitted, or existing service terminated, if the "public convenience and necessity" so require (section 1). Mergers and securities issues are subject to a number of restrictions, but the general standard of the Act is consistency with the "public interest" (section 20a). Congress has sometimes elaborated on the concept of the "public interest" (or similarly broad statutory concepts), but without reducing the level of generality. Thus, the national transportation policy, in accordance with which all provisions of the Interstate Commerce Act are to be administered and enforced, provides:

> It is hereby declared to be the national transportation policy of the Congress to provide for fair and impartial regulation of all modes of transportation subject to the provisions of this Act, so administered as to recognize and preserve the inherent advantages of each; to promote safe, adequate, economical, and efficient service and foster sound economic conditions in transportation and among the several carriers; to encourage the establishment and maintenance of reasonable charges for transportation services, without unjust discrimination, undue preferences or advantages, or unfair or destructive competitive practices; to cooperate with the several States and the duly authorized officials thereof; and to encourage fair wages and equitable working conditions;—all to the end of developing, coordinating, and preserving a national transportation system by water, highway, and rail, as well as other means, adequate to meet the needs of the commerce of the United States, of the Postal Service, and of the national defense. . . .

What are the consequences of these highly generalized legislative standards?

In some instances, they have led to wide-ranging and unwieldy regulatory proceedings. Thus, the *Von's* case, though handled with relative dispatch, was decided in the District Court four and one-half years after it had been commenced, and by the Supreme Court six years after its initiation; other antitrust cases have been more protracted. The licensing of airlines and television broadcasters, the regulation of natural gas producer rates, and the adjudication of railroad mergers, have produced proceedings that rank among the major monstrosities of the law.

To avoid such proceedings, and the threat they pose to the continuation of the regulatory process, efforts have been made to develop subsidiary rules clarifying the impact of the general statutory standards. Thus, under the Sherman Act, only "unreasonable" restraints of trade are unlawful; but price-fixing and other cartel practices have been held to be unreasonable *per se*. In passing on whether "public convenience and necessity" require new services the regulatory agencies tend to focus on the "adequacy" of existing services; in particular contexts, the agencies reduce the area of uncertainty by specifying deficiencies that will render existing services inadequate. In rate regulation, the development of cost and accounting standards (including the substantial resolution of the long-festering dispute over "original cost" and "reproduction cost") has narrowed the area of controversy, although most rate cases continue to present stubborn problems. In almost every context, accretions of regulatory policy have served to particularize the highly general statutory terms.

The remaining question is how these subsidiary standards are to be formulated.

Formulation of Decisional Standards

In *Von's*, the District Court decided the case without explicit reliance on any standard other than the broad generalization of the statute. On appeal, the Department of Justice suggested a more specific standard for application to mergers of competitors in relatively unconcentrated markets. The Supreme Court apparently adopted a fairly specific standard, but one differing significantly from that proposed by the Department. These diverse approaches can be explained in large part by reference to two factors: (a) diverse appraisals of the purpose of the statutory prohibition and the mode of its implementation, and (b) differing views of the role of economic analysis in legal regulation.

THE DISTRICT COURT'S DECISION IN VON'S

The District Court addressed itself to the question of whether the merger was likely to reduce the intensity of inter-firm rivalry in the

Los Angeles retail grocery market, and came to a negative conclusion. In so doing, it relied on a number of propositions of economic analysis—never clearly articulated—which might be stated as follows:

Other things being equal, the rivalry of competing firms in a market is likely to be more intense:

(a) If the number of firms in the market is large.
(b) If each consumer has a choice among a number of firms.
(c) If it is easy for a new firm to enter the market.
(d) If it is possible for small firms in the market to prosper and expand.
(e) If the share of the market controlled by the largest firms is declining (or is not increasing at a substantial rate).
(f) If the identity of the largest firms in the market is changing.
(g) If new methods of merchandising are being introduced to challenge existing channels of distribution.

The propositions are stated here in the disjunctive, for the District Court did not consider them to be mutually dependent. However, the District Court obviously concluded that the cumulative effect of favorable findings under each of these headings (and some others) required a favorable conclusion with respect to the legality of the merger.

These propositions of economic analysis have several features in common:

First, they are statements about the behavior of business firms under differing economic circumstances. As such, they cannot be inferred from statutory texts or previous judicial decisions; their validity depends on some combination of economic theory and empirical study of business behavior.

Second, the District Court employed these propositions without explicit reference to limits or qualifications in their application. Thus, propositions (b) and (d) may state conditions *necessary* for vigorous competition but these may not be *sufficient* to insure such competition if a large proportion of the market is controlled by a few firms following oligopolistic pricing practices. According to oligopoly theory, a market may satisfy conditions (b) and (d)—by giving consumers some choice among firms and by providing a hospitable climate for small firms on the fringe—and still be characterized by fairly rigid price leadership. Similarly, propositions (a), (c), (f) and (g) may state conditions which restrain the pricing power of dominant firms in an oligopolistic market without negating the existence of that power. In sum, the factors enumerated by the District Court may all be relevant in that they state conditions favorable to competition, yet inconclusive in the specific case in not taking account of relevant limitations or qualifications. On the question of concentration, which is most directly related to the oligopoly problem, the District Court's opinion cited trends in the direction of both more and less concentration.

Third, the propositions implicit in the District Court's opinion were qualitative in nature, and scant clues were provided as to their general quantitative dimensions. To be sure, the District Court thought that 4,000 firms was a "large number" of firms; that a "choice" of from three to ten stores was adequate for consumers; and so forth. But the failure to provide more articulate quantitative dimensions for the propositions makes it difficult to test their theoretical and empirical underpinnings, and limits their usefulness in providing a means for resolving future cases in an orderly and systematic fashion.

Finally, the District Court sought to arrive at a result based on a consideration of all the factors involved. No particular weight was assigned to any factor, and no effort was made to relate the various factors to one another. The result was a ticket good for "one ride only;" the decision is of no significant value in any subsequent case involving a different array of factors.

THE APPROACH OF THE DEPARTMENT OF JUSTICE IN VON'S

The Justice Department differed with the District Court in both institutional approach and economic analysis. On institutional approach, the Department emphasized long-term trends in the market, whereas the District Court was more concerned with the immediate consequences of the particular merger. The Department also stressed the need to develop a rule which would permit more predictable and expeditious disposition of merger cases. In economic analysis, the Department relied almost entirely upon the implications of oligopoly theory, which the District Court had apparently ignored. In contrast to the District Court, the Department presented its economic theory in explicit terms, with occasional references to the underlying economic literature, and sought to develop a general approach that could be applied to most, if not all, horizontal mergers occurring in relatively unconcentrated markets. But on one point, the Department's approach was similar to that of the District Court, and ran into similar difficulties. The approach was stated in general *qualitative* terms— holding presumptively unlawful a merger which "appreciably increases" the level of concentration in a market manifesting a "significant tendency" toward "undue concentration." But the test had to be applied to the stubborn *quantitative* facts of the particular case.

In light of the Department's theory, the critical question was whether the Los Angeles retail grocery market was manifesting, or tending toward, oligopoly pricing patterns. The Department maintained that the market was a "loose oligopoly," relying upon: (a) a classification by Professor Bain, an economist, which found some "elements of oligopoly" in industries in which the largest eight firms controlled more than 25 per cent of output and the largest sellers had more than "a few per cent apiece of the market"; and (b) the fact that major firms in the Los Angeles retail food market took account of the pricing practices of their major competitors in formulating their own pricing plans. The Department indicated that any market in which eight firms controlled more than 33 per cent of output could be regarded as oligopolistic.

The Department's approach poses a basic problem. If the Los Angeles grocery market was already unduly concentrated, there was no need to develop any new test to govern the situation. In markets thus concentrated, even small accretions by the leading firms were unlawful under previous decisions. See, particularly, *United States v. Aluminum Co. of America*, 377 U. S. 271 (1964). If, on the other hand, the market was not yet "unduly" concentrated, the Department's proposed test was unworkable without concrete quantitative guides. Three questions appeared to be presented by the Department's test:

(a) What level must concentration reach before it can be considered "undue"?
(b) How pronounced must be the tendency toward such concentration for it to be "significant"?
(c) How much must a merger raise the level of concentration for it to be an "appreciable increase"?

To answer the first question—as to when concentration becomes "undue"—the Department could have turned to empirical studies of the relation between oligopoly pricing and market concentration. The pioneering work in this field was done by Professor Bain, the economist upon whom the Government relied. His investigations—in contrast to his general theorizing—indicate that a critical point is reached where eight firms or less control 70 per cent or more of production in a market defined along fairly broad lines. Others have come to similar conclusions. This measure could have been selected by the Department as an approximation of "undue" concentration.

To answer the second question—as to when a trend toward concentration is "significant"—the Department would have had to be somewhat arbitrary, but it could have cited two factors as influential in the formation of a judgment. First, the answer to the question of "undue" concentration is only a rough approximation, so that in some markets significant oligopoly pricing may set in before eight firms obtain control of 70 per cent of output. Second, trends toward concentration are supposed to be stopped somewhere short of the brink, since the basic purpose of the law is prophylactic; accordingly, some margin of safety is appropriate. In light of these factors, the Department could have suggested that the tendency to concentration is "significant" when (a) concentration is increasing at a perceptible rate, and (b) existing concentration has reached a point halfway toward the stage where pronounced oligopoly behavior becomes likely—i.e., eight firms already control 35 per cent or more of output. Earlier intervention might be justified in a specific situation if there is evidence of oligopoly pricing, but such evidence is difficult to obtain (the Department's argument along this line in *Von's*, pointing to the reactions of the major chains to competitors' pricing policies, was not persuasive).

For the answer to the third question, whether a particular merger results in an "appreciable increase" in concentration, the Department could well have considered the institutional proposition that firms similarly situated should be treated similarly by the law. If one firm is permitted to obtain 5 per cent of a market by merger, it may be difficult to justify suppression of similar mergers by other firms. If a trend is in progress which has brought forth an affirmative answer to the second question, the issue here may be restated to ask: what mergers can be safely ignored notwithstanding that adverse trend? It may be safe to sanction mergers involving small companies which could be duplicated indefinitely by other small companies without transgressing the line indicated by the answer to the second question (8 firms with 35 per cent of output). But it would not be appropriate to sanction a merger which is too large to permit indefinite duplications by other companies. Since eight firms each controlling 5 per cent of the market would have an aggregate of 40 per cent of output, it would appear that 5 per cent for merging firms would be the outer limit in any market exhibiting a significant trend toward concentration.

These are not the only answers that might be given to the questions implicitly posed by the Department in *Von's*. There are, in fact, a number of important objections which would have to be considered before the preceding proposal could be adopted:

(1) The concentration studies of Bain and others are generally consistent in their findings, but there are some variations in the conclusions reached and a few contrary findings. It would be necessary to consider which studies were the most reliable and which findings could be accepted with confidence.

(2) The concentration studies to date have been concerned principally with manufacturing industries operating in national markets. There is some question as to whether their findings can be extrapolated

to retailing industries operating in multifarious local markets. Moreover, antitrust litigation has produced some strange markets—both in size and shape—and an initial issue in making use of concentration studies would be to determine whether the market definition employed in a particular antitrust case is consistent with the definitions underlying the concentration studies.

(3) The proposed test requires the courts to adopt explicit quantitative standards as a means of determining illegality under the antitrust laws. There have been approaches to such a methodology in a few antitrust cases—particularly *Standard Stations*, 337 U. S. 293 (1949), and *Philadelphia National Bank*, 374 U. S. 321 (1963). However, the formulation of quantitative standards generally has been left to legislative and administrative bodies, and there may be objection to their promulgation by judicial tribunals.

The first two objections, which involve the selection and application of economic knowledge, must be met and resolved on the merits. But this presents nothing new: the underlying economic issues are no less relevant because the courts and the parties have tended to talk about "monopoly" and "oligopoly" and "concentration" in loose terms. If, on the other hand, economic knowledge does *not* provide a basis for generalization, the alternatives are (a) rules specifying *per se* legality and illegality, or (b) case-by-case adjudications typified by *ad hoc* judgments on both administrative decisions to prosecute and judicial determinations of violation. The present drift of antitrust opinions indicates that *per se* rules are the most likely prospect, at least at the level of judicial determinations.

The third objection also is related to the question of alternatives. If quantitative standards represent the most rational means of complying with the statutory directives of the Clayton Act, are the courts obliged to adopt less rational techniques? If the judiciary's role in antitrust enforcement has been generally satisfactory, must the courts be abandoned simply because advances in economic knowledge require recourse to quantitative measures?

THE SUPREME COURT'S DECISION IN VON'S

The Supreme Court introduced new elements to both institutional approach and economic analysis; its stance was radically different from either of the preceding approaches to the merger problem.

With respect to institutional approach, the District Court and the Department of Justice differed in emphasis and technique, but apparently agreed that the "competition" to be preserved was the intensive rivalry of competing firms that would redound to the benefit of consumers. To the Supreme Court, the preservation of "competition" was treated as equivalent to the preservation of as many businessmen as possible, without apparent concern about the nature of their rivalry or its impact upon consumers. The merger was disapproved because, in the Court's view, it contributed to the reduction of the number of firms in the market.

The distinctive approach of the Supreme Court is illustrated by its concept of "concentration." In the Court's view, concentration was increasing because the number of firms in the market was decreasing. In a sense this is true, because concentration is not a concept which yields a single number for a given market; rather, "concentration" yields a series of ratios indicating the shares of the market controlled by the largest firms down to a designated, but variable, cut-off point. Thus, for the same market, concentration figures may indicate that the largest firm controls 10 per cent of production, the two largest 15 per cent, the ten largest 50 per cent, the hundred largest 70 per cent, the thousand largest 90 per cent, and the fifteen hundred largest (all in the market) 100 per cent. If the number of firms in the market is reduced from fifteen hundred to a thousand, concentration is increased in the sense that the thousand largest firms now control 100 per cent of output, whereas formerly they had controlled only 90 per cent. And this is true even though the shares of the largest, two largest, ten largest and hundred largest firms remain the same. The important question, however, is whether all changes in concentration ratios are of the same significance.[2]

In oligopoly analysis it is customary to focus on the shares of the largest four firms and largest eight firms and to pay some attention to market shares of firms within the top twenty. The reduction in total number of firms, if confined to attrition of very small firms on the fringe, has not generally been thought to be significant. But for the Supreme Court's purpose, given its concern about the survival of small firms, it was appropriate to focus on the firms on the fringe. On this premise, however, there was no need to talk about "concentration" at all, since the idea of attrition of small firms can be conveyed more precisely by dealing with numbers of firms. Perhaps the Supreme Court had failed to distinguish between the objective of preventing oligopoly—which requires a consideration of concentration ratios—and the objective of preserving small firms—which is not related to concentration ratios as they are normally used.

---

[2] For purposes of this discussion it is assumed that the nature of the market and of the participating firms remain unchanged. This was not true of food retailing in *Von's*. Automobiles greatly enlarged the area served by each store; and supermarkets carried much broader lines of merchandise than the small stores they replaced.

The Supreme Court's approach illustrates several things about the relation of economic analysis to legal regulation. First, the role of economic analysis can be altered sharply by changing the supposed policy objectives of the regulatory legislation. Economic analysis may be useful in distinguishing between diverse policy objectives, and in suggesting the implications of a choice between them. But once a choice has been made by an appropriate political instrumentality, economic analysis is unhelpful in indicating that a given result is desirable or undesirable because it serves or disserves some *other* policy objective which has been rejected. Thus, the oligopoly theory of the Department of Justice became superfluous once the Supreme Court had decided to pursue the policy objective of preserving small firms. Second, it may be observed that there is a tendency for political instrumentalities, such as courts, to manipulate economic concepts to implement the particular policy objectives they have chosen to pursue, even though the concepts may be poorly suited for the purpose. This was true of the Supreme Court's use of the concentration concept in the *Von's* case.

Given that the policy objective in *Von's* was to preserve small firms, economic analysis could have been used to better advantage to resolve the issue at hand. The Supreme Court was troubled by the reduction in total number of business firms in the Los Angeles retail grocery market. It condemned the Von's-Shopping Bag merger as contributing to this development in two ways: (a) the merger, together with other similar mergers, directly reduced the number of firms in the market; and (b) the merger produced a "more powerful" firm, which evidently was regarded as a menace to other firms in the market. Both grounds are dubious.

The unchallenged findings of the District Court made it clear that the principal factor behind the reduction of number of firms in Los Angeles grocery retailing was the technological shift from small neighborhood grocery stores to larger supermarkets located in shopping centers. It is doubtful that mergers played any substantial role in this development, and certainly the Von's-Shopping Bag merger was not part of this general trend.

The menace of the "more powerful" firm appears to be equally unfounded. Again, the unchallenged findings of the District Court indicated that smaller firms could enter, expand and prosper in the Los Angeles grocery market, and that larger firms possessed no distinctive competitive advantages over smaller ones. This point was made, not only by the defendants, but by the Department of Justice. And it was underlined by the position of the National Association of Retail Grocers, an organization composed of 40,000 local grocery operations. The Association urged that the merger should be held lawful, a point of view that is hardly compatible with the idea that mergers of this magnitude create companies that are a menace to their rivals.

Thus, at the very least, the economic reasoning of the Supreme Court required further elaboration to deal with the strong, inconsistent findings of the District Court. And in light of the Supreme Court's prior decisions emphasizing the oligopoly problem, the Court should have indicated why the preservation of small firms on the fringe of the market should be controlling, rather than the prevention of conditions conducive to oligopoly. Perhaps the answer is that the Court did not clearly distinguish between the two, as indicated in its comments about gravitating "from a market of many small competitors to one dominated by one or a few giants."

In *Von's,* the Supreme Court articulated an antimerger rule more stringent than that propounded by the Department of Justice. As the law now stands, apparently any horizontal merger can be proscribed if (a) it takes place in a market characterized by a declining number of firms and some degree of merger activity, and (b) it involves two firms which are neither small nor financially vulnerable. (Whether some minimum size in terms of market share will be required—say 5 or 7.5 per cent—is not clear.) This might be thought to be administratively sound, even though resting on dubious economic grounds, because it clarifies the conditions under which horizontal mergers will be held to be unlawful. In fact, this is not true. The Department of Justice, regarding the Supreme Court's rule as unduly broad—condemning mergers which are innocuous along with those which are economically harmful—has exercised considerable discretion in instituting actions against mergers. And the Department is free to apply its own standards, without meaningful judicial supervision, as long as they are less restrictive than those of the Supreme Court. While this may produce reasonably efficient law enforcement in the short run, it does so by placing essentially unsupervised discretion in the hands of enforcement officials. This discretion may be exercised without formally promulgated standards (or, for that matter, without any standards at all) and without assurance of continuity as one administrative official is succeeded by another. Thus, in the case of horizontal mergers, the attitude of the Supreme Court has created an area of administrative lawmaking where none was indicated by Congress and where, as a consequence, even the most elementary safeguards are lacking. That the officials of the Department may develop sound administrative practices to handle the determinations thus delegated to them, and formulate some minimum of standards and safeguards, hardly excuses the Court for enunciating rules which make possible this pattern of unauthorized and unsupervised administrative lawmaking.

Conclusion

In discussing the formulation of decisional standards, the *Von's* case was singled out for particular attention. But it is hardly unique. Indeed, horizontal mergers present relatively modest challenges in formulating meaningful standards. The problems posed by vertical and conglomerate mergers are more difficult, and the formulation of appropriate standards for evaluation of discriminatory practices under the Robinson-Patman Act is even more troublesome. In the regulated sector, where the degree of government intervention is larger, the scope and depth of requisite analysis is magnified proportionately. Thus although the year 1970 will mark the one hundredth anniversary of commission regulation of railroad rates, federal and state commissions are still struggling with the obstinate problem of determining the appropriate relation of one transportation rate to another—and appear to be making little headway.

If headway is to be made, it is necessary to call upon various aspects of economic analysis in addition to conventional legal reasoning.

First, the objectives and scope of the regulatory program must be clearly defined. This is chiefly an exercise in statutory interpretation. Even so, economic analysis may play a role by indicating the existence of multiple objectives, where a conventional reading might find only one; by suggesting situations in which statutory objectives may be conflicting or internally inconsistent; and by suggesting which of several possible objectives would make the most sense in situations where the legislative direction is unclear and leaves substantial discretion to the courts.

Thus, in *Von's*, although the statute spoke of "competition," the policy objective might be taken to mean the preservation of intensive interfirm rivalry, or the preservation of individual firms, or some combination of the two. In some circumstances, an attempt to increase interfirm rivalry might lead to attrition of individual firms—through failure of the weakest firms when confronted with intensified competition. In other situations, the preservation of individual firms might be important in maintaining sufficient numbers to prevent oligopoly patterns from emerging—although it would be self-defeating to place an "umbrella" over weaker firms in order to prevent an oligopoly from placing a similar "umbrella" over the market. In deciding whether to emphasize the prevention of oligopoly or the preservation of small firms (assuming that the statute and the legislative history afford some latitude), a court might turn to economic analysis to judge the relation of mergers to each of the two possible objectives. The court could also consider the respective advantages and disadvantages to the public of preventing oligopoly and preserving small firms.

Second, once objectives are selected and their relative importance determined, attention should focus on the means by which they are to be attained. Here the issues are almost entirely factual in nature, and economic theory and empirical data must be consulted in order to establish relationships between the various phenomena involved. It must be emphasized that specific cases cannot be resolved solely by investigating the facts of those cases. Without general propositions to serve as a linking mechanism, it is not possible to say whether the events in question will serve or disserve the policy objectives sought. Thus, all of the factors adduced by the District Court in *Von's* are without value unless accompanied by generalizations, express or implied, which indicate how the number of firms, ease of entry, etc., are related to the policy objective of maintaining interfirm rivalry. And the validity of such generalizations can be tested only by resorting to the accumulated knowledge and techniques embraced by economic analysis. Given the range and theoretical complexity of this material, it does not lend itself to easy or uneducated application.

Finally, any standard which is formulated must be administratively workable. The standard must be one that can be implemented by looking to phenomena that can be readily observed and classified. It is pointless to have a rule which requires the impracticable *(e.g.,* a flat prediction that an individual merger will or will not jeopardize interfirm rivalry); or which compels an investigation so broad in scope as to be impossible of repeated regulatory implementation *(e.g.,* the District Court's approach in *Von's*); or which purports to resolve quantitative problems by purely qualitative standards *(e.g.,* the Department's proposed test in the *Von's* case). Administrative considerations —calling for simplification and ease of application—are of principal importance at this stage; but the underlying analytical foundations must be kept in view so that the most significant operative factors are retained in the final regulatory standard. Thus, if the Supreme Court opinion in *Von's* were to be treated as a simplified application of oligopoly theory, it would have to be concluded that the simplification process had distorted the standard beyond recognition.

To function effectively in this area requires a combination of skills: the appreciation of statutory language and policies and a familiarity with administrative and institutional problems—which are part of the general experience of lawyers; but also an understanding of economic analysis—which, though not yet part of the standard equipment of lawyers, is clearly vital in the area of legal regulation.

Adam Yarmolinsky

6

Responsible Law-Making in a Technically Specialized Society

It is a commonplace fact that ours is a technically specialized society in which the technology is every day becoming more specialized and more intricate. One of the effects of this development is that the technical information relevant to decision-making appears to be accessible to decision-makers with diminishing facility and intelligibility. It might seem to follow from this situation that traditional decision-makers, in both private and public institutions and agencies, suffer the risk of ignoring the technicians or of being displaced by them. At the same time, decision-making may become less and less subject to effective review by those to whom the decision-makers are responsible. In the case of private organizations, serious questions are raised about traditional concepts of rights and obligations of those participating in private transactions. In the case of governmental agencies, the reality of government accountability to the public is challenged.

These are serious questions and it is appropriate that there be concern whether responsible law-making (including the "law-

ADAM YARMOLINSKY *is Professor of Law and a member of the Institute of Politics at Harvard University. In public life, Professor Yarmolinsky has been Special Assistant to the Secretary of Defense, Deputy Assistant Secretary of Defense for International Security Affairs, and also served as Deputy Director of the President's Anti-Poverty Task Force. In his private capacity, he has been Public Affairs Editor of Doubleday & Co., Secretary of the Fund for the Republic, and a lawyer in Washington, D. C.*

making" of private organizations) can be satisfactorily sustained in a technologically sophisticated society. Yet the questions and the risk of irresponsibility they imply must be seen in full context. When they are, the significance of technical considerations appears rather different than is often assumed.

Major issues of public policy seldom turn on the resolution of technical questions.

Take two extreme cases. The decision to proceed with the production of the first hydrogen bomb, while it would not have been possible without the application and organization of extraordinary technical skills, was very nearly a "pure" political question. That is to say it turned almost entirely on questions of political judgment and moral philosophy, to which the technician, qua technician, could bring no special expertise.

On the other hand, the decision to produce a single strike aircraft, the TFX, for Air Force and Navy use, and to buy it from the contractor who appeared to be most responsive to the Secretary of Defense's concern with maximum "commonality" between the Air Force and Navy versions of the airplane, was essentially a technical decision in a situation where the "political" forces were sufficiently in balance so that "technical" considerations could be decisive.

Neither decision was made by the direct exercise of the popular will. The process of consultation in the first decision was limited only by the demands of secrecy. In the second decision it was limited by the substantive character of the issues themselves. When asked about the whys and wherefores of the TFX decision, anyone closely involved in the decision might have replied, like the late Senator Connally to the young man who asked after his health, "Are you sure you have time to hear the answer to that question?"

Both decisions have been the subject of a certain amount of after-the-fact review. The transcendental character of the H-bomb decision put the issues beyond the reach of the experts, although more or less expert opinions about the state of the art in Soviet weaponeering and the availability of delivery systems were relevant. And this meant that decisive authority rested where it belonged (given the necessity for secrecy), with the Presidency—the apex of the structure of political responsibility. The TFX decision turned entirely on expertise—engineering expertise about the degree of common design that was feasible between the Air Force and the Navy models, and business expertise about the probable discrepancies between actual and projected costs of the two rival designs in a multi-billion dollar development and production program that would run over a period of years. For those who, like this author, believe that the decisions taken about the TFX—to build a joint-service airplane, and to award the contract to General Dynamics rather than to Boeing—were the correct ones, it seems fortunate that it was the administration that made these choices, and that the McClellan Committee chose to take the opposing view. If the sides had been reversed, the administration would still have won out, since it had the weight of authority on its side, even though the decision would have been wrong, and neither the Congress as a whole nor the informed public could inform itself fully enough to dispute that authority effectively. Again, decisive choice was exercised by the political authority with the broadest responsibility, and in a context in which technical considerations, being so intricate and so finely balanced, could be accorded political significance only by distorting them.

Most cases fall somewhere between these two. In most public policy decisions, non-technical issues are (almost always) paramount, but technical issues are (almost always) relevant and material. Before considering how technical issues can best be presented in public policy forums, it may be worth examining some of the limitations on the role that technical analysis can play in decision-making. These limitations are quite severe.

The Limits of Technical Analysis as a Policy-making Tool

To begin with, there are the internal limitations on technical analysis. Technical analysis, for our purposes, deals with what can be done, as distinct from considerations of what is desired to be done by various constituencies and interest groups. In the days of antiquity, most public issues involved the resolution of conflicts between interest groups that were relatively simple in content. "Technical" questions were most likely to be involved in issues of foreign and defense policy, as in Charles Hitch's famous illustration of the triumph of cruder, but cheaper iron spears over the superior, but more expensive bronze spears (since the cost advantage of the iron spears meant that even common soldiers could be equipped with them).

Although technical analysis is relevant to a much wider range of public policy questions than in former times, its relevance is limited by its own special characteristics.

THE IMPRECISIONS OF QUANTITATIVE DATA

Technical analysis is essentially quantitative analysis. (Political analysis can be quantitative also, as anyone knows who has estimated head counts.) This does not mean that technical analysis depends on the availability of precise numbers. The technical analysis relevant to difficult decisions—which is to say important decisions—usually involves quantitative measures (numbers) of many ranges of precision, and often the consideration of dimensions of a problem for which numbers are theoretically necessary but in fact unavailable. Many quantitative measures therefore are approximations, sometimes approaching guesswork. Technical analysis is not impossible in these circumstances, but its value is limited by the availability and reliability of the data. Not only is a great deal of the data needed for technical analysis of public policy problems simply not there, but what is there often breaks down alarmingly when one begins to inquire about how it was put together—whether it relates to census figures on Negro males living in the ghetto, or to body counts in Vietnam. A large part of the problem of obtaining good data lies in the reluctance of technical people to substitute real technical analysis for simple reliance on traditional approaches to quantitative assessments—a habit that is surprisingly even stronger among civilians in government than among military men.

In this connection, it should be observed that computers don't help with data gathering either. They only make it possible to digest large amounts of data more rapidly. If anything, the remarkable facility of computer data manipulation may impair appreciation of weaknesses in the data that are being manipulated. The succinct maxim of computer experts still applies: "Garbage in; garbage out."

THE POLITICAL CONTEXT

More important than the internal limitations in technical analysis, however, are the external limitations on the role that such analysis can play in decision-making. Alain Enthoven has said,

> The most the analysis can do is to make clear to the decision-maker the difference in cost and effectiveness between the two approaches so that he can make an informed judgment about their weight in relation to the political problems.

But the in-box of the political decision-maker is full to overflowing with problems generated by the political situation in which he must operate. The magnitude and complexity of these non-quantifiable aspects of the question confronting the decision-maker usually overshadow its technical ones, often so much so that technical matters are never reached. He is like the man who observed about a particularly troublesome problem that it didn't keep him awake at night only because he had so many other problems to worry about first that by the time he got around to that one, it was time to wake up.

The technical advisor too often, therefore, finds himself unable to reach the policy-maker with relevant technical material, even where he has whole new concepts for approaching the policy problems, because the policy-maker is simply too busy listening to partisans on all sides of the issue. This being true, the technical advisor is tempted to take his advice directly to the partisans, and doing so may be his best contribution to the over-all problem.

What the experts have to say is still only a small part of the input to political decisions. It will remain a small part so long as available alternatives are limited by what the non-experts—in the bureaucracy, in the Congress, or in the general public—are willing to accept. Technical analysis reaches for the best possible solution. Functional budgeting, for example, is an analytical tool designed to identify all the costs of doing a particular job, whether it is in a weapons system or in a school system. Functional budgeting, taken together with other analytical tools, points toward the best possible solution to a problem. But the political decision-maker starts from the status quo, however inadequate or unfair or dangerous it may be, and he knows (or believes) that in the foreseeable future he can move only a small distance away from it. If the distance between the status quo and the technically optimum solution is great, as it often is, what the technical advisor can provide the political decision-maker just does not get used.

Still another limit on what the technician can get across to the politician is how much the politician can get across to the public. A sub-cabinet official in Washington who was arguing the cost justification of certain domestic programs with a sympathetic senator, pointed out that the cost of these programs over the years had remained steady as a percentage of GNP. "That's too complicated an idea to use," replied the senator. "If you could tell me the cost hadn't risen at all, I could use it."

PROBLEMS OF COMMUNICATION

Technical ideas and facts are hard to explain, not only because of their inherent difficulty, but because attempts to explain them go forward in contention with attempts to explain other complicated problems to distracted politicians and a distracted public. The media are clogged with information, true and false, important and unimportant, relevant and irrelevant. They are many times noisier than they used to be. The Lincoln-Douglas debates, for example, were conducted on no higher plane than some of the contemporary debates about the anti-ballistic missile, or the problems of nuclear proliferation. But they faced a good deal less competition for public attention. It did not detract from the intellectual content of political discourse in the 19th century that it was also designed to provide entertainment. But it wasn't competing with the Johnny Carson Show.

So great are the uses of public information media, indeed, that there is a kind of built-in credibility gap in the contemporary political scene, which makes the communication of technical information proportionately more difficult. Instant access to the media is almost taken for granted by the proponents of any special viewpoint or special interest. At the first meeting of any new group, whether in a ghetto or on a campus, one of the first items on the agenda is the press release (usually accompanied by a press conference). Many press releases go from the mimeograph machine through the mails and straight to the wastebasket, but many appear, without attribution, in the press. And for every formal press release there are a dozen leaks, planned and unplanned, off the record, not for attribution, shallow background or deep background. The problem for the sophisticated newspaper reader, particularly in Washington, is to figure out who inspired what statement in an apparently straightforward news story, and why. Against this background of ploy and counterploy, the problem of conveying even relatively simple technical information to the public is almost insuperable.

Technical data can be subject to instant inflation also, through the immediacy of the mass media. The cranberry scare in the 1950's is an example of this kind of inflation. The discovery by the Department of Health, Education and Welfare that a chemical spray used on cranberry bogs might have left a dangerous residue on the cranberries was so sensationally handled between the press, the agency, and the Congress that it produced a panic among food buyers, an almost cranberryless Thanksgiving, and endless recriminations. The same problem has dogged the footsteps of the Federal Radiation Council, which is charged with monitoring the level of radiation in the atmosphere. Until the adoption of the Atmospheric Test Ban Treaty, the Council had the problem of fixing acceptable levels of radiation for peaceful industrial uses of atomic energy, and of reporting on the effects of weapon testing, ours and other nations'. This dual responsibility required the Council to assess increases in the background radiation level, as a result of testing, which were in excess of permitted industrial levels. The task of explaining that these increases, while they would indeed increase the likelihood of genetic or biological damage, were not large enough to justify special safety measures (like dumping milk, for example) proved to be an almost impossible one. It was of course aggravated by some apparent efforts to use the Council's report for political purposes, but even with the best will in the world, the Council members found that the technical facts were simply too emotionally charged to get them across to the general public in an objective fashion.

Given all these limitations on technical data and analysis as an effective input to political decisions, the question remains: how can the effectiveness of this input be increased, so that the law-making processes are more responsible?

The Uses of Technical Analysis

Most federal law-making originates or wholly takes place in the Executive Branch of the federal government, whether in the form of administration bills, executive orders, departmental regulations, or speeches by the President or Presidential appointees. And the same pattern is likely to occur at the state and local level. The most effective tool yet devised to encourage a more analytical approach to Executive Branch decision-making is the so-called PPBS—Program Planning and Budgeting System—adopted from the Department of Defense and now being applied to other departments and agencies under the guidance of the Budget Bureau, and being picked up by state and local government as well.

THE PROGRAM PLANNING AND BUDGETING SYSTEM

First of all, the Program Planning and Budgeting System is not a panacea, nor a magic formula. What PPBS amounts to, in brief, is an effort to make a system out of a common-sense, long-term approach. It calls on departments and agencies to articulate their long-term policy objectives, to tie these objectives down to operational goals, to ask themselves, "How do we get there from here?", and then to compare the costs and the effectiveness of alternative routes toward the goals. It requires planners to quantify their objectives, in dollars and in units of housing, or employment, or hospital beds, or classrooms— again using ranges of numbers at least as often as definite single numbers. It requires them to plan not just for the current year, or the budget year that they are defending before the Budget Bureau and the Congress, but for stretches of five years or longer, looking ahead as far down the road as they can reasonably see. And it extrudes hidden paradoxes of government policy—for example, that the Interior Department is spending taxpayers' money to reclaim unusable farm land, while the Department of Agriculture is paying farmers not to plant crops on useable acreage.

PPBS is only as good as the people who operate it. Installing the system requires the departments and agencies to take on new men with advanced training in the black arts of systems analysis and cost-

benefit studies. These men are in very scarce supply, and their availability is probably the limiting factor on the installation of the system.
It becomes increasingly critical as the technique is applied at lower
levels of government.

Observers have pointed out that there are built-in disadvantages as
well as advantages to PPBS. What can be quantified tends to be more
highly valued than what cannot be. And the least difficult factor to
quantify is dollar costs. Yet, it has been argued, the United States is
so rich a country that relative costs, particularly of domestic programs
that make up such a tiny percentage of GNP, should seldom dominate
the decision whether to adopt a program or to reject it. It is always
difficult to balance economic cost against such imponderables as individual human dignity or self-respect, or even against the political
costs of a particular course of action. If the one can be quantified and
the other cannot, then there is at least a tendency to give more weight
to economic cost. The answer to this argument, on the other hand,
is that the cost factor is always present at the decision. PPBS only makes
costs clearer and more specific, and alternatives more immediately available.

PPBS tends to surface technical data, and it tends to force the data
into apparently objective form, drawing on observations and calculations that can presumably be replicated. But the data are still only as
good as their original sources. And, while it can thus be a constant
reminder that the data going into decision-making are only as good
as their original sources, PPBS can also result in the fallacy of abstraction—where information in quantitative form is treated as more
reliable than it may deserve to be.

There is an even more fundamental problem, however. Long before
PPBS was invented, completed staff work assumed that the decision-
maker would be presented by his staff with all the available alternatives, and the arguments on behalf of each one. He would be given
the staff's preferred alternative, and the reasons why they preferred
it, together with the necessary pieces of paper that he would have to
sign in order to make the preferred alternative come to pass, carefully
marked with a stiff cardboard tab, so that the harried executive could
turn to the signature page, if he wished, and skip the rest of the
dossier.

The difficulty with this approach is that it doesn't always insure the
fullest consideration by policy-makers of less likely alternatives. PPBS
by itself does very little to cure this weakness in policy-making by
bureaucracies (again using a term in a non-pejorative sense). It does
help to reduce the built-in bias in favor of things-as-they-are, because,
by encouraging system-wide study of available alternatives, it calls

attention to a persistent phenomenon in established programs: an established operating program will tend to be run so that all its characteristics that are not being called into question at a particular time are skewed toward the most efficient operation *without* changing the characteristic that may be at issue. Or, to put it differently, so that it is efficient at the retail level even if not at the wholesale. When these secondary characteristics are examined and made eligible for change, another alternative at the primary or "wholesale" policy level may turn out to be more effective. The size of oil tankers may be limited by the capacity of canal locks, until one considers whether oversize tankers may be more efficient even if they take the long way round. A food supplement program involving direct distribution to the poor may look efficient because it avoids middlemen's overhead, but not so efficient if it becomes evident that the types of food which can be directly distributed—chiefly dried vegetables and starches—are unwanted or less needed by the intended beneficiaries. The SKYBOLT missile, mounted on manned bombers, would have improved the bombers' effectiveness by permitting them to knock out defenses around the target before they arrived over it. But it turned out that the job could be done more effectively and less expensively by using surface-to-surface missiles, so SKYBOLT was abandoned—and a major diplomatic crisis was precipitated. But there is still a need for more adequate consideration of late-blooming alternatives.

The Uses and Limits of the Adversary System

Perhaps the best way to give a fairer hearing to these alternatives—whether latent or simply late-blooming—is to employ the adversary method more extensively throughout the policy process. In fact, the adversary system is more widespread throughout government, outside formal adjudicatory proceedings, than is generally realized. It didn't take the Joint Staff very long to realize that, when the Secretary of Defense had built up a systems analysis staff in his own office, they should stop fighting the problem and begin to build their own systems analysis capability. Issues of international security policy may pit State Department analysts against Defense Department analysts (frequently in unexpected alignments), and issues of foreign economic policy will generate opposing positions among the Departments of State, Treasury, Commerce, Labor, etc., etc. There were of course comparable adversary presentations by the private manufacturers in the TFX problem, and between the House Ways and Means Committee and the Executive in the recent controversy over the proposed tax increase. But there are limits to the effectiveness of the adversary process in these situations. The adversary process may obscure vital questions more than it illuminates them. The adversary positions of private interests are obviously dominated by parochial concerns, and may consciously involve exclusion of possibilities that neither contender wishes to have considered. Struggles such as that over the tax increase may only mask more fundamental but unstated differences, for example differences about the aims and scope of the poverty program or the Vietnam war. The positions taken in controversies between government agencies generally represent bureaucratic interests, and bureaucracies are not inclined to play long shots.

Perhaps policy-makers should stay away from long shots, too. But at least they should be told the combination of circumstances in which ‹ the long shot might just pay off. And here ingenuity is required to get the information pushed up to the policy-making level. Advocates can be designated within a staff to reach out for unlikely ideas and explore them. But these advocates will only survive if they enjoy the continuing confidence of their bosses. The temptation to get back into the mainstream is almost overwhelming, particularly when the mainstream itself is moving at jet speed. Still more effort is required to give strength and status to the advocate of the unlikely within the Executive Branch, at every level of government.

There is a large area of governmental activity, however, in which the clash of ideas is formalized in a variety of hearings, public and semi-public. These forums also have increasingly to deal with technical data of a formidably specialized character. It is a troubling spectacle to see a county board in public session attempting to draft an anti-pollution ordinance, or a congressional committee attempting to review the details of a proposed foreign aid appropriation. One has to conclude, perhaps reluctantly, that a public hearing is simply not a proper occasion for the communication or the analysis of technical data. A public hearing is essentially a dramatic occasion, when the salient conclusions, already reached, can be boldly presented, largely by the choice of appropriate examples, to a large audience. Under optimum conditions, it may serve as a seminar, in which fundamental ideas are explored. But it cannot determine the appropriateness of the examples selected for display, and it cannot be employed to make legislative choices unless and until the issues have been sharpened, as they are in a judicial proceeding before the actual trial or appellate hearing takes place.

Indeed there has developed a whole art of hearing preparation, by no means to be condemned, in which the salient points of the most complex problems and proposals are presented through testimony, colloquy and visual displays, with appropriate changes of pace to hold the interest of the audience. But the perfection of the art raises a question as to how one assures that there is maximum emphasis on the accuracy of the presentation, as distinguished from its dramatic qualities.

Just where does this leave us? One's first conclusion must be that traditional safeguards, as contained in the rules of evidence, are of relatively little value in protecting the hearing process as applied to policy-making. An expert can be properly qualified, but on complicated questions expert opinion is available on all sides of the issue, and qualifying one expert does nothing to indicate his (expert) bias.

One's second conclusion must be that the locus of actual decision-making has moved even further from the public forum than when it moved some time ago from the legislative chamber to the committee room. The shape and fate of legislation is decided not in committee sessions, but when two or three are gathered together. One's third conclusion must be that the quality of staff work and the level of staff competence grow in importance with the increasing importance of the technical questions involved. All these concern matters of political and administrative process and structure, relevant for the law and the lawyer. And it is to be hoped that tender regard for the traditions inherent in rules of evidence, of the right to be heard, and of visible and explicit responsibility of public officials, will not obscure the growing limitations on the effectiveness of these devices to assure that public policy-making is responsible.

The Lawyer's Contribution

A fourth conclusion, perhaps less obvious, is that the lawyer's basic skills—the skills that make the law, in Frankfurter's phrase "the art of the relevant"—are fundamental to the integration of technical data into responsible law-making. As the body of technical information continues to expand, the lawyer's ability to distill out what is essential to a decision grows in importance. It is worth noting, in the interest of minimizing lawyers' smugness, that the approach to professional education that emphasizes learning where to find the information and how to use it, has spread well beyond the law (if it was ever confined to law schools) and is now the new wave in medical education, among other fields.

Lawyers are still the largest source, though by no means the exclusive one, of the kind of government officials who have the quality of "toughness"—as the word was used in the Kennedy administration talent hunt to test the ability of a candidate for high office to resist the pressures from his own staff—to use the technicians instead of being used by them. And one of the best ways to build this quality into the public service turned out to be the recruitment of persons who did not regard government as a permanent career, but who saw themselves as "in-and-outers," coming from a base in private life, in law or business or the universities into government for a tour of duty, and then returning to the private sphere until it might be time for another tour. The development of this pattern as one of the ways of filling top-level jobs in government—and hopefully in state and local as well as in national government—seems one of the most effective ways of securing more responsible decision-making in the face of increasing technical specialization.

Technical specialization increasingly complicates the factual basis for decision-making. Procedural improvements can make decision-makers more aware of the full scope of the alternatives available to them. But procedural improvements cannot significantly increase the narrow restrictions imposed by the political process, nor can they do a great deal to increase the depth of public comprehension. In the last analysis, it is the quality of the men that determines the quality of the decisions. Public judgments of that quality are assisted by the public view of decisions in which the technical content is minimal, although public judgments are obscured by all the devices of publicity. It has been charged that in public life too much emphasis is being placed on style and not enough on substance. But how public men express themselves reflects the quality of their mental processes. How they think about things has a good deal to do with the things they think about. And how they frame the issues affects the shape of their solutions. If the substance of so many decisions is necessarily not open to effective public examination, considerations of public style may not be altogether irrelevant to the measurement of public responsibility.

Murray L. Schwartz

7

Changing Patterns of Legal Services

A Brief History

On January 20, 1513, Balboa, the Spanish Admiral of the Great South Sea, wrote his monarch imploring him that "no bachelors of law" be permitted to come to the New World. A century later, in constitutions, charters and legislation, the English colonists demonstrated the same hostility to lawyers. These early efforts to prohibit, restrict or drastically regulate the practice of law recurred at least until the Civil War, the high-water marks of the opposition being in the immediate post-Revolution period and the Jacksonian era. Indeed, hostility to lawyers and the legal profession is no stranger to the twentieth century. Just a few years ago the voters of Arizona repudiated by a four-to-one majority an effort by the Bar—supported by judicial decision—to keep real estate brokers out of the business of drafting or filling in forms in real estate transactions.

Nevertheless, throughout United States history, the lawyer has been something of a folk hero, a principal source of political leaders, and the symbol of the American dream of upward social mobility. The popular attitude toward lawyers has been and is schizophrenic. Lawyers and the law have been favorite topics of conversation, the subjects of adulation, and the objects of damning indictments.

MURRAY L. SCHWARTZ, who is Associate Dean and Professor of Law at the University of California, Los Angeles, and Reporter, Legislative Revision of the California Penal Code, has been a Consultant to the President's Task Force on the War Against Poverty. He has practiced law, written books and articles, and served as Vice-Chairman of the California State Bar Committee on Group Legal Services.

Yet, despite the high level of visibility of law and lawyers, it was not until this decade that serious effort was undertaken to examine the legal profession critically—to consider its structure from the standpoint of the adequacy with which it performs its role of producing and distributing legal services. It is also fair to say that the marked changes in the structure of the profession which have actually taken place in the past one hundred years will be equalled or surpassed by those that will take place during the next.

In the late nineteenth century, lawyers for the most part practiced alone, or with one partner (one was the "court," the other the "office," lawyer) or clerk. The great majority of Americans lived in rural environments and, correspondingly, the great majority of lawyers practiced in small towns, with clear visibility to their neighbors. The practice, reflecting the economic conditions of the day, centered on real estate transactions and the commercial exchange, although there was no specialization as such and every lawyer would handle just about everything that came his way. The practice of law was truly private and individual, whether viewed from the perspective of the lawyer or of the client.

As the nineteenth century gave way to the twentieth, rural America was replaced by urban America. Real incomes rose and more people had higher standards of living than ever before in human history. Transactions involving wealth became common among larger numbers of Americans. The aggregation of capital in a comparatively few corporate entities was followed by the aggregation of labor in a comparatively few unions. The automobile and the telephone multiplied voluntary and involuntary personal contacts among Americans to unheard-of numbers, and cheap and rapid distribution of the products of printing presses made nearly every American immediately aware of events throughout the world. Government intervention and participation in economic and social affairs increased in an almost continuous geometric curve. The immigrant class progressed from the lowest economic level through the homogenizing melting pot into the great American middle class, but the process of upward assimilation broke down for the urban Negro, who seemed trapped in never-ending poverty.

All of these changes had an inevitable impact upon the structure of the legal profession and the roles of lawyers. What may have worked in the 1870's was not assured of success in the 1970's. If there was a logic to history, it surely pointed to the opposite conclusion.

And the legal profession did change. Thus, industrialization and the concentration of capital stimulated a parallel development in the structure of law firms, which grew larger in size, tended to concentrate in the financial and commercial districts of the cities, turned to the service of corporate organizations, and developed intra-firm specialties, so as to provide better services to the clients whose affairs ranged over the legal spectrum. Increased participation and intervention of government in economic and social affairs developed a greater need for lawyers in government. Correspondingly, more lawyers spent more time for private clients in government-related legal work. Further inroads upon the nineteenth century forms of practice resulted from the more recent tendency of large corporate enterprises to employ their own lawyers on a full time basis as corporate or house counsel.

A profile of the Bar of the middle twentieth century is thus drastically different from that of the Bar of the late nineteenth. Today, over twenty per cent of the lawyers who practice in the United States are "one-client" (government or corporate unit) lawyers, receiving all their income from one source. The number, size and proportion of lawyers practicing in law firms have continued to increase, and, of those lawyers who still practice as individuals, office-sharing and reciprocal arrangements with other lawyers—de facto partnerships—are common. Although a majority of those lawyers who are in private practice are still recorded as practicing in one or two-man law firms, the trend toward aggregation of lawyers into larger units persists; law firms with over 100 lawyers and 200 or 300 supporting personnel have appeared on the scene. More lawyers today are employees—of either other lawyers or of corporate or governmental institutions—than even the most prescient nineteenth-century seer could have predicted.

The adequacy of the structure of the Bar of the twentieth century to provide legal services to business and corporate enterprises as yet has not been seriously questioned. But questions did emerge concerning the adequacy of the structure of the Bar to provide legal services to other groups. It became sharply apparent that one group that had escaped the notice of the legal profession was the poor, and, particularly, those poor who seem unable to break the poverty cycle. Recent attention to their plight, mandated by judicial decision in criminal cases and by federal programs generally, resulted in introspective inquiries within the Bar. Had the Bar, concentrating on affairs of wealth and of corporate enterprise, neglected other responsibilities? And, perhaps more fundamentally, was the Bar's structure adequate to satisfy the legal needs of all Americans in the 1960's and beyond—including not only the poor but the middle and lower-middle income groups as well?

Restraints upon the Providing of Legal Services

The problem of the structure of the Bar has sometimes been stated as the question whether there is an unfulfilled need for legal services, particularly among the middle and lower-middle income groups. Yet, as the American Bar Association's Special Committee on Availability of Legal Services wrote in its 1966 report, this may be asking the "wrong question." The right question begins with the incidence of problems confronting people which lawyers can help to solve. In the words of the Committee,

> the utility and thus the availability and ultimate use of legal services must be considered in the light of alternate resources available to the potential client for assistance in solving his problem. A necessary consequence of any such inquiry is the removal of any impediments to the utilization of legal services to make them at least as freely available as alternate services.

Put in these terms, the more general question can be analyzed into specific elements. Are the existing patterns for providing legal services adequate to: (1) enable the average person to be aware that a problem confronting him has consequences for which the services of a lawyer would be helpful; (2) enable the average person to make an informed decision whether the cost of those legal services is worth paying in the light of the probable benefits of the services; (3) provide him, in appropriate cases, with financial resources to pay those costs; (4) bring him together with a lawyer in whom he has confidence and who has the competence to provide the appropriate assistance.

Thus, what is required is a systematic inquiry into the present patterns of producing and distributing legal services—in the instant context—for the middle- and lower-income groups of the population. For other types of product or service-producing industries, these questions are generally answered by reference to the market mechanism. Products and services are offered and advertised on a basis that is competitive both with respect to alternative products and services and with respect to other producers in the same industry. In the case of legal services, however, as a consequence of professional restrictions neither of these market mechanisms has been operative. Far more than in most enterprises, the potential consumer of legal services has been forced to rely upon his own resources to determine whether he has a problem for which legal services would be useful and which lawyer he should seek to render assistance. The principal relevant professional restrictions are: unauthorized practice prohibitions, restrictions against professional solicitation and advertising, and interdiction of intermediary groups which could serve as channels between potential client and lawyer.

Unauthorized practice—Originating in the barrister tradition of the English Inns of Court and supported by the necessity for competence and expertise in litigation, the conception of unauthorized practice received judicial and statutory reinforcement in the United States. With a few exceptions (administrative agency representation, self-representation, arbitration, small claims courts are leading examples), it is largely uncontroverted today that only lawyers may represent others in litigation. At the same time, to a far greater degree than was ever true of the English barrister, the functions of the American lawyer extend beyond the courtroom to practically every area of economic and social affairs; the number of American lawyer hours spent in litigation-related activities is probably a small fraction of those spent in activities of counselling, drafting, negotiation and the like.

Retrospectively, it was predictable that, as the economic and social changes of the twentieth century made their impact, and as the Bar retained its basically atomistic structure, other organizations would arise to compete with the Bar for the non-litigation portions of the Bar's business. It was also predictable that these organizations would attempt to pre-empt routine transactions which occurred in large numbers with little deviation. Thus arose collections agencies, title insurance companies, real estate agencies and other institutions which specialized in one form of activity and adopted new techniques to handle the volume.

The Bar's response to the rise of these other agencies was not so much to change its own ways of handling its business as to rely upon unauthorized practice doctrines to eliminate the competition. Indeed, the Bar has directed a great deal of energy against the rise of these parallel service agencies which offer to the public, frequently at lower cost, services which lawyers characterize as legal services and therefore exclusively within their own domain.

The issue was clearly joined in the 1930's, significantly a period of depression and of the recognition of the impact of industrialization upon the social order. It was during this period that the Bar, in its war against automobile clubs, insurance companies and the like, adopted the technique of entering into treaties with these organizations— treaties which attempted to delimit the activities of these organizations, or, more accurately, to exclude them from the lawyer's predetermined domain.

The unauthorized practice controversy is, however, far from settled. The viability of the treaties, even if enforced by a militant Bar and favorable judicial decision, is questionable. How long the Bar, with its present structure, can retain its monopoly over these types of transactions against the economic pressure of the parallel organizations, themselves assisted by lawyers, is debatable.

Be that as it may, it seems clear that one consequence of the unauthorized practice restrictions has been to reduce the impact of external

competition upon the structure of the Bar, upon its techniques of
producing and distributing legal services.

Solicitation and advertising—Highly relevant to the unauthorized
practice controversy are the professional restrictions against solicitation
and advertising by lawyers. To the extent that the competitive entities
do solicit and do advertise for business, it is clear that lawyers, as
lawyers, will be at a disadvantage in attempting to obtain and retain
that business, for the rules of the profession restrict or suppress the
use by lawyers of these kinds of devices. Indeed, a frequently voiced
argument in support of the unauthorized practice restrictions is the
unfairness to the Bar which results from the ability of the other
agencies to advertise and solicit.

Deriving from the barrister antecedents of the Bar, and justified by
reference to the evils of stirring up of litigation, fraudulent claims, corruption of public officials, overreaching, overcharging and under representation of clients, and, more generally, to the "deprofessionalization"
of the Bar, the modern restrictions upon lawyers' aggressive business-
getting have, for present purposes, two important consequences. The
first is that, with the exception of the mildest kind of institutional advertising, lawyers as a group do not make their availability known to
the public at large. The second is that individual lawyers or law firms
cannot compete for the middle or lower-middle income client in the
market with other lawyers or law firms for clients on a service or price,
or indeed, on any basis except that of "reputation."

Anti-intermediary restrictions—The third relevant restriction has
been that which prohibits the introduction of an intermediary organization between the lawyer and the potential client. The rule, as expressed in Canon 35 of the American Bar Association's present Canons
of Professional Ethics, is that, while a lawyer may accept employment
from any organization "to render legal services in any matter in which
the organization, as an entity, is interested," this employment "should
not include the rendering of legal services to the members of such an
organization in respect to their individual affairs." Closely related to
the concerns about unauthorized practice and solicitation and advertising, the anti-intermediary restriction incorporates another deeply
felt professional value: unswerving loyalty to the client. In the organized Bar's view, using an intermediary organization as a bridge
between lawyer and potential client carries with it the possibility that
the lawyer's allegiance might be directed more to the organization than
to the client.

Such distinguished leaders of the Bar as Henry Drinker and Roger
Traynor have opposed an interpretation of Canon 35 that prevents
arrangements between organization and lawyer whereby the lawyer

agrees to represent the members of the organization in specified types of legal transactions. But the anti-intermediary rules constituted a substantial barrier to the development of different patterns of providing legal services from those that existed in the 1870's.

The automobile: an instance of accommodation—Concessions in the face of mounting pressures resulting from changing economic, technological and social conditions were, however, made. For the average potential client, the automobile presents a striking illustration of the type of pressures and the accommodations made. Indeed the automobile had almost as profound an impact upon the average American's relation with his lawyer as it did upon his sexual relations. It made the population more mobile, thus breaking the links of visibility between the lawyer and his small town neighbors; it accelerated the trend toward urbanization; and it increased the frequency and gravity of legal problems with which the average citizen was likely to be confronted in his lifetime. Automobile clubs and automobile insurance companies were the natural consequences of this development, and, inevitably, the extent to which those institutions could provide legal services became a major problem for the Bar and the public. The compromise, worked out by treaty and change in the ethical rules, was to exclude the automobile clubs from furnishing lawyers to represent their members, but to permit the insurance companies, which had financial interests of their own at stake, to furnish those lawyers.

THE GENERAL IMPACT OF THE RESTRAINTS

Although changes in the patterns of providing legal services were made where the pressure seemed irresistible as in the case of liability insurance and in the growth of the large law firm, the average citizen was still required to recognize for himself that he had a "legal" problem; other enterprises were prohibited by unauthorized practice doctrines from attempting to reach and to service him in those areas where their services overlapped with those traditionally denominated as legal. Once recognizing that he had a legal problem, the potential client was remitted to the Yellow Pages of the telephone book (where, pursuant to professional restrictions against advertising of specialties, lawyers' unique interest or competence did not appear), to the casual advice of friends or others, or, in some communities, to a Lawyers' Referral Service, which suffered from defects which will be subsequently discussed.

Portents of Change

In these circumstances, it is not surprising that there has been continuing pressure for the creation of new ways for providing legal services; nor is it surprising that the innate conservatism of the Bar and its protection of traditional attributes of professionalism have engendered opposition to the creation of these forms. Yet, the movement for change has begun, stimulated on the legal level by judicial decision and supported by a few voices from the organized Bar.

JUDICIAL INTERVENTION

If it is not the case that all major questions in American life are ultimately referred to judicial solution, it is nevertheless foreseeable that at least problems of providing legal services will be so referred. For the courts (who not only come from the ranks of lawyers but daily deal with them and their clients) have consistently insisted upon their control over the practice of law.

Until 1963, with few exceptions the judiciary had confirmed the previously described professional restrictions, and, impliedly, the existing patterns of providing legal services. But since then the picture has changed dramatically as a result of three decisions of the Supreme Court of the United States.

The NAACP case—The first came in 1963 in a civil rights case, *NAACP v. Button,* 371 U. S. 415 (1963). Virginia had applied its barratry statute to the National Association for the Advancement of Colored People, enjoining the practices by which the NAACP furnished and paid for counsel to represent both its members and nonmembers in civil rights cases. The Supreme Court of the United States struck down the Virginia ruling, holding that the NAACP's activities were protected by the First Amendment to the Constitution of the United States.

The BRT case—Whatever hopes the Bar might have had that the NAACP case was *sui generis,* resulting from the obvious social significance of the litigation stimulated by the NAACP and the equally obvious difficulty in obtaining local lawyers who would handle such cases, were dashed in the second case, *Brotherhood of Railroad Trainmen v. Virginia,* 377 U. S. 1 (1964) . In the *BRT* case, the Supreme Court of the United States again overturned an attempt to prohibit a pattern of providing legal services that deviated from the traditional forms. The Brotherhood developed a national program that divided the country into regions in each of which specific lawyers were designated as Regional Counsel. Members of the Brotherhood injured in their employment who might have claims against the employing railroads under the Federal Employers' Liability Act were referred by union representatives to those lawyers, who had previously agreed upon the contingent fees they would charge, although each lawyer-client relationship was entered into individually. The Supreme Court held the BRT program was also protected by the First Amendment. The state could not prevent the members of the union from getting together to agree to help and advise one another in asserting their rights, including advice about the need for legal assistance, and, in the words of the Court, "most importantly, what lawyer a member could confidently rely on."

The UMWA case—The third case, *United Mine Workers of America v. Illinois State Bar Association*, 88 S.Ct. U. S. 353 (1967), reinforces NAACP and BRT and extends them, among other things by eliminating the possibility that those cases be regarded as limited to legal assistance in matters concerning federal law. The UMWA employed a lawyer on a salary basis to represent members and their dependents in connection with claims for personal injuries and death under the Illinois Workmen's Compensation Act. Whereas in BRT the injured member was personally responsible for the payment of the lawyer's contingent fee, in the UMWA plan the injured member paid nothing; he received the proceeds of any recovery. The lawyer's compensation was derived directly and solely from the union on a salary basis. This was a step beyond BRT the Illinois Supreme Court had refused to permit, for it held that the plan constituted the unauthorized practice of law and enjoined its operation. The reversal of this holding by the Supreme Court of the United States has implications for the traditional forms of providing legal services which are manifestly profound, for it is difficult to conceive of practical and attractive group legal arrangements that would not be protected by the rule it announces.

A FEW VOICES FROM THE BAR

The judicial assaults upon the traditional ethical restrictions have been echoed in expressions of concern from the organized Bar. The first was that of the Group Legal Services Committee of the State Bar of California which, after several years of study, wrote a comprehensive report in 1964, dealing with the subject of "group legal service" plans, defined broadly as any arrangement which contemplated third-party involvement in the financing of legal costs or in retaining attorneys for representation of individuals. The California committee concluded that a substantial number of group legal service plans were actually operating in the state, that they served the public interest, and that the best interests of the Bar would be served, not by attempting to prohibit such patterns of providing services, but by attempting to assure that they satisfied certain professional standards. In its 1966 Report, the American Bar Association's Special Committee on Availability of Legal Services agreed that the principal problem was the establishment of appropriate safeguards to preserve the ethical standards of the pro-

fession and to protect the public, suggesting a dramatic shift of the
Bar's earlier total condemnation of any such plan.

The Functions of New Patterns of Providing Legal Services

Whatever qualifications later decisions may impose upon the
apparent holdings of the three cases, it is clear that there is infinitely
more room today for innovation in the development of new patterns of
providing legal services for the middle and lower-income groups in
the society than has been true in the past. The programs involved in
the three principal cases do not exhaust the possibilities. Each of those
plans did make individuals aware that transactions in which they were
involved had legal implications and that lawyers were available to
assist in the handling of those matters. All three directed the potential
client to a particular lawyer, although under both the BRT and the
UMWA plans the union member was theoretically free to choose a
different lawyer from the one recommended by the union. In the
NAACP and UMWA plans the organization paid the costs of the legal
services; in the BRT plan, the member paid the costs out of his recovery. Significantly, each plan was limited to one particular type of
subject matter—civil rights or occupational injuries. So, too, each plan
was confined to fairly well-defined groups—Negroes with civil rights
problems or union members. Thus none was limitless with respect to
potential client or subject matter.

Each plan responded to a perceived inadequacy in the structure of
providing legal services. It is most likely that new patterns of providing
legal services, whatever form they may take, will also be addressed to
satisfying perceived inadequacies in the existing structure. To re-
capitulate the problems set forth earlier, the underlying question is
whether the existing patterns are adequate to enable the average person to recognize that a lawyer can help him with a problem and to
make an informed decision about the value of those services as against
their cost; to provide him with financial resources to pay those costs;
and to lead him to a lawyer competent to handle the problem. In
general, these questions reduce themselves to questions of awareness,
of cost and ability to pay, and of competence of attorney. Although new
patterns of providing legal services will respond, as did the plans discussed above, to perceived inadequacies in these areas, there exists,
at the same time, the possibility that particular new forms might be so
destructive of professional attributes as to warrant prohibition. This
potential conflict is reflected in the previously cited concerns of both
the California and ABA committees for regulation to accommodate
professional values.

AWARENESS

There is little to say with respect to the problem of awareness. The prospect that excessive use of lawyers' services will turn the population into litigious paranoids is so unlikely as not to warrant discussion. Today's problem is quite the obverse. It is likely that whatever new forms of legal service agencies are developed, one consequence will be wider popular awareness of the legal implications of transactions and of the availability of lawyers for assistance. It is unlikely that new forms will arise solely for the purpose of increasing awareness.

COST

Cost of legal services is another likely perceived inadequacy in the present structure. Yet any attempt to analyze the cost of legal services is troublesome. The legally enforced monopoly of the Bar has, to some degree, reduced the impact of extra-Bar price competition. The internal professional restrictions against solicitation and advertising, together with professional exhortations against price cutting and the publication of minimum fee schedules, have tended to reduce internal price competition within the Bar. Satisfactory criteria for adjudging the reasonableness of existing price structures do not exist.

The average potential client will most probably seek reductions in the cost of legal services and better means of financing them. In general, the legal services he will seek are of two kinds—the emergency or catastrophe situation and the more-or-less routine one.

The classical method of dealing with catastrophe situations is by a spread-of-the-risk, or insurance, principle. In the case of automobile liability insurance, this principle has been applied not only to the potential substantive liability, but also to the cost of legal services, for under the typical policy the insurance company has the obligation to defend the insured in litigation arising out of his use of the vehicle. It is problematical whether the cost of such defensive legal services can be substantially decreased.

A kind of spread-the-cost principle operates in the emergency or catastrophe situation on the plaintiff's side as well. For example, in Workmen's Compensation cases, statutes set maxima for legal fees, which probably results in overcharges in relatively simple cases and undercharges in complex ones. An extreme example of cost-cutting was that of the UMWA plan, where the salary of the lawyer replaced the aggregate cost of the fees which would have been paid had the members of the union sought individual counsel on a more traditional basis. In any event, it is clear that as to its members, the UMWA plan was based on an insurance principle, *i.e.,* each member contributed to the salary of the lawyer whom he might never need, but who was there if needed. The UMWA plan suggests that new arrangements for providing legal services may be directed toward reducing the costs in the emergency situation on the plaintiff's side, now paid for primarily through the contingent fee device. Channelling these types of claims into one processing unit—one lawyer or law firm—will result in pressure to reduce the level of the contingent fee, or, conceivably, to eliminate it altogether.

The second major type of legal event in which the average client will be involved is the more-or-less routine one: divorce, custody, tax, real estate, will, collections, landlord-tenant. Again, it is difficult to assess the adequacy of the present pricing structure for service in these situations, and their relatively low cost makes insurance-type programs comparatively unattractive. On the other hand, it is precisely in similiar types of areas that the Bar's principal competitors— banks and trust companies, public accountants, title insurance companies—have made their greatest inroads upon the business of the Bar. In a substantial sense, this has resulted from the development of standardized methods of handling the great bulk of transactions and the application of modern business techniques to expedite handling and to cut costs.

Whatever the efficiency of these other enterprises, it would seem indisputable that increased use of particular lawyers for particular types of services should result in cost reduction; the marginal cost per new unit of service should decrease as the number of units of service increases. Thus, to the extent that the existing legal cost structure is perceived as inappropriate, it is likely that new patterns of providing legal services will attempt to reduce those costs, in all probability by the aggregation of clients with common problems into one or a few service units.

Another function of new plans may be that of making it possible for the client to pay the cost of the legal service, without any concomitant pressure to reduce that cost. Insurance-type schemes accomplish that objective where an unpredictable risk can be spread. Another trend would be to make better arrangements to finance the costs of legal services. From the lawyer's point of view, the financial problem is that of having to bear the burden of the costs of the service until his client is in a position to pay, either as a result of successful termination of the matter or as a result of the client's diligent saving. At least one plan permits lawyers to discount their clients' notes at a bank, to receive their payment, and to let the financial institution perform its traditional role of financing by loan, repayable in installments or at a later date. This is being tried in

Erie County, New York. It is probably too soon to assess the operations of this program, but it seems clear that such plans are responsive to the Bar's organization for doing business, and are attempts to place the financing of legal services on a different basis than heretofore.

COMPETENCE

A final, and perhaps most troublesome, perceived inadequacy of the present structure of providing legal services has to do with control over the competence of the lawyer. A characteristic of a professional service is that it is extremely difficult for the client to evaluate its quality, at least until long after the event. Particularly is this true with respect to the kinds of legal services rendered the middle class, for in the vast majority of cases these are one-shot affairs; there is no continuing relationship, with numerous transactions, to give the client an overview of the quality of the lawyer's performance.

This difficulty of assessing the quality of the professional service is aggravated, from the client's point of view, by the professional restrictions that prohibit lawyers from designating special areas of interest, if not competence. No system, other than that for initial admission to the Bar, exists for examination or certification of lawyers on a basis of general or special competence. The potential client, with few exceptions, has no professionally approved way of finding a lawyer who is competent to handle his problems or of evaluating the quality of the services his lawyer has performed. It is significant that all three plans that reached the Supreme Court of the United States had the designation of particular lawyers as one essential element. One aim of new patterns of providing legal services will be to enable the potential or actual client, either by himself or through some kind of centralized agency, better to evaluate the competence and performance of lawyers.

It is here that the underlying philosophy of the anti-intermediary rules—the professional values of lawyer dedication to client and lawyer independence—portend the greatest tension between some new legal service patterns and the Bar. Concern about the impact of group pressure upon the lawyer which may affect his handling of an individual case is reflected throughout the literature. Techniques to assure that these values can be retained are needed so that the new patterns will receive broad-based professional support.

Patterns for the Future

If future patterns for providing legal services develop from existing ones, the most likely sources are Lawyers' Referral Services, possibly legal cost insurance plans, and group legal service plans, inasmuch as these seem to be the programs most directly addressed to what have been described as the perceived inadequacies of the structure of the Bar.

LAWYERS' REFERRAL SERVICES

Lawyers' Referral Services differ from place to place but have the common characteristic and function of being designed to bring together a client who thinks he has a legal problem but knows no lawyer with a lawyer who has previously expressed willingness to accept new clients. In some cities these services are little more than truncated classified telephone directories with a telephone answering service; in others, specialties are listed; and, in a few, lawyers are screened before they are permitted to list themselves as specialists. Financed by bar associations and by the fees obtained by the lawyers on the lists, they have had widely varying success, depending in some part on the extent to which their existence is publicized.

To the extent that they are advertised, Lawyers' Referral Services make the public sensitive to the fact that it may have legal problems and that there is a source other than random selection from which to obtain the names of lawyers. Their impact on the pricing structure is uncertain, if indeed they have any impact in this respect. Their existence tends, where they are successful, to perpetuate the atomistic structure of the Bar. Their greatest inherent defect, even where they are well organized, is that the client has no indication of particular competence of the lawyer to whom he is referred. There are no systematized post-audits of the lawyer's performance. Nevertheless, the rise of other forms of providing legal services has given impetus to strengthening Lawyers' Referral Services. The Bar will likely continue to attempt to meet the pressures from both without and within by emphasis on the availability of Lawyers' Referral Services.

INSURANCE

The second major possible source is in the general field of insurance. In the past insurance companies have been uninterested in the possibility of writing legal-cost insurance. Only where the legal services can be calculated as part of the underlying financial liability, as in automobile liability insurance, has such a policy been written. Yet, increasingly the growth and success of hospital and medical insurance plans have raised the question whether it would not be possible to write insurance for legal services generally. The previous discussion suggested that catastrophe, "defensive" insurance might expand in scope, but with no likely reduction in the cost of legal services. Placing the legal cost of "offensive" catastrophe claims— like those for physical injuries or deaths—on an insurance basis may result however, in modifications of the legal fee structure.

When the "routine" legal service is considered, the principal function of legal cost "insurance" is that of a financing mechanism rather than that of a spread-of-the-risk one. The primary advantage would be the removal of financial obstacles to consulting a lawyer, and the possible wider use of lawyers for preventive purposes. This financing function may be accomplished in other ways, however, such as the bank loan. For the poor, one financing mechanism which has been developed is that of Judicare, a system in which the client selects a lawyer and the government pays the lawyer's bill. England has extended this program to provide for government contributions to legal costs where the client has the ability to pay part of those costs. With the exception of the poverty programs, there seems no significant pressure in the United States for government subsidy of legal costs for the non-poor.

In sum, the development of insurance- and financing-type plans is more likely to increase the economic well-being of the Bar than to affect its organization and structure. The only possible qualification to this trend—and it may be a significant one—is the UMWA-type plan, where the contingent fee structure of the personal injury type of litigation is replaced by a time or salary structure. Substantial changes in the patterns of providing legal services are more likely to come from the third source, group legal services.

GROUP LEGAL SERVICES

Every definition of group legal services is so broad as to include almost every conceivable change in the existing patterns of providing legal services. If, however, the strictly insurance features of such plans are excluded, the significant feature is the designation by a group of a lawyer for members of that group. To date, most of the plans have been limited to particular types of legal matters, but there is no theoretical reason why they could not be all-inclusive, or nearly so. Indeed, out of concern that lawyers would form groups solely for the purpose of being able thereby to avoid professional restrictions applicable to them as lawyers, the California Committee on Group Legal Services laid down as an essential condition for approval of a group legal service plan that the group have bona fide purposes other than that of providing legal services.

Inevitably, group legal service plans will vary according to the perceived needs of the affected groups. Because industrial injuries were the dominant concern of the railroad workers and the mineworkers, their plans responded to those concerns. Property owners in a neighborhood afflicted with zoning variances, merchants in trade associations, university professors—all conceivably could have legal problems sufficiently common and numerous to warrant combining for the purpose of entering into arrangements with a lawyer or law firm for the handling of their business.

The principal impact of such arrangements will be the creation of new legal business and the direction and redirection of legal business to fewer law firms than would be sought for legal assistance under the existing patterns. Thus, it is likely that law firms which enter into such arrangements will tend to grow larger to handle the increased volume of business and that the increase in the size of such firms will, in the long run, be accompanied by a decrease in the numbers of individual practitioners.

At the same time, the rise of group legal service plans can be viewed as merely a belated recognition in the legal domain of a phenomenon which has pervasively affected American society, the trend from individual identity to group interest. Dependence upon a group, whether it be union, trade association, political party or other entity, to represent what in an earlier day would have been individual interests, is a feature of American life. Yet, as this dependence has increased, so has the possibility of abuse of the individual member by the group. The general contours of individual rights against groups to which the member may voluntarily or compulsorily belong are in a formative stage. There is room for the individual practitioner to play a creative role; there will be a continuing role in the vindication of individual rights against the group.

Richard W. Nahstoll

8

Regulating Professional Qualification

While the legal profession must be concerned with broad changes affecting our society as a whole, it must also worry about effects of social change on the bar itself. Important among these are the matters of determining the qualifications for admission to practice, and privileges and limitations on practice after admission. The bar has always had rules and procedures governing these matters. Eligibility to practice law depends chiefly upon passing a written bar examination after graduation from law school. And that is practically all there is to it. No jurisdiction has any formal method of determining whether professional competency has been maintained after admission to practice, nor does any have a system for determining or certifying qualifications for special branches of law practice.

The practice of law is more diverse, requires increasingly specialized knowledge and skill, and is less and less localized than a half century ago, or even two decades ago. Yet the regulation of professional qualification has remained essentially unchanged since 1900, when bar examinations had become firmly established. It is time that the profession re-examined its approaches to these problems.

Qualification for Admission to Practice Law

"But," said Alice, "if some people can practice law, and some can't, what's the difference between them?"

RICHARD W. NAHSTOLL *is an attorney at law in Portland, Oregon. A member of the Oregon State Bar since 1947, he has served on its Board of Governors, and as its president (1964–65). In 1964 he won the American Bar Association's Ross Essay Contest.*

The White Rabbit answered arrogantly, "The difference very obviously is that those who can practice law have the piece of paper, and those who can't practice law don't. That's the difference."

"But," Alice persisted, "why do only some have the paper?"

"Because," said the White Rabbit, "only those who have the paper have demonstrated that they are technically proficient and have good moral character."

"And what do you mean 'technically proficient'?"

"Don't be stupid," said the White Rabbit. "If one 'thinks like a lawyer' and is adept at 'legal reasoning,' and has 'legal aptitude,' one is technically proficient; if one doesn't and isn't and hasn't, then he's not."

"How does one prove that he does and is and has?" said Alice.

"By getting into law school; by getting out of law school; and then by showing that he didn't waste his time between getting in and getting out."

"And how does he show that?"

"By writing a paragraph about the Rule in Shelley's Case and another paragraph about Helen Palsgraf."

"Does he do that to get into law school?"

"Certainly not. He's never heard of them at that time. But, he writes those paragraphs to get out of law school and to prove that he did not waste his time."

Alice skwooched up her forehead and ventured quietly, "If he writes the same thing, why does he do it twice?"

"Because," said the White Rabbit, "he may write the same thing, but it's read differently."

"And, I suppose," said Alice, "if he's going to prove twice that he's 'technically proficient,' he might as well prove it three times."

"Oh, of course," said the White Rabbit with a note of triumph, "and, besides, it's easier to do it three times than it is to wonder whether 'technically proficient' means the same thing each time—or whether it really means anything *at all*. But, if we stopped to wonder about that, the game might never get started again."

"I'm not sure I understand about being 'technically proficient,'" conceded Alice, "but perhaps like the grownups, I should stop trying to figure it out. It must be easier to understand what is meant by 'good moral character'!"

"Oh, indeed it is," said the White Rabbit with a confident tug at his gloves, "'good moral character' means 'fitness of character.' And now that that's cleared up, I think I must be going."

Alice called hurriedly to the White Rabbit as he was crawling under the fence, "But, how does anyone find out if he has 'good moral character'?"

"Well," said the Rabbit, brushing his hat, "If three affidavits say he has it, he has it. That's what makes it so easy. No one has to concern himself beyond that."

"And just one more question, please," said Alice. "What if someone thinks there has been a mistake and one who has the piece of paper really isn't technically proficient or is without good moral character after all?"

"Mistake?" said the White Rabbit incredulously. "Mistake, indeed! How could there be a mistake? He has his piece of paper by that time, and the matter is closed. His piece of paper establishes his qualifications and says he can practice law, which he couldn't do unless he was qualified. And that is what I explained to you in the very beginning. And now I'm late. Goodbye."

"Goodbye," said Alice, and in the manner of many before her, she thought the whole problem hardly worth the effort. So, resolved that it could be put off until later, she closed her eyes, forgot her concern, and napped.

The administration of justice, which is what the practice of law in the broadest sense is about, depends for its quality chiefly on the qualifications of those who administer it. To the extent that there is discontent with the administration of justice—and today there is great discontent with the administration of justice—it is appropriate to re-examine the systems for determining those qualifications. And this re-examination must begin with questions concerning the qualifications that are to be looked for. What manner of man can be trusted to handle the lawyer's jobs with tolerable skill and efficiency? How is he to be identified? What is to be done respecting the lawyer whose capacity is once recognized by license but is thereafter found to be lacking or lost?

Historically, and with sound justification in theory, qualification for admission to practice law has involved two standards: (1) technical proficiency, and (2) fitness of character. These standards have about them a tidy illusion of profundity and validity. But, will they survive analysis?

WHAT IS THE ROLE FOR WHICH THE LAWYER SHOULD BE QUALIFIED?

It is surely appropriate that standards of qualification relate to the functions to be performed by the person whose qualifications are to be tested. In short, if a test assumes to measure whether one is qualified to play the role of a lawyer, the role should be understood. The requirements for legal education and the content of bar examinations assume that there is a definable lawyer's role and that the personal equipment required to play it has measurable attributes. This equipment includes acquaintance with legal doctrine, particularly the legal doctrine involved in what are assumed to be the general, usual or common aspects of the "practice of law." The "practice of law" is conceived as centering or at least beginning with the function of appearing in court and directing participation in the litigation procedure. In one respect this is appropriate, for whatever else may be included in the "practice of law," the right to participate in litigation is within the exclusive monopoly conferred by the license to practice law. As a result the bar examination procedure centers on, or at least begins with legal doctrine related to litigation.

Beyond this point, however, there is confusion and difficulty. Participation in litigation does not exhaust the work of a lawyer, nor does the lawyer in performing non-litigation tasks enjoy a professional monopoly. "The work of a lawyer" includes those things which a lawyer does, in common with others, largely because his talents and training are presumed to place these functions within his calling. In common with bankers, realtors, insurance consultants, securities counsellors, and others, the lawyer ventures investment advice and invests the assets of clients. In common with physicians, ministers and social workers, the lawyer gives personal and family advice. In common with accountants, bankers, market analysts, economists and technical persons of all sorts, the lawyer gives business and corporate advice, non-legal in nature. In common with others, the lawyer functions in various ways and situations as a "peacemaker"—negotiating, arbitrating, seasoning his client's demands with a sprig of objectivity or structuring a situation to allow people, essentially desirous of working their way out of a situation which they find distasteful, to "save face" and re-establish communication.

What is the legal doctrine that the lawyer should know to perform *these* tasks? And what examination can be devised that would determine whether he knows enough of it? The process of bar examination assumes, with more confidence than their real difficulty would seem to permit, that there are answers to these questions.

If these questions are difficult, more difficult still is the question whether mastery of doctrine is itself the aspect of the lawyer's technical proficiency that is most important to measure. Fundamental to the broad spectrum of the lawyer's work is the art of communication—communication both sending and receiving, communication in the relatively informal setting of *ex parte* interviewing of clients, witnesses or associates, communication in the relative formality of the courtroom, communication in the negotiation process, communication (perhaps to an unidentified audience) through the written word, whether the document be a letter to be understood on receipt of tomorrow's mail, or a lease or contract to be understood ten (10) years hence. Nor, as we have more recently been made aware, can the subtleties of "non-verbal communication" be ignored.

Compounding the problem for the lawyer performing his broader function is the fact that, generally, he is dealing with people at their psychological and emotional ebb. Their potential for avarice is at full flower and, consciously or unconsciously, their personal stake in the matter at hand influences their participation in the affair and their handling of relevant information. Ideally, the lawyer's handling of these nuances would exact of him a high level of sophistication in several of the behavioral disciplines.

Nor is the lawyer's concern with the humanities of significance only in his one-to-one relationships with other persons. If lawyers are to make meaningful contributions to the solution of the social ills of which the recent riots and unrest are symptomatic, it will be to the extent they are able to appreciate, and hopefully to utilize, the relationship of the law to sociology, anthropology, mass psychology, political science, and perhaps other social sciences.

The failure of the legal fraternity to respect these complexities of its work has contributed to what many now appreciate to be the inadequacies of our admissions system. In default of appreciating the need for and developing procedures for testing whether an applicant is qualified to do a lawyer's work, admissions authorities have quite unimaginatively copied the testing procedures of law schools. They undertake to test essentially, and only, those things which law schools have chosen to recognize and acknowledge as within the scope of legal education. At the same time, by process of anticipation, the law schools in varying degrees organize legal education according to what will appear on the bar examinations. The *Rule in Shelley's Case* is examined on by the bar because it is taught in law school, because it is on the bar examination, because it is what the students have been instructed in. . . .

It is not within the scope of this paper to inquire whether the aspirations of law schools should be different or broader. With some rare exceptions they have disclaimed responsibility for enlarging the scope of law school training or broadening the undergraduate prerequisites for admission to law school. Generally, the position of legal educators has been that their job is so demanding that they cannot concern themselves whether the prior training of the student has left him adequately equipped to spell, to read, to write legibly, to form sentences with a tolerable respect for syntax, and to communicate with clarity and precision—especially to communicate with those to whom his communications will be directed in his years of professional activity.

The preoccupation of legal education with matters of doctrine and formal analysis is a product of the case method of study, which accentuates the development of law at the appellate level. This method treats pertinent facts and conditions as given by hypothesis. It tends to ignore, and even to condition the law student against concern for, the correlation of legal concepts with the marshalling of evidence and the interactions of people, a process which ultimately commands much of the practicing lawyer's time and attention. This is compounded by the fact that legal education is induced by something akin to artificial insemination, through the efforts of teachers who are generally unfamiliar with the workaday role of the practitioner. This statement should not be taken as disparagement of law teachers. By and large, their want of appreciation of the true demands upon the "average" lawyer results from the fortunate fact that the teachers are not "average." To the extent that they have practiced, their manifest intelligence, talents and application have usually earned for them select positions, removed from the general practice of the law and the persons and problems which traffic there.

Whether or not these related but non-legal capacities are matters for law schools to accept as responsibilities was considered at the 90th Annual Meeting of the American Bar Association, Honolulu, Hawaii, August 8, 1967. A joint session of the Section on Legal Education and Admission to the Bar and the National Conference of Bar Examiners scheduled a panel discussion on the subject, "The Right of Law Schools and Bar Examiners to Take Into Account the Inadequacies of Pre-Law College Training in Determining Fitness for Graduation or Admission." But regardless of the different approaches the law schools may take, these deficiencies *must* be of interest and concern to bar examiners and admitting authorities, inasmuch as they make up so large a part of the life to which the lawyer is admitted. And since the concerns of bar examiners and admitting authorities are relevant in the law schools' curriculum planning, the bar must accept part of the responsibility for what the law schools do in the way of legal education.

This plea should not be misunderstood as the oft-heard charge that "law schools don't teach what is 'practical,' " i.e., how to litigate. It is not an expression of common cause with those who believe a law school graduate is ill-equipped if he does not receive a map to the courthouse with his diploma. Rather, it is a plea for recognition that, except those in very refined specialities, a lawyer can do his job only with an arsenal of talents that includes many beyond those developed by contemporary legal education. And if the legal profession is serious in this recognition, it must be correspondingly serious about what it requires in the education of those who are called to the bar.

Part of the bar's policy should concern the pre-legal education of law graduates. In this day and age, it should be beyond question or conjecture that those states which do not yet require an undergraduate Bachelor's Degree should join the trend and raise their standards. (The time-worn argument that this would lose to the bar some latter day

Abraham Lincoln hardly seems still worthy of credence.) A more difficult question is the appropriate content of pre-law education. Presently, most law schools fix no specific requirements and, at most, offer some "suggestions" respecting courses which may be found useful. One who has satisfactorily completed the requirements of a Bachelor's Degree in any major is found academically admissible.

Shouldn't this policy be re-examined? To the extent there is validity to the contentions made earlier that a lawyer needs some demonstrable competence in the communication arts, and familiarity with the behavioral sciences and at least some of the humanities, neither law school nor bar admissions requirements recognize those needs. It may very well be that one whose undergraduate work has been limited to the engineering curriculum can be equipped in law school to practice patent law. But it assumes a great deal to suppose him also equipped to perform the broad spectrum of a lawyer's functions which his license to practice attests. And reconsideration should not be confined to the question whether requirements of substance and subject matter at the undegraduate level bear a relation to predictability of success in law school, nor to the "practice of law" in the limited sense. Rather, the issue should be re-examined in respect to whether such requirements would have validity as equipment to perform a lawyer's broader function. (A recommended starting place is Justice Vanderbilt's article, "A Report on Prelegal Education," *New York University Law Review* 200, April 1950.)

The bar needs also to reconsider whether it is possible by written examinations to test the qualifications required for a reasonably "compleat" lawyer. If written examinations can do only part of the job, then that fact should be faced. Other types of testing may be better— for example, provisional admission. It may also be better frankly to treat the examination for what it really is, a test of reasoning aptitude and not one of technical knowledge or professional skill. That might mean that we couldn't tell whether those admitted were technically proficient, but at least we would no longer be kidding ourselves. As it is, bar examinations are fear-ridden exercises of limited scope that may determine nothing more than the ability to pass bar examinations.

WHAT IS TESTED AS "FITNESS OF CHARACTER"?

Almost without exception, the standards of admission to practice law in the several states include a demonstration of the applicant's "fitness of character" or "good moral character," or some euphonious equivalent. What does this mean? How is it satisfactorily demonstrated? What of those who, once admitted, lose their "fitness of character"?

Generally, the standard, in whatever terms it is phrased, is satisfied by the filing of two, or three or four affidavits by practicing lawyers (who are often uninformed respecting the applicant and are invariably uninformed respecting the standard) to the effect that the applicant satisfies the criterion. In many states this is supplemented by a brief and superficial "interview" with one or more members of the examining board. In many states, the applicant submits his fingerprints so that an FBI report can be obtained as to whether the applicant has ever been charged or convicted of a crime. And there the effort stops. A lawyer member of the examining board would shudder to see the personnel department of one of his large corporate clients employ for a position of substantial trust an applicant of whom he knew so little.

There is little doubt what is hoped to be accomplished by the character evaluation. Our principal objective is to admit only those who will pursue high standards of ethical conduct in their relationships with clients, courts, other lawyers, and members of the public. It is not enough that he "shall not steal" from his client. He owes him affirmatively a full measure of objectivity, candor, diligence, energy, fidelity, time, loyalty, wisdom, patience, concern and judgment founded on emotional balance. And, ideally, he will be one who will devote some meaningful effort and time without hope of financial reward to service of the public in one or more of the ways open to a lawyer. For convenience, we can think of this total package as a sense of professional mission.

The question is how its presence or absence can be tested for. It is unlikely that screening aspirants to the legal fraternity can be done at the law school admissions level. It would be helpful if it could be. But the practical problems loom large. Especially is this true with respect to state-supported schools which are required to make a rather strong case for denying admission to law school—comparable to the burden now imposed on an organized bar disposed to deny admission or to disbar a member. *Willner v. Committee on Fitness*, 373 U. S. 96 (1963).

If, then, screening for fitness of character at the point of bar admission appears ineffectual, and if screening at the point of law school admission probably could not be much better, what can be done? It lends little assistance to protest that we have no method of empirically testing the qualities in question. Whatever they are, the lawyer who lacks them is rather readily identifiable in communities small enough that his conduct is visible. It is a quite usual matter that, within a year or two after he has begun to practice, the consensus of the legal community identifies one who, sooner or later, will be "in trouble with the bar." There is no reason to suppose the situation is any different in large metropolitan areas, except that deficiencies in character are less readily detected. That being so, the profession must assume that each year it admits to its ranks substantial numbers of those about whom it—and the public—will later have regrets.

This condition stands as a strong case for establishing a period of probationary licensing during which some of these shortcomings might become manifest. In any event, it is time for lawyers to cease their incestuous little discussions and search outside themselves for some answers to these problems. If the legal fraternity would climb out of its shell of self-satisfaction and seek the help of other disciplines, it might secure assistance in discovering valid and reliable methods of testing for them these qualities.

It is, perhaps, advisable to insert an important *caveat* in this regard. Any system of testing should allow plenty of opportunity for healthy mavericks to enter the practice of law. We must not deny admission to him who doesn't wear a vest all summer. Combined with the other essential qualities, independence, individuality, vigor and assertiveness are certainly to be encouraged.

A few words should be said about the relation between disciplinary procedures and testing fitness of character at the point of admission. At best, the threat of discipline is a weak re-enforcement of the character standards that admissions testing is supposed to assure. Nor can disciplinary proceedings repair admissions mistakes after they have been made. But a lawyer's continuing qualification to practice can be reviewed in other ways than traditional disciplinary inquiry. The following, for example, could be used to supplement the disciplinary machinery as a means of assuring professional competence:

We need a SOAR (Search Out and Rescue) program—Earlier in this paper it was hypothesized that the lawyer destined for disciplinary trouble could be informally identified soon after his admission. Having identified him, what do we do?—we wait for him to get his tail in the gate, often at the expense of a client, and then discipline him. Is there a sound reason why we don't act earlier? Why can't the disciplinary machinery be supplemented by providing for a lawyer, or group of lawyers, to talk to him and assist him in anticipation of a specific and culpable act of misconduct?

We need an involuntary retirement procedure applicable to the ill and the aged—Currently, we have no provision other than disciplinary procedures for reducing the public risk of practice by those who have grown senile or who have become emotionally unbalanced, alcoholic or otherwise infirm. These are not really disciplinary problems. Governing boards are reluctant to subject the lawyer having such an infirmity to the stigma of discipline. The bar therefore waits prayerfully, hoping that the lawyer's inevitable critical mistake will not do overwhelming damage. The medical profession has the benefit of some supervisory control for these purposes through hospital staffs. The bar has no counterpart of that agency, except as it is effected within firms out of respect for their reputations, affectionate regard for their failing partners and apprehension for their malpractice exposure. We need some sort of involuntary retirement system.

We need provision for a "co-pilot's license"—Everyone who has ever participated in disciplinary procedures is aware of the problem presented by the lawyer who is adequate intellectually but too unstable emotionally to survive the rigors of practice. He will do well functioning as a lawyer on a salaried job where hours are regular and he has no responsibility beyond his emotional capacity. Under our present system, he has no difficulty getting admitted to unrestricted practice. Our only present means of handling his problem is to remove him from all status in the bar. Is it not possible to license him on a limited basis, qualified thereby to perform the jobs for which he is, in fact, suited?

Specialization

In the past fifteen years specialization in the legal profession has been accorded the most written attention with the least tangible results of all matters concerning the functioning of the profession.

In 1954 the House of Delegates of the American Bar Association adopted the following recommendations:

1. That the American Bar Association approves in principle the necessity to regulate voluntary specialization in the various fields of the practice of law for the protection of the public and the bar, and

2. That the American Bar Association approves the principle that in order to entitle a lawyer to recognition as a specialist in a particular field he should meet certain standards of experience and education, and

3. That the implementation, organization and financing of a plan of regulation to carry out such principles is delegated to the Board of Governors, subject to final approval by the House of Delegates.

Thereafter, an ABA Special Committee on Recognition and Regulation of Specialization in Law Practice, under the chairmanship of David F. Maxwell, was created to consider appropriate means of implementing the 1954 resolution. The Maxwell Committee reported back in 1962, proposing a circumspect plan for the "recognition and certification of special proficiency based upon competence, education, experience and compliance with ethical standards as finally approved for each proficiency field" of the practice of law. The proposal, however, failed of adoption by the House of Delegates. With an implication of despair and fatigue, if not of justified pique, the Committee thereafter recommended "that it be discharged and that all efforts to draft an acceptable program be indefinitely postponed." The committee stated as its reason for the recommendation:

> It is apparent to the Committee as it must be to all the delegates that the bar of the country either does not want specialization controlled or is not prepared to accept regulation at this time.

In 1967, the House of Delegates adopted the following resolution:

> That the House of Delegates requests the Board of Governors to further consider the matter of recognition and regulation of voluntary specialists in the various fields of the practice of law for the benefit and protection of the public and of the bar.

This resolution has led to the creation of a new special committee, under the chairmanship of Chesterfield Smith. What will be the nature and fate of its recommendations remains to be seen.

In the interval following 1954, and continuing to the present time, the carousel of formal proceedings has whirled in a blizzard of words. A copious production of papers, articles, and commentaries has evolved, perhaps the most helpful work being the paper, "Specialization," by Mr. Barlow F. Christensen. That report, published in 1967, was distributed prior to the Annual Meeting of the ABA and prior to the action of its House of Delegates referred to above. These studies have been provocative, but they have not resulted in action, either at the national or state level.

While the organized bar has made no progress in defining and regulating specialization, specialization in fact has continued to develop, extend and refine. Firms, which tend to be groups of specialists, have increased in number and in size. Also, the informal recognition of specialized expertise in individual lawyers is now commonplace.

Specialization of practice is developing because it is in the self-interest of lawyers who specialize: specialists make more money. And there is no mystery in the reason for this. Inasmuch as they are working in areas with which they have familiarity and sophistication, they are markedly more efficient. For the same reasons, the client also benefits. He gets more competent service, and at a lower cost per unit of work.

What, then, is so complicated? The complications stem not from specialization as such but from the regulation of it. And these problems boil down mostly to ones of "solicitation" and the ethics of referral.

Specialization in the absence of regulation is merely a self-imposed, and presently authorized, limitation of a lawyer's practice. A lawyer who limits his practice to one field or a few related fields is, to that extent, a "specialist." His competence in that area may increase as a result—but this is not assured. Should the self-anointed "specialist" be permitted to advise the public that his "practice is limited to" his specialty, thus implying that he has some special competence? Few members of the bar are willing to sanction such a self-designation. The alternative, and therefore the issue, is establishment of a system to recognize and certify special competence and proficiency.

The basic question of certification of special competence has been obscured by concern for matters of detail:

1. Would one accorded certification be allowed to practice outside his field of certification?
2. Would one be allowed to qualify for certification in more than one field?
3. How would accreditation be established? a. By examination? b. By examination plus practice in the field? c. What about a "grandfather" clause?
4. What liberty would the certified lawyer enjoy with respect to the advertising of his speciality? a. Only a formal notice to other lawyers? b. Also to established clients? c. To the public? *e.g.,* the yellow pages?
5. On what scale is the certifying to be done? a. National? By boards administered by the ABA? or by separate national boards? b. By the several states where general admissions authority resides? If so, how is tolerable uniformity achieved? Or, doesn't it make a difference?
6. Would the disciplinary authority be jeopardized?
7. What is the risk of fragmentation of the bar into specialty-oriented groups? How can the risk be minimized?
8. What changes are required in the Canons of Ethics to accommodate the concept of certification of special competence?

Serious consideration of the subject has usually disintegrated under the burden of struggling with this welter of details. Yet the central question is itself a difficult one.

Problems of Certification

At least three basic issues need to be faced.

First—The idea of formal certification is most acceptable to those who presently enjoy greatest economic security in the profession. Those who are secure and satisfied with the status quo rather generally are so because they are already in fact specialized in their practice. Typically they are members of firms. Within their firms they now benefit from the equivalent of certification, because they are the recipients of intra-firm referrals from their colleagues. For like reason, they have no particular need of advising the public of their special competence because the public already recognizes (as many lawyers do not) the need for specialization, and recognizes that specialization is the essence of firm organization.

On the other hand, opposition to formal recognition of specialization generally comes from those whose economic benefits from the present system are least—the "general" practitioner practicing solo or in a two or three man firm. Because these lawyers often harvest only a relatively low income presently, for them the prospect of a change in the system which *might* make things worse is forbidding. In economic need of all possible additional income, this group feels it imperative to hold their aprons wide to catch any business which might fall their way. It is beyond their concern that the business may be outside their competence, or might be done more efficiently and at less cost to the client by a specialist in the field.

This group has been sustained in resisting formal systems of certification by the myth of omnicompetence of lawyers—that the general license carries the right to practice general law indiscriminately. Indeed, so far it has not been treated as unethical that a lawyer undertakes to handle work for which he is not reasonably skilled. Moreover, the profession has scrupulously avoided affording the public any help in its effort to identify lawyers having special competence in a pertinent field. The rules on advertising and soliciting are particularly restrictive in this regard. And so, the generalists, often engaged in solo practice, often earning only marginal incomes, dissatisfied with their lot but fearful that it might get worse, resist change. Their resistance is made respectable by being garnished with platitudinous references to "the time-honored traditions of this learned profession" and "the law, a seamless web."

The general practitioner has a very valid role to serve. But it is not the role of attempting to be an expert in every phase of the law, and to compete with, and to withhold clients from specialists more competent than he.

The first order of business should be to define the role of the general practitioner in the "brave new world" of specialization. Dean Niles has seen his role as that of "the captain of the team, the one primarily and ultimately responsible," one who "will have to be the diagnostician in a legal system getting more and more complex." [1] This may be a little visionary. But if the place of the generalist in the new scheme

[1] Russell D. Niles, "Ethical Prerequisites to Certification of Special Proficiency," 49 *ABA Journal* 83 (1963).

of things is thought through, it may be sufficiently attractive that he'll drop his resistance to recognition of specialization.

Second—A system of recognized specialization is functionally important chiefly because it would facilitate intelligent case referral. And here is a rub. No system of inter-office referral of clients will long or successfully function without a fool-proof, reliable, never-fail system to minimize the risk of "client piracy." A referring generalist whose client is not returned by the specialist will remain "once burned, twice shy." If this risk can be removed, the program holds great promise for those lawyers who would prefer to specialize as solo practitioners. The prospect of losing one's client by referral to a firm offering a comprehensive service by a galaxy of specialists is probably greater than by referral to a specialist who is himself a solo.

If protection of the referring lawyer is to be by ethical canons, the sanctions for breach must be certain, and severe. And this is true though it may interfere with the client's freedom of choice of his lawyer.

Third—There is need for prompt and imaginative planning for education in specialized areas. The availability of facilities for specialized training is imperative. It would be a hazardous breach of faith to dangle before lawyers the carrot of certification, and then give them no means of acquiring the necessary proficiency. But, the task is one of major proportions. No doubt the techniques must be revolutionary in conception. Traditional modes and methods of legal education are likely to be totally inadequate.

Training for specialization cannot be accomplished at the location of the established law school. It is too early for a law student to commit himself to a specialty. Thereafter, when he is established in his practice and sufficiently sophisticated to make a selection of specialty, he hasn't the free time to return to the campus for training (however strong might be his inclination).

Moreover, the training techniques must be adaptable to the time available to the specialty-trainee, and adaptable to his individual schedule and rate of application.

Herein is a challenge to pedagogy of truly gigantic proportions. It would be a serious error to delay accepting the challenge until the day, which surely is to come, when formalization of certification is established in the legal profession.

David F. Cavers

9

Legal Education
in Forward-Looking Perspective

Viewed in forward-looking perspective, legal education seems to be in a process of fission, a process that reflects changes taking place in our society, in our government, and particularly, in the legal profession itself. The resulting differentiation in the law schools and their programs can be a desirable, socially important development. It calls for recognition, scrutiny, and encouragement.

In that remote period when I was a law student, viz., in the mid-twenties, legal education was standardized as to scope and purpose, if not as to quality. The curricula of the best law schools did not differ greatly from the curricula of the poorest—and there were some very poor law schools. All sought to prepare for practice conceived much as it had been the generation before. Some few metropolitan centers excepted, practice in the larger cities did not differ greatly from practice in the county seats. The tasks of government were still seen mainly in traditional terms, and lawyers went in and out of government office as traditionally they had done. Of course, signs of change were emerging, signs that hindsight now makes it easier to detect.

I shall not catalogue the changes wrought by the great depression,

DAVID F. CAVERS *is Fessenden Professor of Law at the Harvard Law School and Chairman of its Division of Graduate Studies. His writing and teaching have been chiefly in the fields of conflict of laws, government regulation, and legal education. He is a member of the Executive Committee of the Association of American Law Schools and since 1958 has been President of the Walter E. Meyer Research Institute of Law.*

World War II and its sequelae, by expanding science and technology and an exploding population, or the impact of these on our cities and their ghettos. They have affected legal education, though so far to a surprisingly limited degree. In forward-looking perspective, more radical changes in legal education are to be anticipated, for we must expect that more, and possibly more profound, social and governmental changes will take place bearing directly on the legal profession. As to these, I shall make two assumptions.

Two Assumptions

First, I shall assume that pressures generated by social discontent and governmental malfunctioning in our cities will not relent and, despite probable periods of repression, will lead to major measures and programs, private as well as public, designed to attack, and hopefully to cure, the evils we are now belatedly recognizing. Second, I shall assume that these measures will include some designed to increase the availability of legal services to those who now go without and others designed to socialize and civilize that remnant of medievalism in our communities, the treatment of law-breakers.

My second assumption may prove false. We may permit access to the machinery of justice to remain a perquisite of business, organized labor, and the well-to-do, and continue to relegate the legally indigent to overloaded legal aid services, and to depend for the administration of criminal justice largely on the least reputable, least competent members of our profession, and on other callings. If that happens, then not only will the legal profession find its importance dwindling, but, of more immediate consequence to the law schools, many of their rapidly multiplying graduates will soon have to choose between underemployment and abandonment of the profession of their choice. Should this occur, the planning for larger faculties and student bodies that has been so common among law schools in the past five years will have to be replaced by unwelcome retrenchments.

I make an additional assumption—that the present uncertainties caused by the draft, specifically the recent elimination of student deferment for law students, will be cured by revision of the regulations or by a marked diminution in draft calls. The uncertainties facing law students result in enrollment and program uncertainties for the law schools, and will discourage them from embarking on importantly innovative programs, even though such programs are strongly indicated by longer-run considerations.

Fission in the Bar

The fission in legal education to which I have alluded reflects fission in the American bar. The line of division (which must ignore many exceptions) falls between lawyers organized in the big firms which represent big interests and lawyers practicing "solo" or in small partnerships who serve chiefly small business and small people. I shall call the former "big-firm lawyers," the latter "small-firm lawyers." Bigness, of course, is a relative concept, but I would classify the law firm as big which has attained a size sufficient to permit some division of labor and some specialization, say, at eight or ten lawyers. As for the big firm's clientele, I suggest dimensions big enough to produce a substantial volume of federal problems for the corporate clients and estate planning problems for the individuals. Among corporate and government counsel, a roughly parallel line can be drawn: does the work which the corporate or government lawyer performs resemble more the work of the big-firm lawyer or of the small-firm lawyer?

Are social changes foreseeable that are likely to alter this pattern of the profession? I foresee no marked change in big-firm practice, though its growth rate may diminish as house counsel grows more numerous. Conceivably, an awakened social and professional conscience (quickened by long-term self-interest) will induce big firms to allocate a percentage of their billable hours—or the billable hours of their juniors—to community service in law. This quixotic notion has a distinguished source: Mr. Justice Brennan writing in the *American Bar Association Journal* for February 1968. ["The Responsibilities of the Legal Profession," 54 *A.B.A.J.* 121, 126.]

Solo and small-firm lawyers may feel the pressure of social change severely. In the major cities, many are already underemployed. The handling of routine work by corporate law staffs will cut into their practice more deeply than into the big firms'. Hopefully, reforms in law and public administration will destroy the prospects of politically inclined practitioners for various parasitical employments now open to them. Moreover, the rising tide of law school graduates must turn mainly to the small firms for employment. Of the nation's total of about 300,000 lawyers, big-firm lawyers (including their associates) probably approximate 35,000; corporate lawyers number about 35,000, and government lawyers (including the judiciary), about 42,000, leaving the small-firm and solo lawyers to outnumber all the rest by nearly two to one.[1]

---

[1] For the basis of these estimates, see the Appendix to this chapter.

The expansion in number of admissions to the bar, first registered in 1964, has been substantial. The five years ending in 1968 saw about 20,000 more bar admissions than the number of admissions in the preceding quinquennial, a 37 per cent jump to a five-year aggregate of about 73,000 new lawyers as against 53,510 in the 1959–1963 period. The next five-year period should see the five-year total of new admissions rise to nearly 100,000.[2] The forecast that compliance with *Escobedo* will require 20,000 more practitioners in criminal law does not project a demand that the expanding law schools will find hard to supply.

Fission in the Law Schools

The fission in the bar is paralleled, roughly at least, by fission in law schools. Law schools have been commonly, if somewhat inaccurately, classified as "national," "state," and "local," reflecting what are thought to be the chief sources and destinations of their student bodies. In "Lawyers in the Making," the 1965 report of the National Opinion Research Council by Seymour Warkov with Joseph Zelan, the 124 law schools in which its sample of 1,103 students entering law school in 1961 had enrolled were divided into three categories: "Stratum I," "Stratum II," and "Stratum III." Stratum I was composed of eight (unidentified) laws schools in which the students in the sample had the highest median Law School Admission Test (LSAT) scores; Stratum II, of the 16 schools with the next highest median scores; and Stratum III, of the remaining 100 schools.[3]

Neither classification is satisfactory; the characteristics that may be important in determining the nature of a law school's potential contribution to the legal profession are too numerous to permit a single criterion to dominate. However, I believe most knowledgeable law school professors would identify fifteen to twenty schools as having widely distributed student bodies with high academic credentials, offering curricula pointed to national problems and preparation for federal, corporate practice, being located in universities of high standing with substantial resources, private or public. Though, of course, many of their graduates enter small-firm practice, these are predominantly big-firm schools, and I shall label them such. In contrast, the same commentators would find the obverse of many of these characteristics in from 70 to 80 other law schools. These are predominantly small-firm schools, and so I shall label them. In between, to perplex the categorizer, are 40 to 45 schools, mostly the state university law schools.

[2] For the basis of this prediction, see the Appendix to this chapter.
[3] For further data, see the Appendix to this chapter.

It is easy to draw invidious distinctions between the big-firm and the small-firm schools and to call the former strong and the latter weak. To do so ignores the fact that the schools in one category are coming to perform a function different from the function performed by the schools in the other. Actually, if not avowedly, each is training primarily for service in a distinct branch of the modern American legal profession. Instead of placing all schools in both categories on a single scale and ranking them by a common measure, one may more profitably inquire how the schools in each category can adapt their programs and employ their resources to realize more fully their differing potentialities. Such is the question to which the remainder of this paper is addressed. Let us look first at the big-firm schools.

New Responsibilities for the Big-Firm Schools

Perhaps I am biased or blinded by more than a score of years spent in such a law school, but I think the professional education provided by the schools in this category is more than adequate. They have been doing a first-rate job for the big firms, and this now extends not merely to the top men in their classes but well down in the (grade-determined) ranks. In recent years, they have been adding an international dimension to their curricula, and have been giving to jurisprudence and history more than ceremonial attention.

Can our society ask more of these schools? Certainly. It should deny them the right to view their function simply as professional training. The schools must of course continue to perform that function and to perform it well, but this is not enough. They must furnish for less ordered areas of law that scrutiny, criticism, and innovation they have provided so amply for the judicial process at the appellate level and for the design or interpretation of statutes in certain fields of special consequence to our business establishment: e.g., taxation, commercial transactions, securities regulation, labor relations and restraints of trade.

In any extension of these law schools' concerns, priority should surely be accorded to laws bearing most directly on our cities' troubles —laws dealing with the provision of decent housing, landlord-tenant relationships, urban redevelopment, mass transportation, environmental health and amenities, family disorganization, taxation and public finance, consumer credit and debt adjustments, fair employment, and civil rights. Attention to these needs should not, however, obscure the enhanced recognition that is only now being given in these schools to the criminal law and its administration.

This listing may seem puzzling. Aren't these problems more appropriately the concern of the political scientist (sub-species local government and public administration), economist, sociologist, and social psychologist, the social worker, public health physician, and city planner? Why should the lawyer and the law professor intrude? What skills do lawyers have, to say nothing of law professors, which can aid experts from the disciplines just enumerated in coping with the obdurate troubles of the modern city?

THE NATURE OF THE LAWYER'S CONCERN

As to certain problems in these areas, lawyers' standing and competence should be clear, but I prefer to rest the case for their intervention on a broader base. Their concern goes to the quality of the social order. In many of the areas I have cited, the typical problem confronting the lawyer is how to protect the individual against the bureaucracy. The experts, intent on seeing that their goals will be met, do not often pause to consider whether administrators have been accorded more authority than they can exercise fairly, absent some mode of accountability that the individuals subject to their discretion can invoke. Sometimes, though checks have been provided, there is no one capable of imposing them. In other areas, the typical problem is how to provide a bureaucracy capable of protecting the individual or how to assert the public interest effectively in clashes with private interests that often are more ably represented or more aggressively pressed. These tasks may entail the enforcement of existing law or the creation of new law. Troubles may spring from the obsolescence of legal instrumentalities or procedures which have persisted for want of studies searching enough to reveal their deficiencies. There may be need for social inventions. There certainly will be need for the identification of goals and the articulation of issues where goals conflict.

These problems all give rise to law-jobs, as Karl Llewellyn would have called them, but jobs not likely to be done if we depend on the initiative and resources of individual lawyers or on improvised political action. In our complex communities, a social order in which due process, democratic process, and the equal protection of the laws are actually enjoyed will not come about simply as a result of some lawyers' battles for underdog clients or occasional exposures by crusading journalists. Devising new institutions and procedures to replace outworn or outdated ones, and ascertaining how their ends can be achieved without the sacrifice of values basic to the law, are tasks that can best be assumed by the law schools. Among these, probably the fifteen to twenty big-firm schools can mobilize the most resources, human and financial, and best preserve the continuity, disinterestedness, and relative freedom from pressures that multidisciplinary creative studies in this politically sensitive field require.

Implicit in the foregoing scheme is a departure concerning the place of research in big-firm law schools, and, in turn, the conception of the professional function of their graduates. In the received tradition, law schools are viewed as teaching institutions, whose research activities are essentially incidental. Yet in problem areas I have mentioned, our primary need is not to teach but to learn, and to learn a very great deal. That learning requires major organized investigation, with corresponding costs in manpower and money. And because this is so, the question of priorities will be critical.

Priorities will be determined partly by particular interests of particular faculties, as in the past, and by the directness of the relationship between traditional lawyers' know-how and the problem at issue. These criteria will not, however, be adequately comprehensive if the pressing problem areas are to receive attention they demand. The law schools therefore will have to tackle research, and related teaching, that is outside the special competency of their faculties as now constituted. In determining directions for such departures in law school programs, the conventional tests of preparation for the practice of law may not suffice. In certain of the urban problem areas to which I have referred, the opportunities open to the law-trained men may often differ from those presented by the lawyer's familiar professional role.

Studying and ministering to the cities' many troubles will require enlistment of persons representing a variety of disciplines. Among these, the law man is likely to be the one most concerned with problems of action—social engineering, to recall a term now fallen out of favor. His task is the synthesis of knowledge and skills of diverse other disciplines and professions in formulating policies and planning institutions and procedures, and the translation of academic learning into action.

To discharge this role, the law men cannot complacently depend on quick study; they will need to be literate in the languages and familiar with the methodologies of the social sciences, to be sensitive to their concerns, and to appreciate their potentialities and limitations. Thus equipped, law men should be able to work effectively with the experts and in the process, to instill in the latter a clearer awareness both of values to which they, as spokesmen for the law, are committed and of problems to which their legal training has rendered them alert.

We have had great difficulty developing institutions in universities and in government that relate theories and methodologies of social sciences to the attack on the exigent and long-run problems of our society. It is as a base for institutions concerned with the application of social science that I see a new role for those law schools which can command resources sufficient to perform that function. Their graduates specializing in this area—whose numbers would not be large—would be in much demand both within and without academia.

All this has little relation to what law schools have traditionally done. For institutions that have been fed a steady diet of judicial decisions packaged each week in the advance sheets of the National Reporter System, the notion of finding out what is actually happening to people under laws so obscure that they have never been collected in a service or a casebook must, I realize, seem utopian—or the reverse. The necessity of having to call frequently on the methodological skills or seek the insights and understanding of social and behavioral scientists and other professionals does not make the task seem easier. And the manpower needed is not now at hand, even in the largest law schools.

URBAN LEGAL STUDIES IN FORWARD-LOOKING PERSPECTIVE

Though these jobs are both formidable and unfamiliar, the law schools should not be daunted. Of course, no law school is going to plunge headlong into any such program. Law faculties are inclined by nature and by budgets to the strategy of gradualness. Nonetheless, a series of appointments to instructional and research positions, some temporary, some permanent, reinforced by fellowship and incidental expense funds, could, over a five or six year period, produce a center of urban studies at a law school which, though still small in numbers, had achieved critical mass, to adopt David Riesman's apt borrowing from nuclear physics. The investigators would not be working in isolation (as is typically the plight of the occasional law school researcher straying off the disciplinary reservation). Moreover, their findings would tend to stimulate, support, or challenge the findings of others, provided careful planning had insured against scatteration of effort.

What would be the relationship of such an undertaking to the rest of the law school, still committed to professional training for big-firm practice? If the new development proved to be only a research satellite proceeding on an orbit of its own, it would be an unhappy ending to a bold endeavor. Instruction and research must go hand in hand, the need for knowledge is scarcely greater than the need for knowledgeable people. Moreover, the kinds of inquiries to be pursued would call for student participation—they would gain from the experience, and their help would hold costs down.

The participating students would encounter unfamiliar modes of instruction. Typically a law school emphasizes instruction in relatively large classes (even in the smaller schools), focused on uniform assignments of carefully selected and edited material, designed to pose questions which can be discussed and answered on the basis of that material. The discussion is usually structured by the teacher, often with an art that conceals his art. Urban problems would not often yield questions that could be so neatly packaged. Knowledge would have to be imparted of an unfamiliar environment and its people, their difficulties and discontents. Relevant legal structures and processes would have to be analyzed as systems, and not simply described by inference or assumption. Orientation to a single case, explored by the give-and-take of traditional law school classroom dialogue, would yield in large measure to consideration of the flow of problem cases, explored by exchange and evaluation of information, often in substantial volume. Courses in which human relations problems were central would clearly have much grist for the mills of class discussion. In a developed urban legal studies program, students would doubtless find the greatest stimulus in seminars and workshops and in field studies and clinical work.

The ratio of faculty and staff at all levels to the students would have to be much higher than law schools have thus far felt obliged to maintain. Social and behavioral scientists would be needed in teaching and research positions and collaboration with other professionals as well. Indeed, the urban legal studies program would become a segment of the law school having a pattern of instruction and research resembling more closely that of the graduate schools of arts and sciences than that of the rest of the law school's program. It would in effect represent the "school of applied social science" which David Riesman envisaged in addressing Harvard's Sesquicentennial Celebration.

Would full participation in this program be incompatible with a student's preparation for practice? I submit that, for a student of average ability or better in the big-firm law school, the devotion of about one third of his second year and one half his third year to course, seminar, and field or clinical work in urban studies, plus a summer's internship after his second year, would still leave him with enough conventional learning to pass his bar examination (after the customary cram course) and to practice law successfully in big-firm or small-firm style. Arguably, this would constitute superior preparation for practice. The student would have sacrificed study in fields that probably he would choose to bypass in practice. If the program were achieving its goals, he would have observed the constructive role that law can play in society and also the strategies and tactics of hard-nosed defenders of the status quo. He would be sophisticated in a sense that many law review editors are not.

For students whose appetite was whetted for more knowledge and experience, especially for those with teaching or research careers in view, post-LL.B. studies should certainly have to be more fully developed. The opportunities that some law schools already give for the concurrent pursuit of two degrees—the LL.B. and a master's degree in a social science—could be exploited, though in a sense these are an admission of the law schools' failure to develop their own curricula so as to articulate needed social science instruction with law study and thereby advance the special objectives of law-trained men. More effective, I submit, would be another year of residence in the law school with social science studies designed to enrich field research and clinical experience. This should lead to an LL.M. and, for distinguished performance, an option to a pursuit of a Ph.D. in law.

I specify the Ph.D. for two reasons. First, some, perhaps many, of the students completing such a program might well seek teaching posts outside the law schools. For them a Ph.D. would open more doors than an S.J.D. Second, the S.J.D. and J.S.D. degrees are likely to suffer from confusion with the flood of J.D.'s now being granted for three-year law courses, however pedestrian.

THE STUDENT RESPONSE TO THE PROGRAM

Only a few years ago the idea of a program of applied social science in law schools of high standing would at once have raised the question: Where are the students coming from? The law student was then viewed as a young man with his eye on the main chance, and that was seen in big-firm practice. Whether this was a misjudgment of our students or is a measure of the change in our times (I suspect it may be both), clearly both times and student bodies have changed. In many big-firm law schools, a substantial number of able students do not see a big-firm partnership as a career goal but seek opportunities for public service, especially to the disadvantaged, through the legal profession.

Probably programs of the sort I have sketched would increase the number of such students enrolling in the big-firm law schools, but I doubt their total would ever be absolutely large. At Harvard, for example, I should be surprised if a sixth of today's students would commit themselves to a full urban studies program even though, as in international legal studies, many more would pursue some work in the area. Whether and to what extent this proportion would grow would depend on many factors outside the schools: the actual progress made in coping with city problems; the career opportunities in government and in teaching in law schools and other departments; and the new prospects in law practice.

A program along the lines I have suggested would probably attract to its courses and seminars a much larger number of graduate students in the social sciences than we have heretofore seen in the law schools. They should be welcomed. The new work would be more meaningful to them than law school offerings have heretofore seemed, and they could contribute to it. The long-run effects could be important and beneficial both to their disciplines and to the law.

In choosing the field of urban legal studies (including the criminal law) as the subject of the possible program of "applied social science," I have done so because, in my opinion, national needs entitle that field to priority. But there is nothing to preclude the development of applied social science programs directed to more flourishing areas of our economy. Field studies can be performed on Wall Street and its counterparts and in Washington and the state capitals. If our publications are an index, our knowledge of the actualities of achieving, exercising, and controlling economic power through legal instrumentalities is about as fragmentary as our knowledge of the operation of welfare agencies and public housing administration.

The Challenge to the Small-Firm School

As and if a number of the fifteen or twenty big-firm law schools were to develop applied social science programs, undoubtedly some of the forty to forty-five law schools possessed of the first group's qualifications in somewhat lesser degree would seek to follow suit. They might be content to restrict their programs to particular problems in which their respective faculties were strong or as to which their environments were especially relevant. I shall later consider a special opportunity open to these schools. But what of the other seventy or eighty law schools? For only a few of these would even a limited program of research and education development of the sort I have suggested seem practicable.

One small-firm law school has, to be sure, boldly embarked on a pioneering program in urban law with a considerable research component as well: The University of Detroit School of Law, aided by a substantial OEO grant. However, this venture (which has already produced the excellent *Journal of Urban Law*) has imposed a heavy burden on the school in relation to its resources. Few small-firm schools could hope to emulate its example.

Is not a more realistic alternative for these schools simply the better adaptation of their educational programs to the social needs which their own graduates will be called upon to meet? They should not strive for a place near the end of a procession headed for professional goals remote from those of their own graduates. Schools that produce many of our solo and small-firm practitioners, most of the counsel for our criminal defendants, and probably most of the lawyers who hold state and local legal offices (including judgeships), should recognize the opportunity that these facts afford. They can claim with little, if any, exaggeration that their graduates will have greater responsibility for the well-being of our urban society than will the lawyers who represent great corporations or hold federal office. But how can these schools equip their graduates to discharge this responsibility effectively and well?

This question cannot, of course, be answered with assurance. But we are postulating a society seeking to extend legal services much more widely—not merely to the indigent—a society moving toward revolutionary changes in the treatment of law-breakers, and that is reorganizing the political and administrative structures of our 225 "standard metropolitan statistical areas." On this horizon, we can glimpse some of the directions that change must take.

First, the schools should seek to remove some of the barriers to the extension of legal services. Ways must be sought to awaken students to an appreciation of the importance and the techniques of preventive law, a cause that Louis M. Brown has been advocating to the California bar and to Southern California students for many years. The need to command the confidence of a clientele which has long viewed recourse to law as itself a misfortune indicates the desirability of developing in law students a sense of the lawyer's human relations problems and also of the art of client counseling. And, if the economic barriers to widespread use of legal services are to be lowered, law schools should shake off their inhibitions and devote study and instruction to ways of providing legal services efficiently and at costs acceptable to low- and middle-income clients.

Second, an expanding role for the law-trained man in a newly-conceived system of criminal justice will call for more than courses in criminal law and procedure. He must have some understanding of basic social and psychological factors involved in all phases of the criminal processes from police operations to the prisoner's reassimilation into his community. Law graduates possessing this expertise may hope for posts at appropriate places in the criminal process, though not necessarily qua lawyers.

Third, the engagement of governments at all levels in ministering to our urban maladies has had a minimum of study by law faculties. Their graduates have too little knowledge of urban blight, suburban sprawl, and the intricate entangling of federal, state, and local bureaus. The lawyer likes to see himself as the architect of social structures; he has come close to losing this role by default in the urban scene. A bar educated to a better understanding of today's urban problems, physical, financial, and governmental, would be contributing more of its members to the staffing of governmental machinery and could also be vigilant in assuring respect for the rights of the individual citizen.

Do these lines of development represent counsel of perfection to the small-firm schools? With faculties of limited size, burdened by the need to offer courses thought necessary for both bar examinations and practice, how can small-firm law schools offer instruction in pre ventive law, human relations and client counselling, law office management, the social and psychological problems of criminal justice, and an unidentified group of courses concerned with the correction of metropolitan maladjustments? How can these hard-pressed schools provide time and talent to devise apt methods of instruction (including the clinical) and suitable teaching materials (reflecting local conditions)? Finally, could they take the risk that students not dedicated to practice in these areas might fail to get adequate instruction in more conventional fields of law?

These questions are just. As for the development of new courses, new teaching methods and materials, I think the answer is clear: this should be a task initially for the enlarged faculties of the big-firm schools, aided by the students in their applied social science programs. Their products would not be for export only; I should suppose that ordinarily an innovation would be tested by use in the innovating school or schools. The situation would resemble the pioneering days of the case system when Harvard sent its case-trained graduates out to carry the new technique to other law schools. Before long, about one-quarter of all American law teachers were Harvard graduates, a hazard minimized in the situation I am envisaging by the fact that the missionary role would be assumed by not one but by fifteen or twenty schools, with still other schools joining in the enterprise at various points. Adapting centrally produced course plans and materials to particular states or communities would, of course, have to be a task for the teachers on the firing line, some of them graduates of one of the innovating schools. Feedback from their actual teaching experience would be essential.

Even harder than the task of designing new courses, methods, and materials would be convincing law deans and faculties that they and their students could sacrifice time from the standard courses. I have already viewed this problem optimistically as regards those students

in the big-firm law schools who would be committing a more substantial part of their second- and third-year work to urban studies
than I believe could be expected of students in the small-firm schools.
Efforts to avoid placing the latter in jeopardy from the lag in bar
examinations might induce a more persistent search for methods of
inculcating legal knowledge and understanding in less time than the
case method now requires.

This increase in instructional efficiency could be achieved, I believe,
in many courses by combining challenging text with provocative
problems, adding appellate opinions on selected issues where the pay-
off of case analysis seemed highest. By recourse to this or other means
to the same end, the curriculum could be compressed to the extent
required to permit election of the new offerings. Quite possibly, moreover, the new materials would lead to a greater understanding of the
fewer matters they covered. In law schools where the students' academic records are not strong, too strict an adherence to the traditional
case method may be counter-productive. Moreover, in any assessment
of curriculum coverage by a school serving a large city, recognition
should be accorded the growth of continuing legal education and its
ability to round out as well as to update a body of knowledge which
the law schools have not been able to carry beyond the fundamentals.

An Opportunity for State Law Schools

I have oversimplified the developmental process by under-
casting the role of the forty or so law schools I have viewed as falling
into an intermediate category between the big-firm and the small-firm
schools. Of course, no school is to be irrevocably typed: once confronted by the problems and opportunities I foresee, each school would
have to determine its own role, taking account of faculty interests and
aspirations, its resources, and, especially, the communities and careers
into which its students would be most likely to go.

Many of the law schools in this intermediate category are in state-
supported universities. This circumstance gives them a special, long-
neglected opportunity. I am alluding to the creation of "institutes of
government" in which problems of state and local government and
administration are subjects of continuing study by staffs recruited
mainly from the law schools and the bar, and which also provide
special courses of instruction for officials administering the law and
programs that the institutes have studied. This not only can improve
the quality of governmental services but also can establish two-way
communication between those services and the state's law schools.

The extraordinary success story of the Institute of Government at the University of North Carolina testifies to what can be accomplished by such a body. The Institute at Chapel Hill was created by Professor Albert Coates of the Law School in the darkest days of the great depression. Staffed almost exclusively by law graduates from his own and other law schools, it took root after years of trial and since has flourished. Unfortunately, it has had rather limited connections with the Law School's own educational program, a fact which may reflect the widely-held view that the public laws of state and local governments and their administrations are not really the concern of law faculties. As I look forward, the days of that view seem numbered.

Para-Legal and Pre-Legal Instruction

Still looking ahead, I see two more developments, one yet to be initiated; the other still striving for full recognition. The former is the training of "para-lawyers"; the other, the teaching of law in the liberal arts curriculum. Each deserves more attention than I can give it here, but neither should go unremarked in this context.

"Para-lawyer" is an elegant term for a person trained to perform, under a lawyer's supervision, a variety of legal services not requiring a complete legal education. We have para-lawyers now; they have had apprentice training; we usually call them clerks and secretaries. (We also have lawyers doing the para-lawyer's work.) Given, say, a year's training in a law school or a properly-staffed college, a person who lacked the money, temperament, or some of the qualifications needed for a full legal education, might well attain a more responsible place as a practicing lawyer's aide than that now attained by various assistants who have no formal training. Moreover, extension of legal services to more and more people with low and middle incomes will multiply the occasions for rather routine operations performable by the para-lawyer. Perhaps, indeed, para-lawyers are an economic prerequisite to this extension of legal services.

In this the most law-ridden of all nations, the proportion of university-educated citizens who possess some education in law is probably lower than that in any other country. This is due mainly to the fact that law study here is seen exclusively as professional training, whereas most of the world views some law study as general education. We have paid a price for this professionalization of law study in our citizenry's ignorance of law, even though it has probably led to better legal education.

Happily, the situation is remediable: as a growing body of experience is demonstrating, undergraduate instruction in the role of law as a social institution and in the processes through which law functions can help to bridge the gap between the legal profession and the educated public. One result should be better communication between the lawyer and scholars trained in other disciplines. Another result would be to aid law school curricular developments of the sort I have been suggesting. Among the beneficiaries would be the para-lawyers, who would gain the broader view of the law which their training courses might neglect.

Money

One final aspect of my subject I am not entitled to ignore: money. The big-firm schools pioneering in programs in applied social science concurrently with professional education would have to give up their usual low teacher-student ratios and also incur substantial research costs. Similarly, small-firm schools seeking to modify traditional law curricula and to initiate instruction better adapted to social needs could not escape an increase in costs. Increases in tuition income from larger enrollments could scarcely meet these expenses nor could the continuing generosity of law school alumni. In the long run, the law schools will have to depend on the readiness of the Congress and of foundations to recognize and provide for their increased needs.

Grants and appropriations, even if no more than a fraction of the annual contributions from the same sources to medical education and research, would represent a veritable bonanza for legal education and research. There is some evidence that Congressional largesse may be in prospect. If it comes, there will doubtless remain certain law school needs that the legislation could not be construed to cover. If so, one must hope for foundation support. Should neither respond, the potentialities of legal education when viewed in forward-looking perspective may never be realized. At this juncture, if we close our eyes to the war in Vietnam and the draft, there seems room for optimism. However, if the law schools begin to break ground without waiting on the support they hope for, they will, I predict, increase their prospects of attracting it.

Appendix

Statistics concerning the structure of the legal profession are hard to come by, and my figures are rough estimates. I assume that additions to the bar will have brought the 289,404 listings by states in the Martindale-Hubbell Directory for 1966 close to 300,000 and that the 30,000 lawyers not then listed in the Directory were probably not in lawyers' occupations. In 1966, of 212,662 lawyers in private practice, 78,544 were partners, and 20,845 associates, See Am. Bar Foundation, The 1967 Lawyer Statistical Report, Table 6, in publication. However, there is no breakdown by size of firm. Another source, Smith & Clifton, Income of Lawyers, 1962–1963, 42 A.B.A.J. 1943, 1044, Table v (Nov. 1966) drawing on Internal Revenue data, reports that in the United States in 1963 there were 2,180 law firms with five or more partners, of which only 404 had ten or more partners. Taking averages of 15 partners for the 404 firms and seven partners for the remaining 1,776 firms yields a total of just under 18,500 big-firm (five or more) partners in 1963.

Of 17,395 associates in the Martindale-Hubbell data for 1963, Am. Bar Foundation, The 1964 Lawyers Statistical Report, Table 6, p. 32, (Hankin & Krohnke eds. 1965), certainly not over 10,000 would have been employed by the 2,180 firms with five or more partners. If that figure is taken, then the big firms would have accounted for roughly 28,500 lawyers in 1963. My guesstimate of a total of 35,000 today provides margins for growth and error.

On the basis of the foregoing, small-firm partners and their associates in 1963 accounted for 59,000 of the 200,500 lawyers then in private practice. Am. Bar Foundation, The 1964 Lawyer Statistical Report, supra. Probably they have been continuing to grow at an increasing rate while the solo practitioners have continued to decline in proportion if not in absolute numbers: (Their number, 113,273 in 1966 compared with 113,127 in 1963, was nearly 4,000 fewer than in 1960). Perhaps today the respective figures would be close to 110,000 solo practitioners, 75,000 small-firm partners and associates, and 35,000 big-firm lawyers.

The total number of lawyers in "private employment" in 1966 (including 2,717 employed by educational institutions) came to around 33,200. This (largely) house counsel category has been growing rapidly; probably it will have reached the total 35,000 estimated in the text. The government section in 1966 was comprised of approximately 9,700 in judicial posts and 31,300 in executive and legislative, for a total of about 41,000. Here growth has been uneven; in city and county governments the number was lower in 1966 than in 1951, while the number in state and federal government has doubled since 1951. The 42,000 estimate in the text may well be conservative.

*   *   *

In the five years ending in 1963, new admissions to the bars of the several states numbered: 10,744 (1959), 10,505 (1960), 10,729 (1961), 10,784 (1962), and 10,788 (1963), for a total of 53,550. See 32 The Bar Examiner 99 (1963), 36 id. 99 (1967). In 1964–1966 new admissions numbered: 12,023 (1964), 13,109 (1965) and 14,644 (1966). See 36 id. 99. Data are lacking for the '67 and '68, but new admissions in any year approximate closely the number of third-year students enrolled in law schools the year before. On that basis, I forecast new admissions in '67 of 16,250 and in '69 of 17,250. See 18 J. Leg. Ed. 211 (1965), 19 id. 216 (1966). Adding these to the actual totals for 1964–1966 provides a five-year total of about 73,000 for 1964–1968.

Given the size of the class of '68 which entered in '66 and the draft incentives for them to continue as students, the third-year class in '68–69 may well reach 19,000, pointing to bar admissions at that level in '69. If one ignores the new ground rules for military service and projects moderate growth in succeeding years, the annual number of new admissions might exceed 21,000 by 1973; bringing the aggregate for the 1969–1973 quinquennium to the neighborhood of 100,000.

* * *

The lowest median LSAT score in a Stratum I school was 572; in a Stratum II school, 485. See Warkov & Zelan, Lawyers in the Making, 55 (1965). LSAT scores have been edging upwards, and corresponding scores today would be higher. The study's other indicia point to student bodies of a considerably lower academic caliber in Stratum III schools. *Ibid.* Of course, law schools admitting low-ranking students often eject a substantial proportion of them at the end of the first year. I discussed some implications of the upward sweep in law school enrollments since the NORC study in reviewing the books in 33 U.Chi.L. Rev. 898 (1966).

Abraham S. Goldstein

10

The Unfulfilled Promise
of Legal Education

We have seen law students, somewhat belatedly, joining the dissident chorus on campuses across the nation, giving voice to feelings of unease and discontent about the current state of their educational situation. Far too many of us dismiss these stirrings as more expressive of a generalized dissatisfaction with the course and quality of life in America than of any serious defect in legal education. And the students, as is so often the case in matters of this kind, know better how they feel about the situation than why they feel that way or what to do about it. I should like to add my voice to the students' because I think they have good reason to be unhappy about legal education and that it is long past time for law faculties and the legal profession to sort out which of the causes can be dealt with in the law schools.

The Case Method and Legal Realism

For some time, we have harbored the illusion that the legal realist movement of the '20s and '30s—growing out of an earlier sociological jurisprudence and nurtured by the later writings of the functionalists—brought into being a body of literature, and a style

ABRAHAM S. GOLDSTEIN *is William Nelson Cromwell Professor of Law at the Yale Law School and a former Fellow of Christ's College, Cambridge. He has been engaged in the practice and teaching of law for almost twenty years; and he is the author of many articles and books, including* The Insanity Defense *(1967).*

of legal education, that was well attuned to the contemporary scene. The illusion traces, of course, to the extent to which the case method of law teaching, developed almost a century ago by Dean Langdell of the Harvard Law School, proved an easy target for its critics. That method had begun as an effort to base the study of law upon real cases rather than concepts. But the use of the appellate opinion as the exclusive source of "case" material was soon found to be much too limited a vehicle for learning about the legal rules, much less about the legal system. Drawing intellectual sustenance from sociology, anthropology and psychology, and from the pragmatic tradition in philosophy, the new critics brought within the lawyer's universe the relation of appellate court rules to other parts of the legal process—the trial courts, the informal processes which precede and follow the judicial decision, the legislative and administrative processes. This led in turn to questions about why participants in the process behaved as they did, what effect doctrine had upon them and they upon doctrine, what behavioral assumptions underlay legal rules, and what were the consequences of adopting one rule rather than another. In short, they began a serious effort to convert the study of law from a professional art which was almost entirely textual, literary and analytical to something approximating a science. Of course, the paths traveled by Pound, Llewellyn, Moore, Frank, Lasswell and McDougal in pursuit of these objectives varied greatly. But they all reflected the underlying dream that a body of descriptive material would lead to behaviorally based theories of law and legal institutions and, eventually, to a functional jurisprudence which would enable lawyers to understand how "law" develops, when to invoke it, and through what institutional forms.

It is impossible to touch upon the legal realist period without feeling its excitement and sense of intellectual adventure, its faith in intelligence and the capacity of men to order human affairs. Indeed, this feeling may well have contributed to the illusion that a functional jurisprudence had either come to pass or was ready for creation. But this was to mistake the promise for the reality. Legal realism was a short-lived enthusiasm that in fact has left a legacy of expectation rather than accomplishment.

The lessons of the '20s and '30s have been absorbed hardly at all. The empirical research, the close study of legal institutions, the exploration of behavioral presuppositions, have not come into being. There has been an almost total failure of follow-through. The reasons are, of course, not difficult to find. The Depression, the New Deal and World War II diverted much of the available intellectual energy toward reshaping society. Though this sort of social engineering was, in a sense, the fulfillment of at least part of the legal realist dream, it left little or no time for incorporating the lessons of the laboratory into legal scholarship or research. Law and lawyers were far too busy doing to have much time to study what was being done. Meanwhile, legal institutions were undergoing profound changes and at an increasing rate. As home, church, and ideology began to lose their cohesive force, "law" was increasingly seen as a way not only of expressing pre-existing norms but also of creating them. Both the New Deal and World War II had shown the way and had accelerated the tendency to turn to law to solve the most fundamental problems of the society.

Legal scholarship came into the period following World War II without ever having had the time, the resources, or the constancy of purpose to do what had been called for in the '20s and '30s, much less to extend the call to include the legal and social product of the '40s, '50s and '60s. The movement of course has had an important impact on legal education, but chiefly in the classroom rather than in legal research and scholarship; and this has served to confuse all of us, law faculty and law students, as to the nature and purpose of legal education.

The Case Method in Search of Purpose

Legal realism has infiltrated legal education through the same Langdell case method which had been the object of its attack. But where Langdell used the appellate opinon as a way of finding the "true" rule of law, and of putting that rule in a neat logical fit with other rules, we now assume that task can be learned quickly and easily, that particularly after the first year our students can parse a case and tell us what is holding, what is dictum. Under pressure from the weight and dynamism of an ever-increasing body of law, we have shifted our emphasis and have made "the case" the occasion for a much broader inquiry—one which will enable the lawyer to capture the dynamic of a given field, to cope with the changing legal scene and to call into question the old rules. But because we are not clear which concepts or course of training should be made central, we tend to treat the appellate decision as if it were an all-purpose hypothetical problem leading in any direction the teacher chooses to travel—sometimes to a search for behavioral presuppositions, sometimes to an assessment of impact, sometimes to discerning the lines along which doctrine is likely to develop.

In response to these currents, law teachers have begun to use casebooks and teaching materials which go well beyond the appellate opinion. They use trial transcripts, legislative and administrative materials and extracts from the relevant behavioral sciences in an effort to provide a living context for the rule of law and to illustrate the ranges and variety of settings and problems which must be taken into account. Indeed, many conceal under the old course names impressive efforts to turn legal education toward the institutional or theoretical framework promised by the new jurisprudence. Unfortunately, however, these casebooks rarely press matters far enough. Their utility lies more in sensitizing the law student to the infinite complexity of legal processes than in framing hypotheses for understanding those processes. The reason, of course, is that the full exploration of any case which raises a substantial question is impossible—not alone because time is lacking but because, at every point, it becomes apparent that we do not know how to answer the questions we are raising. We do not have the psychology, the sociology or the political science to fill the many spaces left by legal developments in a welfare state; and we certainly cannot supply what is needed by conceptions of legal education as broad as those held by the legal realists and the functionalists. The result is that law teaching has taken on a hit-and-run quality. The search for principle through appellate opinion has too often given way to bewildered contemplation of the open texture and the growing points, punctuated with reflections on how difficult and unanswerable are the questions we have raised.

Curiously, this method of teaching has provided very good training for the practicing lawyer. As one of the last of the generalists in an age of increasing specialization, he must learn how to move quickly in and out of complex fact situations, how to grasp what is known and what is not in an ever-proliferating variety of fields. He must do this in a setting that is adversary or, if not formally adversary, one which involves parties to a dispute. As a result, he will have been well-trained only if he has become intellectually supple enough to master the art of the hypothetical case, and to join his intelligence and his emotions to one or the other side of the case. What is more, he must be able to apply these arts to a wide variety of roles with regard to a variety of subject matters in a variety of institutional settings—and to do so without too much prejudgment of the merits of any given issue.

The law schools can prepare students for this sort of role only by teaching them how to move into a problem and to separate it into its component parts, emphasizing always what is known and what is not. This method makes the lawyer especially skilled in showing the limits and inadequacies of what is proffered by others. But it has only limited utility for understanding the nature of law, its development or the uniqueness of its institutions and processes. However much we talk the language of legal realism or of functionalism, we are doing so essentially from the inside view of the working lawyer, one which makes little effort to place law and legal institutions and legal decision-makers in a context which would enable us to learn what jobs can be done by law and what cannot.

For the law student, examining doctrine in order to demonstrate its myriad relations to people and institutions falls cruelly short. It draws him into mysteries without giving him the skill or the training adequate to their solution. The fields of law being opened for him require for their comprehension a degree of specialization that he simply does not have. If, for example, he is urged to consider the relevance of perception to the law of evidence, or of social class to prosecutorial discretion, or of the place of the criminal sanction in controlling deviant behavior, he is inevitably brought to the question whether investigation of these phenomena should be undertaken by him or by members of his profession. Why else, after all, is he being called to consider them? Yet he cannot pursue these inquiries very far, at least in his present state of training, for he would soon be heavily involved in problems of social and psychological research lying well beyond his competence.

I mean to suggest not that problems of this sort should be avoided, but rather that they can no longer be addressed by the hit-and-run method. Too many of the law's most interesting questions have only marginal relevance to the work of lawyers-as-professionals to justify the attention we pay them. Addressing them in full dimension can be justified only by a conception of legal education that transcends the professional and places law firmly among those social sciences which search for a body of theory and for a methodology adequate to test the theories.

The unfortunate fact is that we have not yet settled what we are about in legal education. For legal realists, it seemed quite enough to demonstrate that "law" was something more than the words recited in appellate opinions. But for the current generation of law teachers and law students, that lesson has been learned and a new lesson waits to be written. If law is everywhere, and legal rules turn on and relate to everything, then what is legal education to select out as its special province? Can the lawyer-generalist survive under a legal philosophy which presses toward ever more detailed study of legal institutions, particularly when society turns ever more often and more insistently to law to solve its most serious social problems?

Specialization and the Generalist Myth

It is time for the law schools to face the question whether they should continue to pursue the ideal of the lawyer-generalist. The pressure to make the choice comes not only from prevailing legal theory and from the pervasive role of law in America, but also from the new student generations. These students are the product of an increasingly competitive and selective educational process. Many of them come to us at unusually high levels of competence in their major fields and readier than in the past to pursue their studies along "graduate" lines. For such students, many of whom have heard the promise of inter-disciplinary adventure and social action so much in the air these days, it comes as a cruel disappointment to find law school very much like college—except that its organization is more random and archaic.

The law school teaching method is of course likely to be more prob-lem-oriented. Yet it turns out to be curiously abstract, stopping at general speculative propositions without having pursued fully their validity or relevance in a broader content. And it rarely draws in any meaningful way on the considerable competence many students bring with them from fields like economics, political science, history and sociology. In part, this is because the law schools make no effort to dig very deep into any particular area. There are no "majors," no real areas of concentration. Instead, the law student goes from course to course, each related in a loose way to the other but only introductory in nature. When a second year student meets the course in Evidence, for example, he is exposed to the entire field—either through a skim-ming coverage of the whole or through concentration on a number of selected areas. But even when he concentrates, he does little more than touch on the area—learning the case-law, finding the open texture and the major themes, only glancing at the behavioral presuppositions of the rules and the functions they serve.

The fact is that advanced work in a legal field at present is less likely to profit from the study of other law courses than from fields which are not legal at all, in the conventional sense. The criminal lawyer is only marginally interested in the law of corporations. As a professional, he is far more interested in the nature of police and prosecutor, probation and parole officer. As a research worker, he is far more interested in psychology and sociology.

Even if the law schools were to confine their activities to "law," as traditionally understood, it is not at all clear which areas should be selected for treatment or how intensively. Does the fact that lawyers are involved with statutes and regulations dealing with monetary policy, for example, mean that the law schools should teach or en-courage research in that subject? Should the pattern of law dealing with schools, highways, medical care, air pollution, water pollution, etc., be incorporated into the law school curriculum? Until fairly re-cently, of course, the law schools have not had to face the problem because the fields they taught, following the interests of practitioners, were almost entirely private in nature and oriented to the judicial process. Now, however, the situation is quite different. With the advent of legal services organizations and public defenders, with the pressure of the civil rights movement, and with the growth of governmental regulation, the newer areas of public law offer promise not only of novelty but of a working role for lawyers.

The law schools, as they are now constituted, cannot possibly prepare students adequately for these new and intricate areas of law practice any more than they prepare students to fulfill the legal realist dream in the more conventional areas. The law schools retain a curricular model conceived in a day when the lawyer really was a generalist and was called upon by a simpler society to deal with all facets of the law. Today, when the general practitioner in law is as nearly obsolete as the general practitioner in medicine, the law schools still pursue the generalist dream. That dream is as disabling for the lawyer-as-practitioner as it is for the lawyer-as-scholar. In each instance, the dream prevents us from helping him to become master of the materials of an increasingly specialized practice and scholarship.

Several justifications are advanced for retaining the generalist structure of legal education. One, which is widely prevalent, is that the study of the various fields of law, even by persons who are not likely to work in them, provides some sort of "exercise" for the mind, chiefly through the use of analogy, which transfers in unidentifiable ways to the field of real interest. A second is that the lawyers are the engineers of the planned society, uniquely situated to handle the controls which must be relied upon as the welfare state turns to ever new areas. Both justifications are, in my view, misplaced. The first seems to be little more than a rationalization of what history has provided us by way of a curriculum. The second is a conceit which converts the accidental fact that the lawyer is an available social handyman, ready to take on a wide variety of complex assignments, into a basis for supposing he has a competence to deal with ever more complex phenomena.

If we were to surrender the myth of the lawyer as omnicompetent and of legal education as preparing the law student to take on any job coming his way, he might be able to learn what it is that lawyers can do and what they cannot, what legal institutions and processes can do and what they cannot, what the effect of legal doctrine is upon the men and institutions it purports to affect and control. I do not see how we can begin to learn these things when we do not provide within the law school curriculum specialized training that is at least addressed to these questions.

A Proposal for Curricular Reform

The present state of legal education has a turn-table quality. We tell the law student of today, again and again, the things which seemed so revolutionary in the '20s and '30s—that words have many meanings, that doctrine is but a part of an institutional matrix, that everything we say and do must be monitored and affected by the kinds of institutions through which the words must pass. We fight again the battles which led to our conversion, but with students who are already persuaded. Our revolutionary faith is, after all, their tradition. The effect of such exhortation to the already-committed is to exaggerate the extent to which lawyers can address and appraise behavioral and normative questions. This would not be an entirely undesirable development if issues bravely confronted were as bravely explored—not just in the classroom but in social research. How long, for example, will we talk about treatment and deterrence and distribution of risk before we mount serious efforts to investigate these problems?

I do not mean to suggest that questions of this sort are easily answered, or that there are techniques and resources ready at hand to conduct the inquiry. There are not, and that fact underscores the frustrations inherent in our current situation. We regularly exhort our students to address questions which we have not really begun to address ourselves. One has but to scan the legal literature to see how case-bound it still is, how rarely it places the legal problem in a historical perspective large enough to sound the major themes, how occasional is the close exploration either of behavioral presupposition or institutional consequence, how entirely absent is the effort to build on what has gone before in an effort to find laws of growth and development which define the legal situation. As a result, we tend to leave our students with the feeling that law and legal institutions are infinitely manipulable; that if social phenomena point in the wrong direction, we can always rely on law to put them right.

It seems apparent to me that the present structure of the law schools is unsound and that the unsoundness contributes to the delusion that the lawyer-generalist is competent to deal with the increasingly complex areas drawn within legal regulation and control. It is time for us to give up the generalist myth and to develop instead patterns of lawyer specialization adequate to the need. In urging that we give up the myth, I should not like to be understood as saying that we should also abandon the ideal that it is possible to make valid generalizations, and large ones, about law and legal processes. Indeed, my interest in specialization derives in considerable part from my belief that it is only through closer and deeper studies that we will develop the behaviorally based theories which are essential to a valid jurisprudence. Nor do I wish to be understood as urging that the lawyer retreat everywhere from the role of social engineer. My feeling, rather, is that lawyers cannot survive in this age of increasing regulation unless they define their roles more clearly. It is essential for us to determine what we mean by legal skills and where they are central; where, for example, the lawyer should indeed be the generalist who draws other disciplines together and guides the process of policy choice and where he should assume a subordinate role, as one specialist among many—with the generalist role played by someone from another field (*e.g.,* public health or community psychiatry or monetary policy).

In brief outline, I have in mind a course of study which in the first year would pursue a conventional curriculum of the more advanced sort; and in the second and third years, divide equally between general electives and courses in the area of specialization. The content of specialized courses would be appropriate for each specialized area. The nature of these areas might, of course, depend upon whether the law school is "national" or is trying to define a course of study uniquely appropriate to its region and resources. In the so-called Stratum I law schools and those others which are specially favored by unusual students, unusual faculties and rich interdepartmental resources, I would provide, in addition, for research degrees in each of the areas of specialization. The research student would be expected to learn the methods of social research, theory building, etc. Throughout the curriculum, particularly in the second and third years, a significant amount of his time would be allotted to research and writing, to participant observation and field research—all tied as much as possible to the fields of specialization. A judicious amount of clinical and internship experience would be interspersed, as an essential catalyst for making concrete the abstractions inherent in a study of legal rules.

In short, I have in mind adding to legal education a track which incorporates genuinely graduate and research objectives while at the same time sharpening the focus of the professional curriculum. Such a system would require faculty-student ratios which resemble those of graduate schools, on the one hand, and medical schools on the other. Though my own law school already has one of the most favorable faculty-student ratios in the country among law schools, it does not begin to compare with that of the economics department or the political science department. Our 16 to 1 ratio pales beside the exquisite tailoring—*e.g.,* the 6 to 1 ratio—that a genuine graduate program entails.

Implicit in what I have said is the risk of a tremendous conflict between the objective of professional education and the objective of treating law as a branch of political or social science. We should take that risk, because there is a creative tension between the professional model and the graduate model; the professional model forces a degree of responsibility upon the graduate model while the graduate model may draw the professional model away from the smugness and self-satisfaction which has often pervaded it. The challenge we must face is how to bend each of the models to the purposes of the other without sacrificing the professional school as we have known it.

If we have any hope of pursuing the logic of legal realism in the context of a highly expanded body of law, we must give up the myth of omnicompetence which underlies the existing course of study. Until we do so, legal education will resemble entirely too much an antenna careening wildly in search of a signal to give it direction.

Irving F. Reichert, Jr.

11

The Future of Continuing Legal Education

Continuing legal education, commonly called CLE, is legal education that continues after a graduate from law school has been admitted to practice. Its purpose has generally been described as two-fold: to improve the professional competency of lawyers, and to bring about greater professional responsibility. By "professional competency" is meant the ability of the lawyer to perform services for his clients in a technically proficient and sophisticated way as counsellor, planner and advocate. "Professional responsibility," as described in the 1959 Arden House Conference on Continuing Legal Education for Professional Competence and Responsibility, refers to other duties and obligations the lawyer assumes, or should assume, among them: improving the administration of justice; reforming of both procedural and substantive law; providing representation for all persons, including the poor and unpopular; serving in civic and public affairs; participating actively in the work of the organized bar. Most CLE programs have been aimed at the objective of improving professional competency; improvement of professional responsibility, if indeed it can be enhanced by organized educational efforts, in practice has been a secondary objective.

IRVING F. REICHERT, JR., *Assistant Administrator, Continuing Education of the Bar, California, is a former Assistant District Attorney of San Francisco. He is founder of the San Francisco Bail Project and one of the founders of the San Francisco Neighborhood Legal Assistance Foundation. He has served as a special consultant to the Governor's Welfare Study Committee, and is the author of "Relationships Between Welfare and Law Enforcement Agencies in Administering the Welfare Laws of California."*

Continuing legal education undertakes to improve professional competency in five dimensions—which are frequently interrelated because of the nature of the subject matter and the varying levels of experience found among lawyers attending any given program.

The first is "keeping current"—providing fresh information in concise form regarding legislative changes, major new court decisions, changes in rules of procedure, and new administrative rulings of governmental agencies.

The second is "sharing experience"—providing to lawyers who encounter various types of problems only infrequently, the benefit of the expertise in handling such problems that specialists or quasi-specialists have developed.

The third is "refreshers"—providing "brush-up" instruction for lawyers who have lost their familiarity with a field of practice or never really developed it.

The fourth is "new learning"—providing comprehensive instruction in fields with which the lawyer is unfamiliar either because the field of practice is in its infancy (e.g., space law), or because he has no prior experience or education in that area.

The fifth is "advanced training"—providing specialists with further training to handle the more sophisticated and complex problems in their fields.

Written materials invariably accompany each program. The evolution of these has been from sketchy mimeographed lecture outlines to practice manuals that include basic legal doctrine, legal document forms and analysis of the practice aspects of the subject in question. In fully developed form continuing education practice books with their annotated pleading and practice forms, checklists, procedural guides, practical suggestions for handling cases (and avoiding traps for the unwary), pertinent substantive law, and comprehensive indexes, serve as desk reference bibles which enable lawyers to practice on a level of competency that was never before possible.

The potential audience for CLE consists of three groups: the newly admitted lawyer fresh from law school; the general practitioner; and the "specialist." The emphasis in CLE to date has been on programs for the general practitioner, partly because they constitute by far the largest single segment of the potential audience. Indeed, most of the energy in present CLE programs is concentrated in improving the quality and efficiency of the instruction aimed at the general practitioner. To an increasing degree, however, attention has been shifting to continuing education for the fledgling lawyer, the would-be specialist, and the specialist. Before turning to the problems that CLE faces in providing education for these groups, a brief historical note may be helpful to provide context.

A Brief Sketch of the History, Structure, and Function of CLE

The first organized CLE programs conducted by a professional administrator were held in New York under the leadership of Harold Seligson. These classes began in 1933, and were designed to help young lawyers "bridge the gap" between law school and practice. They eventually led to the formation of the Practicing Law Institute of New York, a nonprofit corporation that today offers numerous programs and publications to assist lawyers in keeping current with developments in most fields of legal practice.

At the close of World War II, the American Bar Association and the American Law Institute began giving serious consideration to the need for continuing legal education in all parts of the country. As a result of their interest and efforts, the Joint Committee on Continuing Legal Education of the American Law Institute and the American Bar Association (ALI-ABA) was founded in 1947. The general purpose of the Joint Committee was to develop a national program of CLE and to encourage and assist legal educational efforts at local, state, and regional levels.

As CLE developed in the following decade, however, its thrust was chiefly at the state level. The modesty in development at the local level appears primarily to be the result of insufficient resources: few local bars are large enough to sustain programs of the required technical quality. The modesty of development at the national level can be attributed to the fact that most of the practice of most lawyers is state-law oriented.

Statutes, procedures, and practices vary greatly among the states; a program to improve the competence of an Oregon lawyer in handling a real estate sale, a divorce, or a criminal case should be prepared and conducted by Oregon lawyers familiar with practice in that state. Lecture series or books prepared for a nationwide legal audience that attempt to cover subjects controlled by local rules and statutes may be profitable to the sponsor or publisher but have proved of limited value to the listening or reading audience.

Evidencing the state orientation of CLE is the fact that by the fall of 1967, thirty-one states had programs conducted by full- or part-time administrators. Responsibility for policy and administration varies from state to state. In some states the program is conducted under the auspices of the state bar; in others by one or more law schools; in a few it is a joint effort of law schools and the state bar; in California, the state bar, the law schools and the University of California Extension collaborate to conduct the program.

However, the pre-eminence of the state programs should not obscure the development of CLE programs at the local and national levels. In addition to the programs organized by ALI-ABA, continuing legal education programs are also conducted by a variety of organizations including local bar associations of lawyers who specialize in particular fields of practice.

CLE program quality varies considerably. The success of any given program of course is largely dependent upon the performance of the participants. The search is always for lecturers and writers who are not only experienced in the area of practice but who are also clear and stimulating in their presentation. This combination of talents is not always available. One chronic problem is the speaker whose primary desire is to use any podium as a means of increasing his referral business: as the "Have case, will travel!" attorney regales the audience with an eye-bugging account of the most recent staggering verdict he has obtained, one can almost hear the subliminal computations of fee-sharing by the prospective referring attorneys in the audience. There are also problems with speakers who obviously have failed to prepare their material, who ignore the subject assigned to them and those who drone on from a manuscript. It is impossible to prevent these eventualities from occurring even in CLE programs managed by professional staffs, but in programs run by volunteers who lack the resources and devices to screen speakers and edit writers, they tend to recur with alarming regularity and to threaten the continuity of the general program. The need to provide professional administration, however, leads to important economic problems in the organization of CLE.

The frequency and quality of the programs sponsored by any CLE organization are largely determined by its available resources. These include money, staff, support by the bar, and the number of experienced attorneys who can and will take the time to write or lecture. Moreover, every systematic CLE program tries to accommodate the divergent objectives of "keeping current," "sharing experience," "refreshers," "new learning" and "advanced training." Obviously these objectives cannot all be accomplished in a single program, so that programs pitched at different levels of technical sophistication become necessary. Program proliferation of this kind creates further economic problems, and CLE operations can meet the diverse needs of the potential audience only if they are either based in large states or can be organized so as to surmount the barriers of state-law orientation. This is one of the chief dilemmas in the current CLE situation.

Having briefly examined the past and present of CLE, let us now look ahead.

A Brief Overview of Future Problems

How will CLE of the future differ from that of today? Will major changes in approach and programming be necessary? Is CLE reshaping legal practice so that CLE itself is changing the educational needs of lawyers?

The chief determinant of future CLE will be changes that may take place within the profession itself. The legal profession seems never to have been in greater ferment than at present. Critical aspects of the profession now under reappraisal include the way in which law students are being educated; the qualifications for admission to practice; the feasibility and possible methods of recognizing specialties; the standards for measuring legal competence and professional responsibility; and the instrumentalities for meeting legal needs of those who cannot, under present fee and service arrangements, afford counsel.

How the bar resolves—or fails to resolve—these problems will importantly shape CLE. But CLE programs will play a part in molding these decisions. For example, programs attempting to "bridge the gap" between law school and practice draw in question what the law schools are doing and whether they should be doing something else. Similarly, programs on specialized subjects make it possible for the general practitioner to practice in areas that have previously been occupied by only a few. So also, instruction that increases the knowledge and efficiency of the average practitioner sets new standards of competency to which all attorneys can reasonably be held. There is little sign thus far that the bar as a whole has appreciated these implications or that its traditional resistance to new ideas will permit acting upon them except by halting steps.

Another set of problems, which can be termed administrative, will continue to plague us in the future. Primary among these are program financing and securing and retaining full-time staffs of qualified personnel. A third category of problem is technological—developing educational techniques that utilize the latest scientific developments in audio-visual aids. These include tele-lectures, tape recordings, closed circuit television, and similar media that offer possibilities both of expanding audience coverage and making programs more stimulating and informative. These administrative and technological problems will be dealt with in greater detail, but let us first consider some of the basic objectives of CLE. Both logically and chronologically we start at the point when the law student passes the bar and becomes a lawyer, and CLE is asked to "bridge the gap" that exists between law school and practice.

Educating the Newly Admitted Lawyer

A fairly well-kept secret of the profession is that most law schools teach a student practically nothing about how to practice law. Sidney Post Simpson's statement of two decades ago, is still true today: "A law school graduate who passes his bar examination is not a lawyer. No one knows it better than he, unless it be his law office or his prospective clients." [1] Or, as Judge Jerome Frank put it, law schools are "library law schools" rather than "lawyer schools." To him, law students were "like future horticulturists studying solely cut flowers" or "prospective dog breeders who never see anything but stuffed dogs." [2] Since that time, some changes have been made. In a number of schools, more effort is directed toward training in drafting documents, legal counselling, negotiating contracts, trial techniques, client interviewing and other subjects that help the student to prepare for what he will eventually do as a lawyer. There is considerable disagreement within the law schools whether these developments are appropriate, and how far they should extend. Even at law schools where there is agreement in principle, curricula change is slow owing to cost, vested academic interest, and tensions over the reputability of "practical courses" and their teachers. There is also much disagreement on grounds of principle, opinion diverging not in two directions but several.

The attitude of many "prestigious" schools seems to be expressed by Professor Alexander Bickel of Yale, who is quoted by Martin Mayer as stating, "we very consciously *don't* fit somebody to hang out a shingle and try a case." The position of these schools is that the most effective job they can do in three years is to train students to "think like lawyers" and to analyze a problem in a legal manner. Another view holds for more practical instruction in the law schools so that a graduate has had some experience in interviewing clients, in drafting contracts, wills, trusts and business agreements, and has become familiar with trial preparation, courtroom procedures and trial work. Still other schools hold that it is impossible for a three-year

---

[1] Simpson, "Continuing Education of the Bar," 59 *Harvard Law Review* 694 (1946).

[2] Jerome Frank, *Courts on Trial* (Princeton, New Jersey: Princeton University Press, 1949), p. 227.

course adequately to cover the practical knowledge and procedures required in practice, and therefore that more time should be spent on courses that will familiarize the student with the political, social, and economic dynamics of our complex society.[3] Many law school curricula reflect attempts to accommodate all these points of view.

From all this, one thing is clear: the task of continuing legal education in "bridging the gap" will be affected by what the law schools do in the future. If they become more practice-oriented, the gap between law school and practice may be narrower though it will probably never disappear. If the schools continue their present system of education, or become even less practice-oriented, the need for "continuing" education at the point of admission to practice will become more acute. At all events—whether in law school, in law offices, in CLE programs or in a combination of them—newly admitted lawyers must be given more efficient training in handling the practical work that is the daily business of the law office.

Those of us in CLE are realistic enough to know that years of practical experience are necessary for the mastery of any profession and that instructional programs cannot instantly transform a neophyte into an omniscient practitioner. Many types of programs are being conducted to hasten and alleviate the pain of this metamorphosis. They vary widely in their ambition and scope. Some, typically a few days in length, consist of talks by practicing lawyers who sketch out problems commonly encountered in probate, domestic relations, criminal law, organizing small businesses, and other areas of practice in which the neophyte is most likely to encounter his first cases. During these sessions, the group may visit the local courthouse where the local judge explains elementary court procedures and the county clerk shows what legal papers look like and where and how they are filed. In some states, there are programs of greater depth which are accompanied by bridging-the-gap materials, ranging from mimeographed syllabi to more sophisticated and detailed hardbound or looseleaf volumes containing forms, checklists, interview sheets, and similar practice guides. Other states are experimenting with skills training courses of several months duration; in some of these, such courses are a prerequisite to admission to practice.

The programs have not been evaluated for their effectiveness, nor is it easy to see how they could be in a reliable way. All of them have been subject to skeptical criticism, part of it attributable to an insatiable anxiety in the bar that the young lawyers—and their clients—be protected from the blunders of elemental incompetence. Because of

[3] See, for example, Irwin C. Rutter, "A Jurisprudence of Lawyer's Operations, 13 *Journal of Legal Education* 301, 1961.

the diversity in the law school training and the initial practice experience of young lawyers, it is not easy to create a training program that is tailored to the needs of all. But the fact remains that for many, a fairly elaborate training program is essential or helpful and that such programs remain to be implemented in most jurisdictions. If the bar could establish a clearer concept of what a neophyte lawyer needs to know to practice, it would be easier to decide what he ought to be taught—in law school or in CLE—in order to do so.

Experienced Practitioners as Law School Teachers

Related to the question of what law students should learn in law school is the question of who should be law teachers. The "gap" between law school and practice is as much attributable to the style and viewpoint in law teaching as it is to course content, and perhaps more so. It will not be narrowed unless law school faculties comprise professors who have experience in private practice or are willing to learn the workaday problems of the legal practitioner. To both suggestions there is a great deal of resistance in the schools themselves.

Many law schools appear to have a supercilious attitude toward the practice of the law. As a result, comparatively few really experienced practitioners are found as full-time faculty members in many leading law schools. The reluctance to hire experienced practitioners cannot be based on the practicing lawyer's lack of teaching experience—few, if any, law professors have any background in teaching when they are first hired. Rather, faculty recruitment policy shows a discernible preference for specific types—law review at a leading law school, clerkship with an appellate court judge, then a year or two with a government agency or a large law firm. Irving M. Mehler, then Assistant Professor of Law at the University of Denver, reported the results of an ABA section study which showed that, of teachers listed on 15 consecutive pages of the Association of American Law School's Teacher's Directory, 34 had no experience in practice.[4]

This recruitment policy no doubt staffs our law schools with brilliant professors having superlative scholastic attainments. But it is questionable whether this is appropriate for schools whose task is to prepare their students for a profession that is extraordinary in its practical orientation; one imagines a barber college whose faculty has never cut a man's hair. Moreover, an unfortunate by-product, as Mehler states, is the "lack of admiration and regard for law teachers on the part of practicing lawyers. They do not consider law teachers, lawyers

[4] Mehler, "Medical Education: A Guide for Law Schools," 44 *A.B.A. Journal* 869 (1958).

in the real sense of the word." Mehler's statements are borne out by the experience of continuing education organizations. Repeatedly, we receive requests that we use experienced practitioners not professors, as our instructors. (Actually, the ideal CLE speaker is a practice-oriented professor.) My experience both in practice and in CLE compels me to add support to the view that law students will become better oriented and equipped for practice if they are trained by men who are aware of the problems which they will face.

Professors as CLE Instructors

One way in which the "gap" between law school and practice can be at least partially bridged is for the law faculties to begin bridge building themselves. This can be achieved by legal academicians undertaking to acquire practice experience after entering teaching, to gain not merely new skills and sophistication but also an appreciation of the professional perspective that their students will have. It is to be hoped that more law teachers will see the utility in doing so, and that law firms will accommodate them by making temporary tours of duty in practice more accessible.

Yet another means to this end is for law teachers to participate more widely in CLE.

For this to happen, there must be a change of attitude on the part of a number of law school deans. As Professor Casner of Harvard has pointed out, there is still strong feeling in academic circles that professors who engage in CLE work are "people who are performing second-class roles in the legal education community." In many schools, writing for the practicing bar in CLE books is beneath the dignity of a professor and not worthy of serious consideration in the annual review of his accomplishments. Lecturing or conducting classes for CLE is looked upon in the same fashion as writing for CLE—not necessarily with disfavor, but with the attitude of "that's interesting, but what has he done that's important?"

This is not to derogate the importance of the types of research and writing that law professors traditionally do. Nor would I attempt to minimize the significance of their work as consultants to legislative bodies, governmental agencies, and the nonprofit legal reform organizations that vie for their time. I say only that working with CLE can be of great significance not only to the bar but also to the professor. An academician who is willing to instruct lawyers, as well as law students, finds himself confronted with questions more practical, more current, more sophisticated and more intellectually challenging than he suspected, and he gives considerable thought to their solution. He finds that he enjoys the experience of trying to find practical answers to challenging situations. Moreover, in working them through, he does so with an audience of lawyers, judges and legislators who can exert influence toward the law reform that is typically his chief interest and concern. And, what he learns from his CLE experience is reflected in his teaching.

Educating the General Practitioner

If the principal unresolved problem of CLE is still that of "bridging the gap," its principal concern has remained the education of the general practitioner. In this CLE has suffered trials, which are perhaps becoming more acute, arising from the fact that the "general practitioner" is in some sense a hypothetical character. Although the practice of law is known to be widely various, there have been few studies of what lawyers actually do, and none that is particularly reliable. In an American Bar Foundation report on specialization a few years ago, the authors pointed out that the results of surveys concerning specialization—which presumably is the obverse of general practice—are ambiguous, not comparable one with another and discrepant or dubious in their sampling procedures. In addition, in all such surveys the lawyer-respondents "made their own determination as to whether they were specialized," combining the weakness of self-evaluation with those of imprecise definition.[5] The extent and characteristics of specialization in law practice thus remain substantially an unknown quantity. And by the same token so do the professional characteristics and work of the "general practitioner."

In this state of affairs, it is little wonder that discussion of aims and methods of CLE for the general practitioner is conspicuous for its ambiguity and confusion. Yet it is both possible and necessary in CLE to establish working definitions, so as to select program subject-matter and the methods of presentation.

The working definitions prove only partially satisfactory, being reworked by trial and error in program development, but they exist: a "general practitioner" is a lawyer who will handle most types of cases that his clients bring him and who does not concentrate his practice in any one particular field; a "specialist" is one whose practice is largely confined to one field or a few closely related fields of practice. These necessarily loose definitions generally correspond with the way in which lawyers think of themselves, and will suffice for our purposes.

[5] Greenwood and Frederickson, *Specialization in the Medical and Legal Professions.* A report of the American Bar Foundation (Chicago, Callaghan & Co., 1964), 56, 99–119.

In this definitional frame of reference, the future of CLE undoubtedly lies in specialized training. For however "general practice" is defined, it seems to be in steady—perhaps even rapid—decline. Today no single lawyer—and comparatively few firms—can stay abreast of all developments in the law any more than a doctor can completely master every branch of medicine and surgery. So far as many a lawyer does try to perform a comparatively wide range of professional services, CLE will try to help him, but at best it will represent efforts at "keeping up to date" with subjects that he most frequently encounters. As this objective becomes more and more impossible of realistic achievement, its significance in CLE will undoubtedly decline.

The emphasis in CLE as regards the "general practitioner" will likely shift, as it seems now to be shifting, to programs designed to assist the general practitioner to develop a specialty or cluster of related specialties. This responds to the expressed interest and desire of the bar itself. A 1967 survey of the California bar is indicative.

A survey of 900 lawyers who enrolled in a California Continuing Education of the Bar Program on Evidence showed that 16 per cent would like to specialize in one field of law and that 48 per cent wanted to specialize in more than one field. Presumably this means that substantially over half of those surveyed wanted to concentrate their practice in fields where they could establish particular competence.

This desire reflects the practical exigencies of contemporary professional life in the law. A true "general practitioner" today might, in the course of a few days, be called upon to give advice about the purchase of a business, handle a three-party real estate exchange, evict a tenant, stop the Air Force from creating sonic booms, set up a revocable trust, get his client's son out of juvenile hall, find and collect child support from a delinquent father, draw a lease, handle an adoption, take a deposition, prepare an appellate brief, make several routine appearances in court, try a personal injury case and appear in a workmen's compensation hearing. To do so, he would have to study the applicable substantive law and the procedural steps on matters he has never encountered and to refresh his learning on those he has not handled for some time. In addition to this, he would have to read advance sheets from state and federal courts, study the weekly tax reports service, attend meetings of one corporation board and three civic groups, and try to find a replacement for his secretary who just had a nervous breakdown. Since there are few who can contemplate this array of tasks, let alone master them, the erstwhile general practitioner limits his commitments, and thereby becomes a specialist. Few lawyers in practice today can do otherwise.

This being the problem of choice confronting the lawyer, a corresponding one confronts CLE. It must either develop programs in variety and depth of subject-matter that correspond to the specializations and would-be specializations of its lawyer audience or cease to be relevant. The only serious question at present is how long CLE will entertain the idea that it can do otherwise.

Recognizing Specialization

It does not require great powers of prophecy to see that if the bar is specialized, and its post-admission educational system is likewise specialized, then more or less formal methods of identifying specialization will follow. Problems of client referral and intra-professional communication will make such methods of recognition a practical necessity. And when that point is reached, one important problem will be the relation between CLE training and recognition of specialty.

Specifically, it is fairly safe to assume that successful completion of an acceptable course may be one of the prerequisites that will entitle a lawyer to be recognized as a specialist. This will bring about a great demand for such courses, but it will obviously create many new problems. Who will develop such courses and who will decide whether they are adequate? Who will give the courses? Will satisfactory completion of the course entitle a lawyer to recognition as a specialist, or will he have to take a special examination similiar to the bar examination in order to qualify? And when specialties are recognized, will the general practitioner be forbidden to handle a case that falls within an area designated as a specialized field of practice?

How soon the great demand for such courses will come and how successfully that demand will be met depends upon many factors.

One factor certainly will be the speed with which the bar acts in recognizing specialties and in determining the qualifications that a specialist must have. This is a subject on which much has been written but little has been done. The problem is exceedingly complex, but cannot be postponed indefinitely, and action may be compelled sooner than we think. The problem of specialties is closely associated with two other problems that the bar has yet to solve: (1) setting standards of competency that a lawyer will have to meet in order to maintain his license, and (2) limiting a lawyer's practice to cases which he is reasonably competent to handle. It does not appear that within the foreseeable future changes in licensing will occur. At present there is no continuing check by the bar to make certain that an attorney maintains any standard of competency. Efforts to establish such checks are likely to meet almost unanimous resistance in the bar. But there is no legitimate reason why lawyers should not be compelled periodically to complete courses or examinations that provide some measure of assurance in this regard. Depending on the courses or examinations that he has successfully completed, his license might allow him to handle certain types of cases unaided; he might be required to associate a specialist with him if he undertakes other matters; and he might be barred from handling some cases.

Such a scheme seems remote at the present time, but I believe that eventually the profession will have to develop such a plan if it is to enjoy the respect and confidence of the public. Certainly, if any such plan develops, CLE will play an important part in providing the post-law school education and training that will be required.

Impact of Anti-Poverty Programs

The time for action on both specialization and setting standards of competency may well be hastened by the development of the new legal services that are part of the anti-poverty program. For the first time we are seeing the poor becoming organized—and they are demanding and getting better job training, better food, better medical care, better housing, better education, and bettter legal assistance. The new leaders of the poor are not content with legal representation that consists of overworked, understaffed and underfinanced public defender's offices, legal aid societies, and assigned legal counsel who are often inexperienced and unqualified. They want proper legal care, and the indications are that sooner or later, come Republicans or Democrats, they will get it. I suspect that they will constitute a primary force in compelling the legal profession to face, much sooner than we anticipate, a plethora of problems about which we have long been aware but with which we have yet to come to grips.

Because government-funded neighborhood legal service offices are not permitted to handle cases that generate a fee, such cases are generally referred to lawyer reference panels conducted by local bar associations. Under most present referral arrangements, the client is referred to from one to three attorneys whose names are at the top of a rotational list. If the lawyers to whom referral is made have had experience with the client's particular type of problem, it is purely fortuitous. Even where referral panels are broken down into specialties, there is little screening under our present system to make certain the lawyer has expertise or even experience in the specialty. (How can there be effective screening when we can't agree on the qualifications of a specialist?)

This arrangement cannot persist. It seems plain that when the

leaders of the poor discover that their fellows are being turned over
to lawyers in this fashion, a howl will arise that this is second-rate
representation occasioned solely by the poverty of the client. They will
not accept the honest but unbelievable answer that the reference panel
system gives the same hit-and-miss treatment to rich and poor alike.
Pressure to change this system will mount, and will be supported by
the public that is largely ignorant of lawyer referral's present weaknesses. Because the system is anachronistic, a long overdue change will
take place. To change the reference panel systems will require establishing standards of competence and correlated educational programs that
will enable lawyers to meet these standards—and it will be to CLE that
the bar will eventually turn for training.

Financing CLE Programs

Whether CLE becomes more closely tied in to specialization or
not, it seems clear that the growing complexity and rate of change in
the law will require CLE to put on an increasing number of programs
which, because of the demands of the bar, will have to keep improving
in quality and thoroughness. One of the main problems that will
accompany this growth is that of obtaining adequate financing. A few
observations about the existing financial structure may help put the
problem in sharper focus.

In California, we are fortunate to have a large legal population,
and, more significantly, a legal population that will support programs
designed to aid them. We are able to publish practice books, make
occasional motion pictures, send teams of lecturers throughout the
state, and engage in other activities that are expensive to produce.
These programs are paid for solely by enrollment fees; there is no
financial burden on the taxpayers and no general subsidy from the state
bar. But even in California, the cost of putting on programs and
publishing practice materials of the quality we seek is so great that a
vital consideration in selection of programs is whether they will be
self-supporting.

Programs that are not self-supporting have to be offset by those
that make up the deficit. Yet the breadth of financial base on which
CLE operates, even in so large a state as California, is so thin that the
margin for error, and therefore of experimentation, is slim. As Felix
F. Stumpf, Administrator of the California Continuing Education of
the Bar, pointed out to the National Conference on Continuing Legal
Education in May of 1967, most CLE organizations are operating on
shoestring budgets, are undercapitalized, and are in constant fear
of financial disaster.

If I am correct in foreseeing increased specialization, and a demand for more courses designed both to create specialists and keep them up to date, the financial problems of CLE will be intensified. Even a large staff of programmers, editors, and book produc͟ion specialists can produce only a limited number of programs each year. These comparatively few courses (in California we now offer from eight to fourteen programs a year) must attract large audiences if financial solvency is to be maintained. And to achieve large enrollments, we must produce programs that appeal to the broad sector of general practitioners. If most general practitioners become specialists, the number of programs will have to go up while the size of the average enrollment or subscription goes down, with corresponding cost problems. In addition, courses that are designed to train lawyers to become specialists will be particularly expensive to develop. The lawyers, specialists and professors who alone can prepare these materials and instruct the classes will have to be adequately compensated for their time. Particularly in the smaller states, the fees charged will have to be higher than now, at least until the instructional materials have been developed, tested, and proved adequate. Even so, first-rate specialist-oriented education can never be cheap. Pooling of funds and preparing the materials at a national level would be possible for a few courses, but past experience shows that effective programs must be geared to local laws and procedures. If pilot funds can be found and the programs established, will enough lawyers—particularly younger attorneys—be willing and able to pay the fees that are necessary if the programs are to be self-supporting? If not, who will make up the deficit?

Technological Advances and CLE

As scientific advances are made in the field of electronics, the present methods of education may substantially change. It would be unrealistic to believe that the live lecture, panel discussion, or classroom will ever disappear completely, for there are obvious advantages that come from men getting together and being able to exchange ideas and experience. But it is not always convenient or possible for lawyers to attend classes. Distances between urban centers, the pressure of daily practice, and sheer physical and mental exhaustion make participation in "live" CLE difficult and sometimes impossible.

In the future, many types of programs may be presented on video tape and offered for rental or sale so that attorneys can receive instruction at their own convenience at any time they wish. In California, we have taken a step in this direction. We tape-recorded a live twenty-hour lecture program on Significant Developments in California Substantive Law, given by B. E. Witkin, one of California's leading legal writers and lecturers. Approximately 1600 lawyers attended the live program presented in Los Angeles and San Francisco. Over 600 lawyers, including a number of those who attended the live lectures, purchased the tapes and the hardbound syllabus which Witkin prepared for the course. Four other live programs have since been similarly offered on tape. Lawyers have been listening to the tapes at their convenience, alone or with other lawyers in group discussion sessions. Unsolicited letters to us indicate great enthusiasm for this type of programming. We are now planning special programs designed solely for the tape audience.

We have no idea how taped programs will work out in the long run, nor what effects they will have on attendance and enrollments for live programs. If education by audio tapes is successful, and I think it will be, the next step may be video tapes, particularly for home and office use—when the technology makes production economically feasible. Films have of course been made—we have made four in California—but they have been so expensive that their production has been very limited. The cost of video-taping and video tapes will lie somewhere between the cost of audio tapes and films; the cost, not the effectiveness of the technique, will determine how widely they can be used in the future.

Resolving the problems of costs and financing will depend on how strongly the legal profession recognizes its need for continuing education. At present, recognition of the need is more fully expressed than acted upon. If the rate of obsolescence of professional knowledge continues to rise, it may well be that effective CLE in the future will require radical changes in the relationship between basic legal education and subsequent formal instruction. It is not incautious to predict that post-admission legal education, rather than initial law school training, will achieve a place of predominant importance in the life of the profession. The question is whether the institutional and financial arrangements will have been made to sustain CLE in that place.

Alex Elson

12

General Education in Law
for Non-Lawyers

*It is scarcely possible to enslave a Republic
where the Body of the People are well instructed in their Law, Rights and Liberties.*
— Ezra Stiles (1777)

To every generation of Americans leaders have said that knowledge of law is of crucial importance to non-lawyers. In the past 15
years there has been response to this appeal in demands for teaching
law to university and college students, to school children in the
elementary and secondary grades, to graduate students in other disciplines, to related professions, to businessmen, union leaders and
the public generally.

Why Lay Knowledge of the Law?

A wide variety of reasons have been assigned in support of
this demand. Some are simplistic, as where ignorance of the law is
advanced as the explanation for such social ills as juvenile delinquency,

ALEX ELSON *is engaged in the practice of law in Chicago. He has held a number of governmental positions, has been active in the organized bar and
continues to serve in a voluntary capacity for governmental and social service
agencies. He has taught law to graduate and law students at the University of
Chicago, Northwestern and Yale universities. He is an advisor to the Walter
E. Meyer Research Institute and recently wrote a report for The Ford Foundation on educating school children in the law.*

business crimes, absence of moral values, cynicism and apathy toward legal process. Yet beneath these oversimplifications is the more substantial proposition that in a social order heavily dependent on law it is important that not lawyers alone have an appreciation of what the law is, how it works and what are its limits as a device of social ordering.

THE SOCIAL FUNCTIONS OF LAW

What we ask from law in our society is usually couched in generalities reiterated so often as to become clichés: "Ours is a government of laws, not men"; "Ignorance of the law is no excuse"; "A government by consent of the governed"; "Equal justice under law."

Implicit in these generalities are some of the basic assumptions about a democracy. A democratic society places an enormous burden on the law, the legal process and its institutions. A legal democracy requires an elaborate apparatus for determining and effectuating majority will at various levels and sectors of government. The apparatus is complicated by the fact that any given "majority" is a changeable collection of minorities, by the necessity to distinguish long-run interests from short-run ones, and by postulates that put some matters beyond the power of the majority to change except by extraordinary constitutional process. At the same time, a social democracy implies fluidity in such matters as belief, tradition, and social class. It thus cannot rely on the stabilizing effect these influences have in less fluid societies, and must depend more heavily on formal—i.e., legal— processes for establishing community direction and consensus. We are or should be constantly engaged in balancing—between individuals and groups, between group and group, between public and private activity. Our democracy's survival depends on its ability to adjust the scales so delicately that each weight is accorded due measure and no more.

Partly in response to these fundamental considerations we have evolved a legal system more far-reaching and complicated than any in history, one that mirrors the enormous complexity of our society. The maze of constitutions and statutes, court decisions, administrative regulations, local laws and private regulations is beyond the ken of the layman. Indeed, in technical detail it is beyond the general practitioner, as witness the growth of specialization in the law.

That the increased complexity of law puts it beyond the comprehension of the general public contributes to the crisis of confidence in the social order. One can support on faith what one does not understand, but not for long. The high incidence of crime, violence and looting in the cities, the pervasive incidence of "white collar" crimes and wrongs, and other evidence of mass disaffection seem symptomatic of a serious estrangement between government and governed. To be sure, the causes of estrangement go much deeper than ignorance of the law, but that ignorance is part of the general feeling that the law is something apart from society and its membership.

THE GENERAL QUEST FOR JUSTICE

There is still another basis for the demand for lay knowledge about law. In Edmund Cahn's phrase, we are all "consumers of justice." Few nations so exalt justice as a primary value as does the United States and a society asserting such interest needs to know whether the value it prizes is being realized.

Lawyers as professionals know well the forms in which our society fails to realize its aspirations to justice. For every bad decision reversed on appeal, how many bad decisions are not appealed? How many injustices are overlooked because the cost of bringing the wrongdoer to book exceeds the value of restitution or the monetary resources of the victim? How often does the financial irresponsibility of the wrongdoer abort legal action against him? How much injustice has been done by the sovereign itself under the cloak of sovereign immunity? And how much by interminable delays in trial, sheer ineptness of counsel, and mediocre or incompetent judges? These are defects in the legal system itself. Yet we know also that the people may be deprived of justice, in the narrow sense or broad, out of ignorance of laws and procedures for securing relief, or even out of ignorance of the law's elementary features.

PRESERVATION OF THE LEGAL ORDER

What is it we want people to understand about law? It will not do, as is so often done, to extol the virtues of law, presenting the ideals but not the hard facts. We cannot dissipate popular apathy by a course that nourishes popular cynicism. The legal institutions as they exist should be presented with their strengths and weaknesses and in appreciation of the manifold difficulties that stand in the way of achieving justice. If our democracy is to succeed, indeed if it is to survive, our task must be to develop a citizenry demanding and expecting a true realization of better standards of justice.

Achieving this task is no easy objective. To explore the inadequacies of our legal system risks repelling those who believe it is in good working order and alienating further those already alienated. The risks must be taken, however, because effective general reform requires public sophistication of a fairly high order. The task of educating the public about the law is thus a challenge to the legal order all by itself.

The Current State of Public Education about the Law

COLLEGES AND UNIVERSITIES

The challenge is only beginning to be met. Less than fifteen years ago there were only a dozen universities and colleges offering a general course in law; today more than a hundred colleges and universities do so as part of general education. These courses differ from those taught for many years in political science, economics, history and business departments, such as constitutional history, constitutional law, administrative law, international law, business organization and corporate finance, labor law, and governmental regulation of business. They are also to be distinguished from custom-tailored courses devoted to special interests, such as the law relating to the press (libel, slander and copyright) designed for journalism students, and business law courses in schools of business. Their theme is neither vocational nor technical, but liberal in the classic sense. Their objective is to transmit an appreciation of the concepts and processes of the legal order.

Promotion of courses affording such general approaches to law has been the mission of the Committee on Teaching Law Outside the Law Schools of the American Association of Law Schools. Under its auspices there have been three extended conferences for teachers of these courses. With its encouragement, at least five course books have been published for the purpose. And there are many less formal enterprises aimed in the same direction.

These efforts, expectedly, have not been met with unalloyed enthusiasm. A recent evaluation of the five books criticized them all as too technical in their content and as contemplating courses that would teach liberal arts students as though they were to be lawyers.[1] The social science orientation of the books was also rejected in favor of a humanities approach, a criticism of perhaps more dubious validity if taken without qualifications.

It is somewhat more difficult to appraise the criticism of the use of technical language. We should not underestimate undergraduate students' level of comprehension, nor forget that neither the humanities nor the behavioral sciences are free of esoteric vocabulary. And there is something to be said for exposing students to intricacies of the law's language as a means of comprehending the problems of the law. On the other hand, it is difficult even for the most talented law teachers

---

[1] Barkman, "Law in the Liberal Arts: An Appraisal and a Proposal for Experimentation," 19 *J. Legal Ed.* 1–40 (1966). Recently issued in a second edition, the most widely used book of those reviewed is Berman and Greiner, *The Nature and Functions of Law* (Brooklyn: The Foundation Press, Inc., 1966), pp. xi, 974.

to speak in language readily understood by laymen. The problem is compounded when it is recalled that most courses in law in colleges and universities are taught by non-lawyers, and that almost all teaching at the elementary and secondary level will be by laymen.

Another problem recognized by the American Association of Law Schools Committee is the need to provide training for non-lawyers teaching legal courses. A primary purpose of the seminars sponsored by the Association has been to give to the participants guidance in the teaching of such courses. It may help that law-trained people will be more widely available as teachers as the need is recognized, but in that case teacher training may be necessary to modify the tendency to teach law as a technical discipline rather than a liberal art. An overview of the law teaching now under way in our universities and colleges indicates the following needs: re-working of materials to simplify language; broadening the course perspective to include material from the humanities as well as the social sciences; orienting and training both lay and law-trained teachers in the special problems of teaching law in a way that is sophisticated but not professional in the narrow sense of the term. Not alone lawyers but educators, sociologists, political scientists, psychologists, psychiatrists, and others as well should be drawn into this effort.

GRADUATE AND PROFESSIONAL SCHOOLS

Development of general education in law and legal institutions has been slower in professional schools. The emphasis continues to be on courses specifically relevant, or thought to be, to the professional discipline in question: courses such as commercial law, taxation, economic and trade regulation in schools of business and accounting; forensic law in schools of medicine; courses in welfare legislation, family law, and juvenile court jurisdiction and procedure in schools of social work; and libel and slander and copyrights in schools of journalism. The need for a more generalized approach to law, however, has been recognized in some schools of business administration and schools of social work. Should general education in law of the undergraduate level become more widely available, the need to provide it at the graduate level may of course diminish.

ELEMENTARY AND HIGH SCHOOLS

Most interesting, and probably most important, of the efforts to provide education in law to non-lawyers are those that seek to introduce law into the curriculum in high schools and elementary schools. These efforts have burgeoned in the last five years. Lawyers, educators, and, to a lesser extent, academicians and professionals drawn from other disciplines have been involved. The principal problems—teacher training and the formulation of suitable instruction materials—are being systematically explored, notably in California, Chicago and New York.

The programs for elementary and secondary schools vary considerably in objectives, content, and teaching method. Many center on teaching the Bill of Rights. A few are more directly oriented to political science. Most make use of case materials and emphasize the value of the Socratic method of teaching, and have the primary objective of enhancing the capacity of students to engage in rational thinking by confronting them with the value conflicts inherent in law. A secondary objective is to acquaint students with the judicial system and to impart some general knowledge of fundamental legal concepts.

About half of the projects concentrate on teacher training, particularly in the use of the inductive teaching technique. This requires overcoming the traditional authoritarianism that characterizes most pre-collegiate instruction. Beyond this is the task of imparting to the teachers a knowledge of material almost completely new to them. Like most adults who have gone through our school systems, teachers are generally unfamiliar with the law and its underlying concepts, and have no experience with judicial precedents, statutes, and constitutional provisions. The teacher training programs are not law courses, but there is a danger that teachers will be inclined with their new knowledge to try to play lawyer. Though some untoward misfortunes will occur before this illusion is completely dissipated, the risk is unavoidable and seems not too serious. A related risk is that teaching materials will drift toward emphasis on rules of substantive law. Stress should be on the conceptual and philosophic rather than specific rules of law.

Most of the programs are weak in relating course objectives and hence course content to students and their environment. There are vast differences in cultural and intellectual backgrounds of children in our schools, particularly between those living in slum areas and those of middle class background. The programs typically presuppose students with middle class values and experience, but even in this regard are not systematically geared to the conditions and problems that confront students rather than adults. There has been some polling of students as to their views on civil liberties issues, but this information is of limited value.

It would be more to the point to learn what exposure children and their parents have had to the law and legal problems. Children in the inner city schools and their families have more contact with police, juvenile probation officers and the staffs of public assistance and other social welfare agencies than their peers elsewhere. Problems with landlords, creditors, city social workers, and domestic relations police do not generally beset middle class families. The child of the slum is more likely to have witnessed or been involved in violent fighting, and for him and his contemporaries petty theft may be accepted as a way of life. Unlike his more favored contemporaries in middle class city or suburban communities, he is apt to be a member of a minority group and to know discrimination firsthand. What he may learn from law education programs is the extent to which his legal rights have been transgressed. No program I have reviewed specifically and directly takes into account the great cultural, environmental and intellectual gap that separates the child of the inner city schools from his peers in other parts of the city.

At the same time, there is corresponding obliviousness to the students' legal environment even in programs designed for middle class children. "Due process" is treated as a matter concerning criminals, and not procedural fairness in school disciplinary matters. "Free press" is a problem of political censorship and not censorship or "supervision" of school newspapers. Juvenile matters are treated as though they occur somewhere else. One of the difficult problems is whether the law courses will be permitted to ventilate these issues, given the anxiety about them that typifies attitudes among parents and teachers in middle class schools.

This deficiency in orientation is an aspect of a variety of other problems that appear from a review of the programs. These include the lack of evaluation—the modest present efforts being limited to unsystematic self-evaluation; the lack of communication among those who are trying to develop programs, so that both effort and mistakes are frequently repeated; the fragmented state of programs to train teachers to teach courses about law; the absence of much involvement of relevant non-legal disciplines in working up the curricula; and the almost total disregard of possibilities for adult education in law through the public schools. These problems are difficult and far-reaching, but they will remain so until faced. It perhaps might help if a special institute could be established to assist in these regards, serving simultaneously as a clearinghouse, information resource, and intermediary in program planning, development and evaluation.

The Need for Interdisciplinary Efforts

Thus far the focus has been on making law part of a general education. But other objectives are involved. The most significant concerns education at the graduate level in disciplines to which the law is relevant. If it is true that law-trained people should know more about the social and physical sciences and their methods, it is equally true that both social and physical scientists ought to include acquaintance with the law and its processes. But beyond this, it is crucial to involve these disciplines in the study and development of law. Substantial progress has been made since 1952 when Brainerd Currie observed that too many scientists regarded law as "mere vocational stuff devoid of respectable intellectual aspects." The past decade has witnessed extensive research in legal institutions by lawyers and social behavioral scientists, joint consideration by lawyers and physical scientists of crucial policy decisions concerning our environment, the development of interdisciplinary journals and expanded discussions and interchange between the legal profession and the medical profession, particularly with scientists. Even so, much remains to be done to open the eyes of other disciplines to the law and to open the doors of the law schools to them.

What is required is not a self-conscious systematic approach to mutual education, for that would be self-defeating. The educational exchange should aim at the free association of ideas generated from widely different backgrounds and approaches. As was observed by the Chairman of the Special Committee on Science and Law of the Association of the Bar of the City of New York, in regard to a major study of privacy in which it was involved:

> There was little of the purposeful legal inquiry. Our test of success was not measured in terms of blueprints for reform or technical proposals for legislation. We sought rather to widen our own perceptions and, possibly, those of the scientists who collaborated with us.
>
> This shared experience was productive. It suggests a model for wider use not only by the bar, but by all the professions. Cooperative interdisciplinary examination, by practitioners, not just scholars, into items of common concern could be rewarding in a large number of areas. A dialogue between the working lawyer and the religious leader, the practicing accountant and his legal counterpart, between the priest and the physicist, the moralist and medicine, are suggestive of the richness of the opportunity.[2]

The Promise of a Public Understanding of Law

Making the study of law a professional pursuit in professional law schools has resulted in what seems clearly to be a superior level of training for lawyers. But it has also isolated law as a body of knowledge from other disciplines and from education generally. It is not

[2] Oscar M. Reubhausen, in Foreword to Westin, *Privacy and Freedom* (New York, Atheneum 1967), p. ix.

necessary to forsake the professional law school tradition to recognize that systematic study of the law should not be exclusive to the law schools. The movement to extend law knowledge to non-lawyers ought to be nurtured, not merely in the special fields of law that are germane to other professions and callings, but as an aspect of general education. Indeed, technically oriented legal training for students who have no intention of becoming lawyers may do more harm than good. But education about the role of law in our social order and in our legal institutions is an essential part of a general education and should be brought into the curriculum at all levels of learning. Substantial progress has been made in the past decade in developing materials and teaching methods for use in colleges, universities, elementary and secondary schools, but much remains to be done. Cultivating interest in law outside the professional precinct should broaden public understanding of how the law and legal institutions function in the real world and holds great promise for improving the service of law in our social order.

Roger L. Price

Appendix:
Population and Economic Projections

With noted exceptions, the statistical foundation of this paper is based on three sources: Current Population Reports, *Population Estimates, Series P-25 No. 359 (February 20, 1967),* U.S. Department of Commerce, Bureau of the Census, U.S. Gov't. Print. Off. *1967; Donald Bogue,* The Population of the United States *(The Free Press, Glencoe, Ill., 1959); Hans Landsberg, Leonard Fischman, and Joseph Fisher,* Resources in America's Future *(The Johns Hopkins Press, Baltimore, 1963). Because the different sources use different assumptions for their projections, some of the predictions are in this discussion inconsistent.*

Predictions about today made a generation ago have been wide of the mark. Thus, "at the risk of seeming irresponsible and extravagant," one author, late in 1949, suggested that by 1980 the population of the nation would be at least 175 million and that the national product would reach $416 billion with $569 billion well within the range of

ROGER L. PRICE *is a third-year student at the University of Chicago Law School, and an Associate Editor of* The University of Chicago Law Review. *He obtained his Bachelor of Arts degree, with high distinction, from the University of Michigan in 1965.*

possibilities.[1] While these levels have long been passed, the author's prediction of a thirty-hour week has yet to materialize.

If there have been underestimates of the nation's capacity to produce, there have also been overestimates of its capacity to progress. At the General Motors exhibit at the 1939 World's Fair, the ideal city of the future was described as follows:

> . . . the city itself with its quarter-mile-high towers, huge glass, and soaring among them four-level, seven lane directional highways on which you can surely choose your speed—100, 200 miles an hour. The city of 1960 has abundant functions: fresh air, fine green parkways, recreational centers, all results of plausible planning and design. No building's shadow will touch another. Parks will occupy one-third of the city area.[2]

Nevertheless, predictions are useful. This report is concerned with projections of population trends and economic development, since information concerning these two factors is more available and reliable than that about future technology or ideology. The projections which follow are all based on three assumptions: that there will be no crippling war; that economic recessions, if any, will be temporary and of minimal impact; and that historically dominant social, political, and economic philosophies will continue.

Population Growth

The only agreement in population forecasts is that the population of the nation will increase substantially in the next 33 years. The projections of the Department of Commerce are based on assumed net-immigrations of 400,000 a year and a steady, low mortality rate. On variable fertility rates, these projections in millions are:

Table 1

Year July 1	Series A	Series B	Series C	Series D
1966	197	197	197	197
1975	228	224	214	215
1980	250	243	235	228
1990	300	287	271	256
2000	361	336	308	283

[1] Sumner Slichter, "How Big in 1980," in *Outside Readings in Economics,* Arleigh Hess, Jr., *et al.* eds. (New York: Thomas Y. Crowell Co., 1951), p. 540.

[2] This prediction was recalled by Daniel Bell during a symposium on "The Nature and Limitations of Forecasting," which is to be found in *Daedalus* (Boston: American Academy of Arts and Sciences, Summer, 1967) p. 947.

Numbers alone create for the future the peril of proximity. As reported in *The New York Times* (July 24, 1966, p. 23, col. 1), the Hudson Institute contends that man like other animals has a minimum space requirement, without which normal social relationships are disrupted and stress is created. At the least, more people means more conflicts with which law enforcement and judicial units must deal. In addition, better education results in an awareness of one's rights, and within a growing economy more people will be financially able to enforce those rights. Thus, the legal system will be strained to handle a growing number of complaints with efficiency and care.

Turning now to the composition of the population, the rate of increase for non-whites (Negroes, American Indians, Orientals and others) will be faster than that of the white population. This is due in part to reduction in the differential in mortality rates between whites and non-whites and, more importantly, to a significantly greater fertility rate among non-whites. There is some evidence of a convergence of the non-white birth and death rates with Caucasian rates. Nevertheless, the non-white population will increase its share of the total population. Using the projections of the Department of Commerce, and assuming a high rate of population growth, the following estimates are available.

Table 2

Year	Total (millions)	Non-white (millions)	Per Cent Non-white
1960	181	20.7	11.5
1970	209	25.8	12.2
1980	250	33.9	13.6
1990	300	44.5	14.5
2000	361	55.0	15.5

Thus, by 2000 the non-white population will likely approximate in absolute numbers the total population of the nation in the early 1880's. Whatever the absolute numbers of non-whites, the percentage of the non-white population will rise at about the rate of one percentage point a decade.

The population will also become more youthful. This may be surmised from the growing relative size of the under twenty-one group, as well as the decline in median age. Adopting some of the Department of Commerce's figures and Bogue's (pp. 768–69) assumptions, I have derived the following table illustrating two elements of the nation's age composition.

Table 3

Year	Per Cent Under 21	Median Age (in years)
1950	35	30.2
1960	40	29.2
1970	39	26.1
1980	45	25.2
1990	43	25.5

Here, again, changes in fertility strength would alter the projections considerably. In the late sixties, the infants born in the post World War II boom will be marrying and beginning another round of population growth. In the mid-1980's, the third generation baby boom will begin and as noted by Bogue (p. 769), "really fantastic amounts of population growth will begin to occur unless fertility is reduced."

These age and racial factors indicate that the nation can look forward to increased social disruption. Even if the rates of juvenile delinquency remain stable, there will be greater numbers of young people living in those age brackets most susceptible to involvement in crime. Juvenile facilities and penal institutions, as well as the judicial system, will be severely strained. Continued immigration of Negro youth from rural areas into strange and hostile urban settings will perpetuate or increase delinquency rates. Continued substandard care for and prejudice toward immigrants, the poor and minority groups will provide added incentive to act outside of the system.

The farm population will decline, not only relatively but in absolute size. In the last fifty years, rural-farm population has decreased by 50 per cent, from over 32 million in 1910 to about 16 million in 1966. A further decline to near 11 million by 1980 is projected. As these persons enter the urban areas further social tensions will be felt.

Conversely, persons sixty-five and over will be an increasingly large factor of the society. Estimated proportions of the population 65 or over are as follows:

Table 4

Year	Percentage
1940	6.9
1950	8.1
1960	8.8
1970	9.8
1980	10.1
2000	10.0

Moreover, if fertility rates decline—as many observers hope—the proportion of aged will increase markedly. In sum, the latter third of the twentieth century will be vitally concerned with two problems which have been emerging in the sixties: providing facilities and care for the aged and programs and opportunities for the young.

Having touched on some aspects of the composition of the population, we turn to an aspect of its quality. Between 1965 and 1980, elementary and high school enrollment should level off to 35 million and 15 million respectively, following the sharp rate of increase since World War II. College and professional school enrollment will continue to grow, although the expansion stress on schools of higher education is likely to be most severe between now and 1971. Another cycle of increasing primary school attendance should develop again in the early 1990's with the oncoming third generation of post World War II babies, unless fertility rates decline.

Although school systems will be strained, the nation will continue to make steady and substantial gains in all levels of educational attainment. By 1980, the percentage of college graduates will rise from 7.6 per cent in 1960 to 11.0 per cent of the total population 25 and over. While in 1960 only one of three persons had completed high school, by 1980 half of the nation will have had at least twelve years of basic education. Over the same period, the relative size of the functionally illiterate class, defined as those persons with less than five years of schooling, will decline from 8.1 per cent in 1960 to 3.9 per cent. This will still leave another 7 per cent of the population with only a grade school background.

Some implications of this development are not difficult to foresee. Thus Bogue (pp. 779–80) anticipates increases in the awareness and understanding of current events, manifesting itself, *inter alia*, in more critical voting behavior as well as civic activity; in interest, support and participation concerning cultural activities, community groups, and leisure and recreational activities; and in compensation for or mechanization of disagreeable unskilled positions because of an increased aversion to those positions; as well as an increasingly better equipped labor force to work within a sophisticated and technically oriented economy. Moreover, he predicts reductions in social and ethnic class differentials regarding educational attainment and social orientation, and in educational differentials between age groupings, as more elderly people are better educated.

If the population will be growing, it will also be shifting. Although demographic changes are even less predictable than total population changes, short range projections are feasible. They indicate greater than average growth for the Mountain and Pacific states and a relatively slow growth rate for the Southern states (except those on the Atlantic coast), New England, and the North Central plains states. Arkansas, Oklahoma and Mississippi may even diminish in absolute size of population.

Most of the population shifts, both intra and interstate, will be to the large metropolitan (urban and suburban) centers. Unless there are some new incentives brought to bear to alter the tide, urban population which comprised 64 per cent of the nation in 1950 and 68 per cent in 1960, should approach 70 per cent in 1970 and 73–75 per cent in 1980, or between 160,000,000 and 170,000,000 people. By 1980, moreover, it is estimated that there will be 165 cities with a population of 100,000 or more, compared with 106 such cities in 1950. There will be twice as many metropolitan areas (30) with over one million population in 1980 as in 1950 (14). Projections for a Los Angeles or New York megalopolis are staggering: the latter will comprise 20,000,000 inhabitants.

Presently non-urban areas such as the South and West will urbanize, and a more even national distribution of the urban population will be achieved. Along with regional decentralization will come tremendously increased growth of suburban areas, in which an estimated 60 per cent of the metropolitan inhabitants of 1980 will live. In sum, the importance of particular urban centers will decline as more and larger urban areas grow throughout the nation. Moreover, within each metropolitan area, dependence on the central city will diminish as industry, trade, services, and the more affluent move to surrounding areas.

Generally, as commercial and cultural centers are redistributed within and around the central city, and as the population becomes even more mobile, the characteristics, tastes, and consumption habits of the people become more homogeneous. However, at the same time the economic and social power of older central cities is declining, in the absence of major changes in housing patterns, the exploding suburbs will be populated by relatively wealthy white citizens, leaving a large, if less socially and economically significant, central city to the non-white population. Alterations in the present structure of suburban governmental organization appear imminent, as does increased cooperation between and within local and regional areas, especially concerning health and welfare services and transportation.

Economic Growth

As important as the question of personnel is that of material —whether there will be adequate natural resources, products and services to support economic growth and to insure national survival.

Projections concerning demand and supply of economic factors are susceptible to even greater uncertainty than are population trends. While components of population—fertility, mortality, net immigration—are fairly stabilized, predictions about economic development in the United States must be based on often unpredictable technological advances, including new energy sources, products, and product substitutes, and on economic developments in other nations.

While the majority of people of this nation currently enjoy unprecedented prosperity, they also support an extended military program, explorations of outer space and ocean life, and assistance to foreign countries. Although there may be shifts in priorities in these latter categories, the demand for a better standard of living—better goods, more opportunities to advance and enjoy—will continue. In general, our national resources should be sufficient for the balance of the century, and a long time thereafter. With regard to specific resources, especially in and from particular geographic areas, however, shortages will occur. At the same time, there are vast untapped sources of material and energy, for example, oil from shale and tar sand, minerals on the ocean floor, tropical forests. The question seems not to be whether the resources are available but whether the nation is willing to pay the price necessary to conserve old sources and exploit the new.

The following interrelated projections are made by Landsberg (pp. 56–57) for resource and economic growth:

Table 5

	1960	1980	2000
Population (millions)	180	245	331
Labor force (millions)	73	102	142
Households (millions)	53	73	99
Gross National Product (billions)	$504	$1060	$2200
Personal Consumption expenditures (billions)	$359	$ 662	$1320
Government expenditures (billions)	$100	$ 242	$ 551
Net exports (billions)	$ 3	$ 3.1	$ 17.8
Private investment (billions)	$ 72	$ 167	$ 361
Kinds of Output			
Agricultural production (billions)	$ 21	$ 29	$ 38
Industrial production (Index 1957 = 100)	108	249	564
Services (billions)	$189	$ 415	$ 909
Construction (billions)	$ 57	$ 130	$ 281

Two particularly relevant statistics cited by Landsberg (p. 57) reflect the growing congestion in community life:

New dwelling units (millions)	1.5	2.6	4.2
Auto production (millions)	6.7	12.6	25.9

When one realizes that the number of automobiles actually in use will rise from 59 million in 1960 to 120 million in 1980 and 244 million in 2000, safety requirements and insurance regulation take on added meaning. So, too, does land use planning if America is to be made livable for its inhabitants.

Under the above assumptions for population and economic growth, the following requirements are projected by Landsberg (pp. 6–7, 31, 56–57) for metals, timber, and energy.

Table 6

	1960	1980	2000
Metals (million tons steel equivalent)	81	145	250
Timber (billion cubic ft. of roundwood)	11	19	32
Electricity (billion Kilowatt hours)	845	2229	4711
(quadrillion BTU's)	(9.3)	(20.8)	(37)
Hydro and atomic power (bil. Kilo. Hrs.)	149	683	2763
(quadrillion BTU's)	(1.6)	(6.4)	(21.7)
Fuel (quadrillion BTU's)	44	73	114

While the nation has the capacity to meet these requirements, great strains will be placed on two fundamental factors: first land, then water. Requirements for grazing (700 million acres), non-producing farmland (45 million acres), and commercial forest land (484 million acres) are expected to remain stable, at about 60 per cent of the nation's land. On the other hand, demands on land for recreation, urban growth, transportation and conservation will intensify dramatically. Typical projections indicate a land "deficit" of about 50 million acres for the 48 contiguous states. If a modest 60 million acres of unusable

Table 7

Land Use (in million acres)	1960	1980	2000
Cropland	447	443	476
Recreation (excluding reservoir areas and city parks)	44	76	134
Urban (including city parks)	21	32	45
Transportation	26	28	30
Wildlife refuge	15	18	20
Reservoirs	12	15	20
Remaining land	110	63	−50

land—mountain, desert or swamp—is eliminated, the deficit rises to 110 million acres.

One example of the severe pinch on land use is the potential national requirements for forest products. The estimated demand for these items will find the country short some 300 million acres of forest land unless there is increased product substitution, fire and disease control, improved management and waste utilization. Similarly, intensified use of grazing land, which accounts for a third of national acreage, becomes increasingly important.

In addition, our supply of water is becoming scarcer and dirtier. Yet the need for water increases. In fact, our water withdrawal depletion, which was 84 billion gallons per day in 1960, should rise to 107 and 149 billion gallons per day in the years 1980 and 2000, respectively. However, local and regional water stringencies should not be long lasting, given large public and private efforts to treat and store water. In the East, amidst relatively heavy rainfall and population and industrial concentrations, the basic problem will be the quality of water. Maximum available water supplies are more than ample in the near future. In the West, except for the Pacific Northwest, however, requirements are four times as large as in the East and the supply is only one-fifth as much. By 1980, combined Western demand may exceed maximum supply. Better allocation of water, desalinization and long-distance transportation are becoming crucial concerns.

Within this century, the great test for our nation will be the maintenance of quality in our lives. Sprawling urban growth, delinquency, racial tension, transportation accidents and congestion, and air and water pollution, are only some of the problems. With advanced automation (and more people), the four day week and thirteen week vacation are, perhaps, not too far away. Similarly Landsberg suggests (p. 7) that visits to outdoor recreational areas should increase markedly from 1960's 393 million to 1980's 1,405 million and 5,170 million in 2000. For all his training and wealth, the man of tomorrow may well question what to do with himself each day.

Index

The American Assembly

The American Assembly holds meetings of national leaders and publishes books to illuminate issues of United States policy. The Assembly is a national, non-partisan educational institution, incorporated in the State of New York.

The Trustees of the Assembly approve a topic for presentation in a background book, authoritatively designed and written to aid deliberations at national Assembly sessions at Arden House, the Harriman (N. Y.) Campus of Columbia University. These books are also used to support discussion at regional Assembly sessions and to evoke consideration by the general public.

All sessions of the Assembly, whether international, national, regional or local, issue and publicize independent reports of conclusions and recommendations on the topic at hand. Participants in these sessions constitute a wide range of experience and competence.

American Assembly books are purchased and put to use by thousands of individuals, libraries, businesses, public agencies, nongovernmental organizations, educational institutions, discussion meetings, and service groups.

The subjects of Assembly studies to date are:

Second Editions: